# Rick S

# GERMANY, AUSTRIA & SWITZERLAND
# 1998

**John Muir Publications**
**Santa Fe, New Mexico**

**Other JMP travel guidebooks by Rick Steves**
*Asia Through the Back Door* (with Bob Effertz)
*Europe Through the Back Door*
*Europe 101: History and Art for the Traveler* (with Gene Openshaw)
*Mona Winks: Self-Guided Tours of Europe's Top Museums*
(with Gene Openshaw)
*Rick Steves' Best of Europe*
*Rick Steves' France, Belgium & the Netherlands* (with Steve Smith)
*Rick Steves' Great Britain & Ireland*
*Rick Steves' Italy*
*Rick Steves' Russia & the Baltics* (with Ian Watson)
*Rick Steves' Scandinavia*
*Rick Steves' Spain & Portugal*
Rick Steves' Phrase Books: German, French, Italian, Spanish/
Portuguese, and French/German/Italian

Thanks to my hardworking team at Europe Through the Back Door;
the many readers who shared tips and experiences from their travels;
the many Europeans who make travel such a good living; and most of
all, to my wife, Anne, for her support.

John Muir Publications, P.O. Box 613, Santa Fe, NM 87504
Copyright © 1998, 1997, 1996, 1995 by Rick Steves
Cover copyright © 1998 by John Muir Publications
All rights reserved.

Printed in the United States of America
First printing January 1998

Previously published as *2 to 22 Days in Germany, Austria & Switzerland*
copyright © 1987, 1988, 1989, 1992, 1993, 1994

For the latest on Rick's lectures, guidebooks, tours, and public television
series, contact Europe Through the Back Door, Box 2009, Edmonds,
WA 98020, tel. 425/771-8303, fax 425/771-0833, Web site: www.rick-
steves.com, or e-mail: rick@ricksteves.com.

ISBN 1-56261-386-3
ISSN 1085-7222

Distributed to the book trade by
Publishers Group West
Emeryville, California

**Europe Through the Back Door Editor** Risa Laib
**John Muir Publications Editor** Krista Lyons-Gould
**Research** Brian Carr Smith
**Production** Mladen Baudrand, Nikki Rooker
**Design** Linda Braun
**Cover Design** Janine Lehman
**Typesetting** Marcie Pottern
**Maps** Dave C. Hoerlein
**Printer** Banta Company
**Cover Photo** The Berner Oberland, Switzerland; Leo de Wys
Inc./Adrian Bake

*Although the author and publisher have made every effort to provide
accurate, up-to-date information, they accept no responsibility for loss, injury,
loose stools, or inconvenience sustained by any person using this book or eating
strudel recommended herein.*

# CONTENTS

# Top Destinations in Germany, Austria, and Switzerland

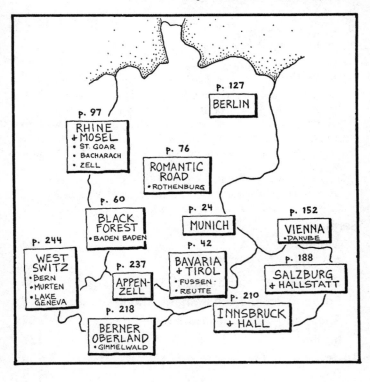

# INTRODUCTION

This book breaks Germany, Austria, and Switzerland into their top big-city, small-town, and rural destinations. It then gives you all the information and opinions necessary to wring the maximum value out of your limited time and money in each of these destinations.

If you plan a month or less in this region and have a normal appetite for information, this lean and mean little book is all you need. If you're a travel-info fiend like me, this book sorts through all the superlatives and provides a handy rack upon which to hang your supplemental information.

Experiencing this region's culture, people, and natural wonders economically and hassle-free has been my goal for more than 20 years of traveling, tour guiding, and travel writing. With this book, I pass on to you the lessons I've learned, updated for 1998.

*Rick Steves' Germany, Austria & Switzerland* is your friendly Franconian, your German in a jam, a tour guide in your pocket. The book includes a balance of big cities and tiny villages, mountaintop hikes and forgotten Roman ruins, sleepy river cruises, and sky-high gondola rides. It covers the predictable biggies and mixes in a healthy dose of Back Door intimacy. Along with visiting Rhine castles, Mozart's house, and the Vienna Opera, you'll ride a thrilling Austrian mountain luge, soak in a Black Forest mineral spa, share a beer with Bavarian monks, and ramble through traffic-free Swiss Alpine towns. I've been selective, including only the most exciting sights. For example, it's redundant to visit both the Matterhorn and the Jungfrau. I take you up and around the better of the two.

The best is, of course, only my opinion. But after more than two busy decades of travel writing, lecturing, and tour guiding, I've developed a sixth sense of what stokes the traveler's wanderlust. Just thinking about the places featured in this book makes me want to slap-dance and yodel.

## This Information Is Accurate and Up-to-Date

This book is updated every year. Most publishers of guidebooks that cover a country from top to bottom can afford an update only every two or three years (and even then, it's often by letter). Since this book is selective, covering only the places

I think make up the top month or so in Germany, Austria, and Switzerland, I am able to personally update it each year. Even with an annual update, things change. But if you're traveling with the current edition of this book, I guarantee you're using the most up-to-date information available. This book will help you have an inexpensive, hassle-free trip. Use this year's edition. I tell you, you're crazy to save a few bucks by traveling on old information. If you're packing an old book, you'll understand the gravity of your mistake . . . in Europe. Your trip costs about $10 per waking hour. Your time is valuable. This guidebook saves lots of time.

## Planning Your Trip

This book is organized by destinations. Each destination is covered as a mini-vacation on its own, filled with exciting sights and homey, affordable places to stay. In each chapter you'll find:

**Planning Your Time**, a suggested schedule with thoughts on how to best use your limited time.

**Orientation**, including tourist information, city transportation, and an easy-to-read map designed to make the text clear and your arrival smooth.

**Sights** with ratings: ▲▲▲—Worth getting up early and skipping breakfast for; ▲▲—Worth getting up early for; ▲—Worth seeing if it's convenient; No rating—Worth knowing about.

**Sleeping and Eating**, with addresses and phone numbers of my favorite budget hotels and restaurants.

**Transportation Connections**, including nearby destinations serviced by train and route tips for drivers, with recommended roadside attractions along the way.

The **Appendix** is a traveler's toolkit, with a climate chart, telephone tips, rail routes, and German survival phrases.

Browse through this book, choose your favorite destinations, and link them up. Then have a great trip! You'll travel like a temporary local, getting the absolute most out of every mile, minute, and dollar. You won't waste time on mediocre sights because, unlike other guidebook authors, I cover only the best. Since lousy, expensive hotels are a major financial pitfall, I've worked hard to assemble the best accommodations values for each stop. As you travel the route I know and love, I'm happy you'll be meeting some of my favorite Europeans.

## Trip Costs

Five components make up your trip cost: airfare, surface transportation, room and board, sightseeing, and shopping/entertainment/miscellany.

**Airfare:** Don't try to sort through the mess. Get and use a good travel agent. A basic round-trip U.S.A.-to-Frankfurt flight should cost $600 to $1,000, depending on where you fly from and when. Always consider saving time and money in Europe by flying "open jaws" (flying into one city and out of another).

**Surface Transportation:** For a three-week whirlwind trip of all my recommended destinations, allow $650 per person for public transportation (train pass and buses) or $600 per person (based on two people sharing the car) for a three-week car rental, parking, gas, and insurance. Car rental is cheapest when reserved from the U.S.A. Train passes are normally available only outside of Europe. You may save money by simply buying tickets as you go (see Transportation, below).

**Room and Board:** You can thrive in this region on $60 a day per person for room and board. A $60-a-day budget per person allows $10 for lunch, $15 for dinner, and $35 for lodging (based on two people splitting the cost of a $70 double room that includes breakfast). That's doable. Students and tightwads do it on $40 a day ($15–20 per bed, $20 for meals and snacks). But budget sleeping and eating requires the skills and information covered later in this chapter (and in much more depth in my book *Europe Through the Back Door*).

**Sightseeing:** In big cities, figure $5 to $10 per major sight, $3 for minor ones, $30 to $40 for bus tours and splurge experiences (e.g., concert tickets, Alpine lifts, conducting the beer-hall band). An overall average of $20 a day works for most. Don't skimp here. After all, this category directly powers most of the experiences all the other expenses are designed to make possible.

**Shopping/Entertainment/Miscellany:** This can vary from nearly nothing to a small fortune. Figure $1 per postcard, $2 per coffee, beer, and ice-cream cone, and $10 to $30 for evening entertainment. Good budget travelers find that this category has little to do with assembling a trip full of life-long and wonderful memories.

## Exchange Rates

I've priced things throughout this book in local currencies.

> 1 deutsche mark (DM) = 60 cents, and 1.7 DM = $1.
> 1 Austrian schilling (AS) = 8 cents, and 12 AS = $1.
> 1 Swiss franc (SF) = 65 cents, and 1.5 Swiss francs = $1.

To convert to dollars, subtract one-third from prices in DM and SF (e.g., 60 DM or 60 SF = about $40). For AS, drop the last zero and subtract one-fifth (e.g., 450 AS = about $36). So, that 40-DM cuckoo clock is about $25, the 15-SF lunch is about $10, and the 800-AS taxi ride through Vienna is . . . uh-oh.

## Prices, Times, and Discounts

The prices in this book, as well as the hours and telephone numbers, are accurate as of late 1997. Europe is always changing, and I know you'll understand that this, like any other guidebook, starts to yellow even before it's printed.

In Europe—and throughout this book—you'll be using the 24-hour clock. After 12:00 noon, keep going—13:00, 14:00, etc. For anything over 12, subtract 12 and add p.m. (14:00 is 2:00 p.m.)

This book lists peak-season hours for sightseeing attractions. Off-season, roughly October through April, expect generally shorter hours, longer lunchtime breaks, and fewer activities. Confirm your sightseeing plans locally, especially when traveling between October and April.

While discounts for sightseeing and transportation are not listed in this book, seniors (60 and over), students (only with International Student Identity Cards), and youths (under 18) often get discounts—but only by asking.

## When to Go

Summer (peak season) has its advantages: best weather, snow-free Alpine trails, very long days (light until after 21:00), and the busiest schedule of tourist fun. The disadvantages of summer travel are minor. A few places charge more in the height of summer, but this is rare. In general, tourism is down. Crowds are generally not a concern, and finding a room (especially if you call a day or two in advance) should be no problem. Nearly every place will hold a room until late afternoon if you call that morning or the day before.

In "shoulder season" (May, June, September, and early October) travelers enjoy minimal crowds, more comfortable weather, plenty of harvest and wine festivals, and the ability to grab a room almost whenever and wherever they like.

Winter travelers find local concert seasons in full swing, with absolutely no tourist crowds, but many sights and accommodations are either closed or run on a limited schedule. The weather can be cold and dreary, and nighttime will draw the shades on your sightseeing before dinnertime. The weather is predictably unpredictable, but you may find the climate chart in the Appendix helpful. Pack warm for the Alps no matter when you go.

## Sightseeing Priorities

Depending on the length of your trip, here are my recommended priorities.

| | |
|---|---|
| 3 days: | Munich, Bavaria, Salzburg |
| 5 days, add: | Romantic Road, Rhine castles |
| 7 days, add: | Rothenburg, slow down |
| 10 days, add: | Berner Oberland (Swiss Alps) |
| 14 days, add: | Vienna, Hallstatt |
| 17 days, add: | Bern, Danube Valley, Tirol (Reutte) |
| 21 days, add: | West Switzerland, Baden-Baden, Mosel Valley, Köln |
| 24 days, add: | Berlin, Appenzell |
| 30 days, add: | Black Forest, slow down |

(The map on page 7 and suggested three-week itinerary on page 6 include everything in the top 30 days except Berlin.)

## Red Tape and Banking

Currently you need a passport but no visa and no shots to travel in Europe. Even as borders fade, when you change countries, you still change money, telephone cards, postage stamps, and *unterhosen*.

Bring traveler's checks in dollars as well as plastic (ATM, credit, or debit cards) with a pin number. Regular banks have the best rates for cashing traveler's checks. For a large exchange, it pays to compare rates and fees. Post offices (business hours) and train stations (long hours) usually change money if you can't get to a bank.

To get a cash advance from a bank machine you'll need a

## Germany, Austria, and Switzerland Best Three-Week Trip

| Day | Plan | Sleep in |
|---|---|---|
| 1 | Arrive in Frankfurt | Rothenburg |
| 2 | Rothenburg | Rothenburg |
| 3 | Romantic Road to the Tirol | Reutte |
| 4 | Bavaria and Castle day | Reutte |
| 5 | Reutte to Munich | Munich |
| 6 | Munich | Munich |
| 7 | Salzburg | Salzburg |
| 8 | Salzkammergut Lakes District | Hallstatt |
| 9 | Mauthausen, Danube to Vienna | Vienna |
| 10 | Vienna | Vienna |
| 11 | Vienna to the Tirol | Hall |
| 12 | Tirol to Swiss Appenzell | Ebenalp |
| 13 | Appenzell to Berner Oberland | Gimmelwald |
| 14 | Free day in the Alps, hike | Gimmelwald |
| 15 | Bern, west to French Switzerland | Murten |
| 16 | French Switzerland | Murten |
| 17 | Murten to Black Forest | Staufen |
| 18 | Black Forest | Baden-Baden |
| 19 | Baden-Baden, relax, soak | Baden-Baden |
| 20 | Drive to the Rhine, castles | Bacharach |
| 21 | The Mosel Valley, Berg Eltz | Bacharach/Zell |
| 22 | Cologne and Bonn, night train to Berlin, or fly home | |

*Note: While this itinerary is designed to be done by car, with slight mod-*
*ifications it works by train. For the best three weeks by train, sleep in*
*Füssen rather than Reutte, sleep on the train from Vienna to the Swiss*
*Alps (skipping Hall and Appenzell), skip French Switzerland, skip the*
*Black Forest, and add two days in Berlin, connecting it by night trains.*

four-digit PIN (numbers only, no letters) with your bankcard.
Before you go, verify with your bank that your card will work,
then use it whenever possible. But beware that the distances
between these machines can be great, and bring enough traveler's checks as backup.

## Best Three-Week Trip

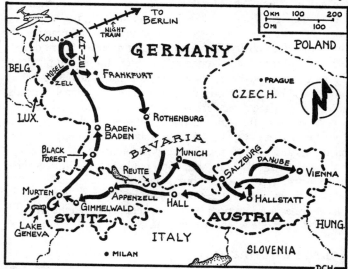

Just like at home, credit (or debit) cards work easily at larger hotels, restaurants, and shops, but smaller businesses prefer payment in local currency.

Don't be petty about changing money. The greatest avoidable money-changing expense is having to waste time every few days returning to a bank. Change ten days' or two weeks' worth of money, get big bills, stuff it in your money belt, and travel!

**Germany:** Banks are generally open Monday through Friday from 8:00 to 12:00 and 14:00 to 16:00.

**Austria:** Bank hours are roughly Monday through Friday from 8:00 to 15:00 and until 17:30 on Thursday. Austria charges exorbitant commissions to cash traveler's checks (about $8). Bring plastic. As a backup, carry American Express checks and cash them at American Express offices (no commission).

**Switzerland:** Bank hours are typically Monday through Friday from 8:00 to 17:00.

## Travel Smart

Upon arrival in a new town, lay the groundwork for a smooth departure. Reread this book as you travel, and visit local tourist information offices. Buy a phone card and use it for reservations and confirmations. Enjoy the hospitality of the Germanic people. Ask questions. Most locals are eager to point you in their idea of the right direction. Wear your money belt, pack along a pocket-size notebook to organize your thoughts, and practice the virtue of simplicity. Those who expect to travel smart, do. Plan ahead for banking, laundry, post office chores, and picnics. To maximize rootedness, minimize one-night stands. Mix intense and relaxed periods. Every trip (and every traveler) needs at least a few slack days. Pace yourself. Assume you will return.

As you read through this book, note special days (festivals, colorful market days, and days when sights are closed). Sundays have pros and cons, as they do for travelers in the U.S.A. (special events, limited hours, shops and banks closed, limited public transportation, no rush hours). Saturdays are virtually weekdays (with most places open until lunchtime). Popular places are even more popular on weekends. Most sights are closed during one weekday (often Monday).

## Tourist Information

The tourist information office is your best first stop in any new city. Try to arrive, or at least telephone, before it closes. In this book, I'll refer to a tourist information office as a TI. Throughout Germany, Austria, and Switzerland, you'll find TIs are usually well-organized with English-speaking staff.

As national budgets tighten, many TIs have been privatized. This means they become sales agents for big tours and hotels and their "information" becomes unavoidably colored. While the TI has listings of all the rooms and is eager to book you a room, use their room-finding service only as a last resort. Across Europe, room-finding services are charging commissions from hotels, taking fees from travelers, blacklisting establishments that buck their materialistic rules, and unable to give hard opinions on the relative value of one place over another. The accommodations stakes are too high to go potluck through the TI. And with the listings in this book, there's generally no need to do so.

## Tourist Offices, U.S.A. Addresses

Each country's national tourist office in the U.S.A. is a wealth of information. Before your trip, get their free general information packet and request any specific information you may want (such as regional and city maps, and schedules of upcoming festivals).

**German National Tourist Offices:** 122 East 42nd Street, 52nd floor, New York, NY 10168-0072, tel. 212/661-7200, fax 212/661-7174; 11766 Wilshire Boulevard, #750, Los Angeles, CA 90025, tel. 310/575-9799, fax 310/575-1565. Web site: www.germany-tourism.de, e-mail: gntolax@aol.com. Very helpful, stocked with Germany maps, Romantic Road maps, city maps, and Rhine schedules.

**Austrian National Tourist Office:** Box 1142 Times Square, New York, NY 10108-1142, tel. 212/944-6880, fax 212/730-4568, Web site: www.anto.com, e-mail: antonyc@ix.netcom.com. Ask for their "Vacation Kit" map. Fine hikes and Vienna material.

**Swiss National Tourist Offices:** 608 Fifth Avenue, New York, NY 10020, tel. 212/757-5944, fax 212/262-6116; 150 North Michigan Avenue, #2930, Chicago IL 60601, tel. 312/ 630-5840, fax 312/630-5848; 222 North Sepulveda Boulevard, #1570, El Segundo, CA 90245, tel. 310/335-5980, fax 310/335-5982. Web site: www.switzerlandtourism.com, e-mail: stnewyork@switzerlandtourism.com. Great maps and rail and hiking material.

## Recommended Guidebooks

You may want some supplemental information, especially if you'll be traveling beyond my recommended destinations. When you consider the improvements they'll make in your $3,000 vacation, $25 or $35 for extra maps and books is money well spent. Especially for several people traveling by car, the weight and expense are negligible.

Students, backpackers, and those interested in the night scene should consider either the hip Rough Guides (British researchers, more insightful but not updated annually) or the Let's Go guides (by Harvard students, better hotel listings, updated annually). Lonely Planet's *Germany, Austria,* and *Switzerland* are well-researched and mature. The popular, skinny, green Michelin Guides to Germany, Austria, and Switzerland are excellent, especially if you're driving. They're known for their city and sightseeing maps, dry but concise and helpful information on all major sights, and good cultural and historical background. English editions are sold locally at gas stations and tourist shops.

## Rick Steves' Books and Videos

*Rick Steves' Europe Through the Back Door* (John Muir Publications, 1998) gives you budget travel tips on minimizing jet lag, packing light, planning your itinerary, traveling by car or train, finding budget beds without reservations, changing money, avoiding rip-offs, outsmarting thieves, hurdling the language barrier, staying healthy, taking great photographs, using your bidet, and much more. The book also includes chapters on my 37 favorite "Back Doors."

**Rick Steves' Country Guides** are a series of eight guide-books covering Europe, Britain/Ireland, France/Belgium/Netherlands, Italy, Spain/Portugal, Scandinavia, and Russia/Baltics, just as this one covers Germany, Austria, and Switzerland. These are updated annually and come out each January.

*Europe 101: History and Art for the Traveler* (co-written with Gene Openshaw, John Muir Publications, 1996) gives you the story of Europe's people, history, and art. Written for smart people who were sleeping in their history and art classes before they knew they were going to Europe, *101* really helps Europe's sights come alive.

*Mona Winks* (also co-written with Gene Openshaw, John Muir Publications, 1996) gives you fun, easy-to-follow, self-guided tours of Europe's top 20 museums (in London, Paris, Madrid, Amsterdam, Venice, Florence, and Rome).

*Rick Steves' German Phrase Book* (John Muir Publications, 1997) is a fun, practical tool for independent budget travelers. With everything from beer-hall vocabulary to sample telephone conversations (for making hotel reservations) to a handy menu decoder, you'll be glad to have this useful book.

My television series, *Travels in Europe with Rick Steves*, includes 11 half-hour shows on Germany, Austria, and Switzerland—including two brand-new shows on the Swiss and Austrian Alps. Check your local public television station or Travel Channel for viewing times. The shows are also available as information-packed videotapes, along with my two-hour slideshow lecture on Germany, Austria, and Switzerland (call us at 425/771-8303 for our free newsletter/catalog).

## Maps

The maps in this book, drawn by Dave Hoerlein, are concise and simple. Dave, who is well-traveled in Germany, Austria, and Switzerland, has designed the maps to help you locate recommended places and get to the tourist offices, where you can pick up a more indepth map (usually free) of the city or region. European bookstores, especially in tourist areas, have good selections of maps. For drivers, I'd recommend a 1:200,000- or 1:300,000-scale map for each country. Train travelers can usually manage fine with the freebies they get with their train pass and at the local tourist offices.

## Transportation

### By Car or Train?
The train is best for single travelers, those who'll be spending more time in big cities, and those who don't want to drive in Europe. While a car gives you the ultimate in mobility and freedom, enables you to search for hotels more easily, and carries your bags for you, the train zips you effortlessly from city to city, usually dropping you in the center and near the tourist office. Cars are great in the countryside but a worthless headache in places like Munich, Bern, and Vienna.

### Trains
The trains are punctual and cover cities well, but frustrating schedules make a few out-of-the-way recommendations (such as the concentration camp at Mauthausen) not worth the time and trouble for the less determined. For timetables, log onto http://bahn.hafas.de/english.html.

If you're doing a whirlwind trip of all of my recommended destinations, a three-week first-class Eurailpass for $698 is worthwhile—especially for a single traveler (available from your travel agent or Europe Through the Back Door—call 425/771-8303 for our free newsletter/catalog). You can save about $60 by managing with the "any ten days out of two months" Eurail Flexipass, but it will require some streamlining. The "Europass" (e.g., five days in two months) which covers Germany and Switzerland with an Austria add-on, is especially good when two travel together (since the "partner" pays only 60 percent). Each country has its own individual train passes. Patchworking several second-class country passes together (for example, a ten-day-in-a-month German railpass, a three-days-in-15 Austrian pass, and an eight-day Swiss pass) may be cheaper than a single first-class Eurailpass for the total traveling time, but the $50 savings isn't substantial and you'll be going second class.

Eurailers should know what extras are included on their pass—such as any German buses marked *Bahn* (run by the train company); city S-Bahn systems; boats on the Rhine, Mosel, and Danube Rivers and Swiss lakes; and the Romantic Road bus tour. Those traveling in the Swiss Alps (where many scenic rides are not covered by rail passes) should consider the various Alps passes (sold at Swiss train stations). The Swiss Family Card allows children under 16 to travel free with their parents (20 SF at Swiss stations or free with Swiss train passes when requested with purchase in the U.S.A.).

If you decide to buy train tickets as you go, look into local specials. Seniors (women over 60, men over 65) and youths (under 26) can enjoy substantial discounts. While Eurailers (over 26) automatically travel first class, those buying individual tickets should remember that second-class tickets provide the same transportation for 33 percent less.

Hundreds of local train stations rent bikes for about $5 a day (discounted for train-pass holders, ask for a *Fahrrad am Bahnhof* brochure at any station).

### Car Rental

It's cheapest to rent a car through your travel agent well before departure (rather than in Europe). You'll want a weekly rate with unlimited mileage. For three weeks or longer, leasing is cheaper (because it saves you money on taxes and insurance). Comparison shop through your agent. DER, a German company, often has the best rates (tel. 800/782-2424).

Expect to pay about $700 for a small car for three weeks with unlimited mileage, and CDW (collision damage waiver) insurance. I normally rent a small, inexpensive model (e.g., Ford Fiesta). For a bigger, roomier, and more powerful inexpensive car, move up to the Ford 1.3-liter Escort or VW Polo category. If you drop your car off early or keep it longer, you'll be credited or charged at a fair, prorated price.

For peace of mind, I splurge for the CDW insurance (about $14 a day). A few "gold" credit cards cover CDW; quiz your credit-card company on the worst-case senario. With the luxury of CDW, you'll enjoy the autobahns knowing you can bring back the car in shambles and just say, "S-s-s-sorry."

### Driving

Every long drive between my recommended destinations is via

# Cost of Public Transportation

## 1998 GERMAN RAILPASS

|  | 1st cl | 1st twin | 2nd cl | 2nd twin | Junior |
|---|---|---|---|---|---|
| 5 days in a month | $276 | $138 | $188 | $94 | $146 |
| 10 days in a month | 434 | 217 | 304 | 152 | 200 |
| 15 days in a month | 562 | 281 | 410 | 205 | 252 |

Discounted "twin" pass is for the companion of anyone who buys a full price pass in the same class (must travel together at all times). "Junior" passes are for those under 26. Covers all the Eurail bonuses in Germany (boats on Rhine and Mosel, Romantic Road bus tour, etc).

**Germany & Switzerland:** Point-to-point 1-way 2nd class rail fares in $US.

## 1998 EUROPASSES

All Europasses include France, Germany, Switzerland, Italy and Spain.

|  | 1st. class | Partner* | Youth 2nd. |
|---|---|---|---|
| 5 days in 2 months | $326 | $196 | $216 |
| With 1 add-on zone | 386 | 232 | 261 |
| With 2 add-on zones | 416 | 250 | 286 |
| With 3 add-on zones | 436 | 262 | 301 |
| With 4 add-on zones | 446 | 268 | 309 |

**Europass add-on days:** Add up to 10 extra days.

| Price per day: | $42 | $25 | $29 |
|---|---|---|---|

**Europass add-on zones**
Choose from:
- ◆ Austria/Hungary
- ◆ Belgium/Netherlands/ Luxembourg
- ◆ Portugal
- ◆ Greece.

**"Partner"** is price for 1 companion traveling with a full-price Europass holder.

## 1998 SWISS PASS AND SWISS FLEXIPASS

|  | 1st cl | 2nd cl | 1st cl twin | 2nd cl twin |
|---|---|---|---|---|
| 4 consec. days | $264 | $188 | $158 | $112 |
| 8 consec. days | 316 | 238 | 190 | 142 |
| 15 consec. days | 368 | 288 | 220 | 172 |
| 21 consec. days | 403 | 320 | 241 | 192 |
| 1 month | 508 | 400 | 304 | 240 |
| 3 days in 15 flexi | 264 | 176 | 158 | 106 |
| Add'l rail days (6 max) | 30 | 24 | 18 | 14 |

Covers all trains, boats and buses with 25% off on the high mountain rides. Kids under 16 travel free with parent.

## 1998 AUSTRIAN FLEXIPASS

|  | 1st cl | 2nd cl |
|---|---|---|
| Any 3 days out of 15 days | $145 | $98 |
| Add-on days (max 5): | 21 | 15 |

Kids 4-12 get 1/3 off. Bonuses include 50% off on Danube ships and on Lake Constance. These passes are available in the USA or at train stations in countries outside of Austria.

**Austria:** Point-to-point 1-way 2nd class rail fares in $US.

the autobahn (super-freeway), and nearly every scenic back-country drive is paved and comfortable.

Drivers over 21 need only their U.S. driver's license. For Austria, you'll need a sticker for your rental car (buy at the border or car rental agency)—70 AS for one week, 150 AS/2 months, or 550 AS/one year. To use the autobahn in Switzerland, you'll pay a one-time 40-SF fee (at the border, gas station, or rental agency).

Learn the universal road signs (explained in charts in most road atlases and at service stations). Seat belts are required, and two beers under those belts is enough to land you in jail.

Use good local maps and study them before each drive. Learn which exits you need to look out for, which major cities you'll travel toward, where the ruined castles lurk, and so on. For parking, you can pick up the "cardboard clock" (*Parkscheibe*, available free at gas stations, police stations, and *Tabak* shops) and display your arrival time on the dashboard so parking attendants can see you've been there less than the posted maximum stay (blue lines indicate 90-minute zones on Austrian streets).

In Europe the shortest distance between any two points is the autobahn. Signs directing you to the autobahn are green in Austria and Switzerland, blue in Germany. To understand the complex but super-efficient autobahn (no speed limit, toll-free) pick up the "Autobahn Service" book-let at any autobahn rest stop (free, lists all stops, services, road symbols, and more). Learn the signs: *Dreieck* means a "Y" in the road; *Autobahnkreuz* is an intersection. Exits are spaced about every 20 miles, and often have a gas station, restaurant, a mini-market, and sometimes a tourist informa-tion desk. Unleaded (*Bleifrei*) gas is everywhere. Exits and intersections refer to the next major or the nearest small town. Study the map and anticipate which town names to look out for. Know what you're looking for—miss it and you're long autobahn-gone. When navigating, you'll see *nord*, *süd*, *ost*, *west*, or *mittel*. Don't cruise in the passing lane; stay right.

Get used to metric. A liter is about a quart, four to a gal-lon; a kilometer is six-tenths of a mile. I figure kilometers to miles by cutting them in half and adding back 10 percent of the original (120 km: 60 + 12 = 72 miles).

# Telephones and Mail

Smart travelers learn the phone system and use it daily to
reserve or reconfirm rooms, get tourist information, or phone
home. Many European phone booths take cards rather than
coins. Each country sells phone cards good for use in that
country's phones. (For example, you can use a Swiss phone
card to make local and international calls from Switzerland, but
it won't do a thing for you in Austria.) Buy a phone card from
post offices, newsstands, or tobacco shops. Insert the card into
the phone, make your call, and the value is deducted from your
card. If you use coins, have a bunch handy.

**Dialing Direct:** You'll usually save money by dialing
direct. You just need to learn to break the codes. When calling
long-distance within a country, first dial the area code (which
starts with zero), then dial the local number. For example,
Munich's area code is 089, and the number of my favorite
Munich hotel is 264-349. To call it from Frankfurt, dial
089/264-349. When dialing internationally, dial the international access code (of the country you're calling from), the
country code (of the country you're calling to), the area code
(without the initial zero), and the local number. To call the
Munich hotel from the U.S.A., dial 011 (U.S.A.'s international
access code), 49 (Germany's country code), 89 (Munich's area
code without the zero), then 264-349. To call my office from
Munich, I dial 00 (Germany's international access code), 1
(U.S.A.'s country code), 425 (Edmonds' area code), and 771-
8303. For a listing of international access codes and country
codes, see the Appendix.

**U.S.A. Direct Services:** Calling home from Europe is
easy from any kind of phone if you have an AT&T, MCI, or
Sprint calling card. Each card company has a toll-free number
in each European country which puts you in touch with an
English-speaking operator. The operator asks for your card
number and the number you want to call, puts you through,
and bills your home phone number for the call (at the cheaper
U.S.A. rate of $3 for the first minute and $1.25 per additional
minute, plus a $2.50 service charge). You'll save money on calls
of three minutes or more. Calling an answering machine is an
expensive ($5.50) mistake. First use a small-value coin or a
German, Austrian, or Swiss phone card to call home for five
seconds—long enough to make sure an answering machine is
off so you can call back, using your U.S.A. Direct number.

European time is six/nine hours ahead of the east/west coast of the U.S.A. For a list of AT&T, MCI, and Sprint operators, see the Appendix. Avoid using U.S.A. Direct for calls between European countries; it's much cheaper to call direct using coins or a European phone card.

**Mail:** To arrange for mail delivery, reserve a few hotels along your route in advance and give their addresses to friends, or use American Express Company's mail services (available to anyone who has at least one Amex traveler's check). Allow ten days for a letter to arrive. Phoning is so easy that I've dispensed with mail stops all together.

## Sleeping

In the interest of smart use of your time, I favor hotels and restaurants handy to your sightseeing activities. Rather than list hotels scattered throughout a city, I describe two or three favorite neighborhoods and recommend the best accommodations values in each, from $10 bunks to $120 doubles.

While accommodations in Germany, Austria, and Switzerland are fairly expensive, they are normally very comfortable and come with breakfast. Plan on spending $70 to $120 per hotel double in big cities, $40 to $60 in towns and in private homes. Swiss beds are 20 percent more expensive than those in Austria and Germany.

A triple is much cheaper than a double and a single. While hotel singles are most expensive, private accommodations (*Zimmer*) have a flat per-person rate. Hostels and dorms always charge per person. Especially in private homes, where the boss changes the sheets, people staying several nights are most desirable. One-night stays are sometimes charged extra.

In recommending hotels, I favor small, family-run places that are central, inexpensive, quiet, clean, safe, friendly, English-speaking, and not listed in other guidebooks. I also like local character and simple facilities that don't cater to American "needs." Obviously a place meeting every critieria is rare, and all of my recommendations fall short of perfection— sometimes miserably. But I've listed the best values for each price category, given the above criteria. The best values are family-run places with showers down the hall and no elevator.

Rooms with private bathrooms are often bigger and renovated, while the cheaper rooms without bathrooms will often be on the top floor or not yet refurbished. Any room without a bathroom has access to a bathroom in the corridor (free unless otherwise noted). Rooms with tubs often cost more than rooms with showers. All rooms have a sink. Towels and linen aren't always replaced every day—drip dry and conserve.

Unless I note otherwise, the cost of a room includes a continental breakfast. The price is usually posted in the room. Before accepting, confirm your understanding of the complete price. The only tip the hotels I've listed would like is a friendly, easygoing guest. The accommodations prices listed in this book should be good through 1998. I appreciate feedback on your hotel experiences.

## Sleep Code

To save space while giving more specific information for people with special concerns, I've described my recommended hotels with a standard code. Prices listed are per room, not per person. When a range of prices is listed for a room, the price fluctuates with room size or season.

**S** = Single room or price for one person using a double.
**D** = Double or twin room. Double beds are usually two twins pushed together—comfortable for non-romantic couples.
**T** = Three-person room (often a double bed with a single bed moved in).
**Q** = Four-adult room (an extra child's bed is usually cheaper).
**b** = Private bathroom with toilet and shower or tub.
**t** = Private toilet only (the shower is down the hall).
**s** = Private shower or tub only (the toilet is down the hall).
**CC** = Accepts credit cards (**V**=Visa, **M**=MasterCard, **A**=American Express). If no CC, assume they accept only cash.
**SE** = Speaks English. This code is used only when it seems predictable that you'll encounter English-speaking staff.
**NSE** = Does not speak English. Used only when it's unlikely you'll encounter English-speaking staff.

According to this code, a couple staying at a "Db-120 DM, CC:V, SE" hotel would pay 120 deutsche marks (around $80) for a double room with a private bathroom. The hotel accepts Visa or German cash, and the staff speaks English.

## Making Reservations

It's possible to travel at any time of year without reservations, but given the high stakes, erratic accommodations values, and the quality of the gems I've found for this book, I'd highly recommend calling ahead for rooms a day or two in advance as you travel. If tourist crowds are down, you might make a habit of calling between 9:00 and 10:00 on the day you plan to arrive, when the hotel knows who'll be checking out and just which rooms will be available. I've taken great pains to list telephone numbers with long distance instructions (see the Appendix). Use the telephone and the convenient telephone cards. Most hotels listed are accustomed to English-only speakers. A hotel receptionist will trust you and hold a room until 17:00 (5:00 p.m.) without a deposit, though some will ask for a credit-card number. Honor (or cancel by phone) your reservations. Long distance is cheap and easy from public phone booths. Don't let these people down—I promised you'd call and cancel if for some reason you can't show up. Don't needlessly confirm rooms through the tourist offices; they'll take a commission.

If you know exactly which dates you need and really want a particular place, reserve a room well before you leave home. To reserve from home, call, fax, or write the hotel. Phone and fax costs are reasonable, and simple English is usually fine. To fax, use the form in the Appendix. If you're writing, add the zip code and confirm the need and method for a deposit. A two-night stay in August would be "two nights, 16/8/98 to 18/8/98"— European hotel jargon uses your day of departure. You'll often receive a letter back requesting one night's deposit. A credit-card number and expiration date will usually be accepted as a deposit, though you may need to send a signed traveler's check or a bank draft in the local currency. If your credit card is the deposit, you can pay with your card or cash when you arrive; if you don't show up, you'll be billed for one night. Reconfirm your reservations a day in advance for safety.

### Camping and Hosteling

Campers can manage with the Let's Go listings and help from the local TI (ask for a regional camping guide). Your hometown travel bookstore also has guidebooks on camping in Europe. You'll find campgrounds just about wherever you need them. Look for "Campingplatz" signs. You'll meet lots of Europeans—camping is a popular middle-class–family way to go. Campgrounds are cheap ($4–5 per person), friendly, safe, more convenient than rustic, and very rarely full.

Hostelers can take advantage of the wonderful network of

hostels. Follow signs marked "Jugendherberge," with Trian-gles, or the "tree next to a house." Generally, those without a membership card ($25 per year, sold at hostels in most U.S. cities and through ETBD) are admitted for a $5 extra charge.

Hostels are open to members of all ages (except in Bavaria, where a maximum age of 26 is strictly enforced). They usually cost $10 to $20 per night (cheaper for those under 27, plus $4 sheet rental if you don't have your own) and serve good, cheap meals and/or provide kitchen facilities. While many have cou-ples' or family rooms available upon request for a little extra money, plan on beds in segregated dorms—four to 20 per room. Hostels can be idyllic and peaceful, or school groups can raise the rafters. School groups are most common on summer weekends and on school-year weekdays. I like small hostels best. While many hostels may say they're full over the tele-phone, most hold a few beds for people who drop in, or they can direct you to budget accommodations nearby.

## Eating

Germanic cuisine is heavy and hearty. While it's tasty, it can get monotonous if you fall into the schnitzel- or wurst-and-potatoes rut. Be adventurous. My German phrase book has a handy menu decoder which works well for most travelers, but galloping gluttons will prefer the meatier *Marling German Menu Master*. Each region has its local specialties which, while not the cheapest, are often the best values on the menu.

There are many kinds of restaurants. Hotels often serve fine food. A *Gaststätte* is a simple, less-expensive restaurant. Ethnic restaurants provide a welcome break from Germanic fare. Foreign food is either from the remnants of a crumbled empire (Hungarian and Bohemian—from which Austria gets its goulash and dumplings) or a new arrival to feed the many hun-gry-but-poor guest workers. Italian, Turkish, and Greek food are good values. The cheapest meals are found in department-store cafeterias, *Schnell-Imbiss* (fast-food) stands, university cafe-terias (*Mensas*), and hostels. For a quick, cheap bite, have a deli make you a *Wurstsemmel*, a meat sandwich.

Most restaurants tack a menu onto their door for browsers and have an English menu inside. Only a rude waiter will rush you. Good service is relaxed (slow to an American). When you want the bill, ask, "*Die Rechnung, bitte.*" Service is included, although it's common to round the bill up after a good meal.

To wish others "Happy eating!" offer a cheery "*Guten Appetit!*"

For most visitors, the rich pastries, wine, and beer provide the fondest memories of Germany's cuisine. The wine (85 percent white) is particularly good from the Mosel, Rhine, Danube, eastern Austria, and southwestern Switzerland areas. Order wine by the *Viertel* (quarter-liter) or *Achtel* (eighth-liter). You can say, "*Ein Viertel Weisswein* (white wine), *bitte* (please)." Order it *süss* (sweet), *halbe trocken* (medium), or *trocken* (dry). *Rotwein* is red wine and *Sekt* is German champagne.

The Germans enjoy a tremendous variety of great beer. The average German, who drinks 40 gallons of beer a year, knows that *dunkles* is dark, *helles* is light, *Flaschenbier* is bottled, and *vom fass* is on tap. *Pils* is barley-based, *Weize* is wheat-based, and *Malzbier* is the malt beer that children learn on. *Radler* is half beer and half lemonade. When you order beer, ask for *ein Halbe* for a half-liter or *eine Mass* for a whole liter. Some beer halls serve it only by the liter (about a quart). Menus list drink size by the tenth of a liter or by the deciliter.

## Stranger in a Strange Land

We travel to Europe to enjoy differences—to become temporary locals. You'll experience frustrations. Truths that we find "God-given" or "self-evident," like cold beer, ice in drinks, bottomless cups of coffee, hot showers, body odor smelling bad, and bigger being better, are suddenly not so true. One of the benefits of travel is the eye-opening realization that there are logical, civil, and even better alternatives. A willingness to go local ensures that you'll enjoy a full dose of local hospitality.

## Send Me a Postcard, Drop Me a Line

If you enjoy a successful trip with the help of this book and would like to share your discoveries, please fill out and send the survey at the end of this book to me at Europe Through the Back Door, Box 2009, Edmonds, WA 98020. I personally read and value all feedback. Thanks in advance—it helps a lot.

For our latest information, check our Web site: www.ricksteves.com. My e-mail address is rick@ricksteves.com. Anyone can request a free issue of our Back Door quarterly newsletter.

Judging from all the happy postcards I receive, it's safe to assume you're on your way to a great vacation—independent, inexpensive, and with the finesse of an experienced traveler.

Thanks, and *Gute Reise*!

# BACK DOOR TRAVEL PHILOSOPHY
## As Taught in *Rick Steves' Europe Through the Back Door*

*Travel is intensified living—maximum thrills per minute and one of the last great sources of legal adventure. Travel is freedom. It's recess, and we need it.*

*Experiencing the real Europe requires catching it by surprise, going casual . . . "Through the Back Door."*

*Affording travel is a matter of priorities. (Make do with the old car.) You can travel—simply, safely, and comfortably—anywhere in Europe for $60 a day plus transportation costs. In many ways, spending more money only builds a thicker wall between you and what you came to see. Europe is a cultural carnival, and time after time you'll find that its best acts are free, and the best seats are the cheap ones.*

*A tight budget forces you to travel close to the ground, meeting and communicating with the people, not relying on service with a purchased smile. Never sacrifice sleep, nutrition, safety, or cleanliness in the name of budget. Simply enjoy the local-style alternatives to expensive hotels and restaurants.*

*Extroverts have more fun. If your trip is low on magic moments, kick yourself and make things happen. If you don't enjoy a place, maybe you don't know enough about it. Seek the truth. Recognize tourist traps. Give a culture the benefit of your open mind. See things as different but not better or worse. Any culture has much to share.*

*Of course, travel, like the world, is a series of hills and valleys. Be fanatically positive and militantly optimistic. If something's not to your liking, change your liking. Travel is addicting. It can make you a happier American, as well as a citizen of the world. Our Earth is home to nearly 6 billion equally important people. It's humbling to travel and find that people don't envy Americans. They like us but, with all due respect, they wouldn't trade passports.*

*Globe-trotting destroys ethnocentricity. It helps you understand and appreciate different cultures. Travel changes people. It broadens perspectives and teaches new ways to measure quality of life. Many travelers toss aside their hometown blinders. Their prized souvenirs are the strands of different cultures they decide to knit into their own character. The world is a cultural yarn shop. And Back Door travelers are weaving the ultimate tapestry. Come on, join in!*

# GERMANY
## (DEUTSCHLAND)

- Germany is 136,000 square miles (like Montana).
- Population is 77 million (about 650 per square mile, declining slowly).
- The West was 95,000 square miles (like Wyoming), with 61 million people. The East was 41,000 square miles (like Virginia), with 16 million people.
- 1 deutsche mark (DM) = 60 cents, and 1.7 DM = $1.

Deutschland is energetic, efficient, and organized, and Europe's muscleman—economically and wherever people are lining up. Its bustling cities hold 85 percent of its people, and average earnings are among the highest on earth. Ninety-seven percent of the workers get one-month paid vacations, and during the other 11 months, they create a gross national product that's about one-third of the United States' and growing. Germany has risen from the ashes of World War II to become the world's fifth-biggest industrial power, ranking fourth in steel output and nuclear power and third in automobile production. Germany shines culturally, beating out all but two countries in production of books, Nobel laureates, and professors.

While its East-West division lasted about 40 years, historically Germany has been divided north and south. While northern Germany was barbarian, is Protestant, and assaults life aggressively, southern Germany was Roman, is Catholic, and enjoys a more relaxed tempo of life. The American image of Germany is beer-and-pretzel Bavaria (probably because that was "our" sector after the war). This historic north-south division is less pronounced these days as Germany becomes a more mobile society. The big chore facing Germany today is integrating the wilted economy of what was East Germany into the powerhouse economy of the West. This monumental task has given the West higher taxes (and second thoughts).

Germany's tourist route today—Rhine, Romantic Road, Bavaria—was yesterday's trade route, connecting its most prosperous medieval cities. Germany as a nation is just 120 years old. In 1850, there were 35 independent countries in what is

# Germany

now Germany. In medieval times there were more than 300, each with its own weights, measures, coinage, king, and lotto.

Germans eat lunch and dinner about when we do. Order house specials whenever possible. Pork, fish, and venison are good, and don't miss the bratwurst and sauerkraut. Potatoes are the standard vegetable. Great beers and white wines abound. Go with whatever beer is on tap. Service and tips are included in your restaurant bills. Gummi Bears are local gumdrops with a cult following (beware of imitations—you must see the word "Gummi"), and Nutella is a chocolate-hazelnut spread that may change your life.

# MUNICH
# (MÜNCHEN)

Munich, Germany's most livable and "yuppie" city, is also one of its most historic, artistic, and entertaining. It's big and growing, with a population of more than 1.4 million. Just a little more than a century ago, it was the capital of an independent Bavaria. Its imperial palaces, jewels, and grand boulevards constantly remind visitors that this was once a political and cultural powerhouse. And its recently-bombed-out feeling reminds us that 50 years ago it lost a war.

Orient yourself in Munich's old center with its colorful pedestrian mall. Immerse yourself in Munich's art and history—crown jewels, Baroque theater, Wittelsbach palaces, great art, and beautiful parks. Munich evenings are best spent in frothy beer halls, with their oompah bunny-hopping and belching Bavarian atmosphere. Pry big pretzels from the no-nonsense, buxom beer maids.

## Planning Your Time

Munich is worth two days, including a half-day side trip to Dachau. If necessary, its essence can be nicely captured in a day (walk the center, tour a palace and a museum, and enjoy a beer-filled evening). Those without a car and in a hurry can do the castles of Ludwig as a day trip from Munich by tour. Even Salzburg can be done as a day trip from Munich.

## Orientation (tel. code: 089)

The tourist's Munich is circled by a ring road (which was the town wall) marked by four old gates: Karlstor (near the train station), Sendlinger Tor, Isartor (near the river), and Odeonsplatz (near the palace). Marienplatz is the city center. A great pedestrian-only street cuts this circle in half, running nearly from Karlstor and the train station through Marienplatz to Isartor. Orient yourself along this east-west axis. Most sights are within a few blocks of this people-filled walk. Nearly all the sights and hotels I recommend are within about a 20-minute walk of Marienplatz and each other.

## Tourist Information

Take advantage of the TI in the train station (Monday–Saturday 9:00–20:00, Sunday 10:00–18:00, Bahnhofplatz 2, tel. 089/233-30-256). Have a list of questions ready, confirm sightseeing plans, and pick up brochures, the excellent free city map, and a subway map. Consider buying the 2.50-DM *Monatsprogram* for a German-language list of sights and events calendar. The free twice-weekly magazine, *In München*, lists in German all the movies and entertainment in town (available at TI or any big cinema till supply runs out). The TI can refer you to hotels for a 10-DM fee, but you'll get a better value with my recommended hotels—contact them directly. If the line at the TI is bad, go to EurAide (below). The only essential item is the TI's great city map (also available at Euraide).

**EurAide:** The industrious, eager-to-help EurAide office in the train station is an American whirlpool of travel information ideal for Eurailers and budget travelers (daily in summer 7:45–12:00, 13:00–18:00; closes at 16:00 weekdays, 12:00 on Saturday, and all day Sunday in winter; in Room 3 along track 11, tel. 089/593-889, fax 089/550-3965, Web site: www.cube.net/kmu/euraide.html, e-mail: euraide@compuserve.com). Alan Wissenberg and his staff know your train travel and accommodations questions and have answers in clear American English. The German rail company pays them to help you design your best train travels. They make reservations and sell train tickets, couchettes, and Eurailpasses (for $20 over U.S.A. price, next day service). They can find you a room for a 6-DM fee; and offer the city map and a free newsletter (which gets you the best exchange rate). They sell a "Czech Prague Out" train pass, convenient for Prague-bound Eurailers, which is good for train travel from any Czech border station to Prague and back to any border station within seven days (comes in first, second, and youth versions; to save money, buy in U.S.A.: call 630/420-2343, fax 630/420-2369). Every Wednesday in June and July, EurAide provides an excellent "Two Castle"

tour of Neuschwanstein and Linderhof that includes
Wieskirche (frustrating without a car).

## Arrival in Munich

**By Train:** Munich's train station is a sight in itself—one of
those places that can turn an accountant into a vagabond. For
a quick orientation in the station, use the big wall maps of
the train station, Munich, and Bavaria (through the center
doorway as you leave the tracks on the left). For a quick rest
stop, the Burger King upstairs has toilets as pleasant and
accessible as its hamburgers. Next door, the post office
(which has handy metered phones) is less crowded than the
main P.O. across the street. Sussmann's Internationale Presse
(across from track 24) is great for English-language books,
papers, and magazines, including *Munich Found* (informative
English-speaking residents' monthly, 4 DM). You'll also find
two TIs (the city TI and EurAide, see above). The station is
connected by U-Bahn, S-Bahn, and buses to the rest of the
city (though many hotels listed in this book are within walking distance of the station).

**By Plane:** Munich's airport is an easy 40-minute ride on
the S-Bahn (13 DM or free with train pass), or catch the
Lufthansa airport bus to (or from) the train station (15 DM,
3/hr, 45 min, buy tickets on bus or from Euraide).

## Getting Around Munich

Much of Munich is walkable. To reach sights away from the
city center, use Munich's fine tram, bus, and subway system.
Taxis are expensive and needless.

**By Public Transit:** Subways are called U- or S-Bahns.
Subway lines are numbered (e.g., S-3 or U-5). Eurailpasses are
good on the S-Bahn (actually an underground-while-in-the-
city commuter railway). Regular tickets cost 3.40 DM and are
good for two hours of changes in one direction. For the shortest rides (one or two stops) get the smallest 1.70-DM ticket
(*Kurzstrecke*). The 8-DM all-day pass is a great deal (valid until
6:00 the next day). The Partner Daily Ticket (for 12 DM) is
good for up to two adults, three kids, and a dog. Get a pass,
validate it in a machine, and you have Munich-by-rail for a day
(purchase at tourist offices, subway booths, and in machines at
most stops). The entire system (bus/tram/subway) works on
the same tickets. You must punch your own ticket before

boarding. (Plainclothes ticket-checkers enforce this "honor system," rewarding freeloaders with stiff 60-DM fines.)

**By Bike:** Munich—level and compact, with plenty of bike paths—feels good on two wheels. Bikes can be rented quickly and easily at the train station at Radius Touristik (daily May–mid-October 10:00–18:00, near track 30, tel. 089/596-113). The owner, Englishman Patrick Holder, rents three-speed bikes (5 DM/hour, 25 DM/day, 30 DM/24 hours, 45 DM/48 hours; credit-card imprint, 100 DM, or passport for a deposit). Patrick dispenses all the necessary tourist information (city map, bike routes), including a do-it-yourself bike tour booklet full of information and history (3 DM).

## Helpful Hints

Most Munich sights (including Dachau) are closed on Monday. If you're in Munich on Monday, you could visit the Deutsches Museum, BMW museum, or churches; take a walking tour or bus tour; climb high for city views (below); stroll the pedestrian streets; have lunch at the Viktualien Markt (see Eating below); rent a bike for a spin through Englischer Garden; daytrip to Salzburg or Ludwig's castles; or hoist a beer at Oktoberfest (in fall, below) or any of the many beer gardens open year-round.

## Sights—Central Munich

▲▲**Marienplatz and das Pedestrian Zone**—The glory of Munich will slap your face into a smile as you ride the escalator out of the subway and into the sunlit Marienplatz (Mary's Place): great buildings bombed flat and rebuilt, the ornate facades of the new and old city halls (the Neues Rathaus, built in neo-Gothic style from 1867 to 1910, and the Altes Rathaus), outdoor cafés, and people bustling and lingering like the birds and breeze they share this square with. From here the pedestrian mall (Kaufingerstrasse and Neuhauserstrasse) leads you through a great shopping area, past carnivals of street entertainers, the twin-towering Frauenkirche (built in 1470, rebuilt after World War II), and several fountains, to Karlstor and the train station. Europe's first pedestrian zone enraged shopkeepers when it was built in 1972. Today it is "Munich's living room." Nine thousand shoppers pass through it each hour . . . and the shopkeepers are very happy.

Drop into St. Michael's church. One of the first great

Renaissance buildings north of the Alps, its interior is decorated Baroque and has interesting photos of the bombed-out city center.

The twin onion domes of the 500-year-old Frauenkirche (Church of Our Lady) are the symbol of the city. While the church was destroyed in WWII, the towers survived. Gloriously rebuilt since, it's worth a visit. The church was built Gothic, but money problems meant the domes weren't added until Renaissance times. These domes were inspired by the typical arches of the Venetian Renaissance. And the church domes you'll see all over Bavaria were inspired by these.

Mary's Place is the city center surrounded by the 100-year-old "new town hall" (with the *glockenspiel*), the gray and pointy old town hall, and the oldest church in the city, St. Peter's. The not-very-old glockenspiel "jousts" on Marienplatz daily through the tourist season at 11:00, 12:00, 17:00, and 21:00.

▲▲City Views—The highest viewpoint is from a 350-foot-high perch on top of the Frauenkirche (elevator, 4 DM, 10:00–17:00, closed Sunday). There is also a fine view from the Neues Rathaus (3 DM, elevator from under the Marienplatz glockenspiel, Monday–Friday 9:00–19:00, weekends 10:00–19:00). For a totally unobstructed view, but with no elevator, climb the St. Peter's Church tower just a block away. It's a long climb, much of it with two-way traffic on a one-way staircase, but the view is dynamite (2.50 DM, Monday–Saturday 9:00–18:00, Sunday 10:00–18:00). Try to be two flights from the top when the bells ring at the top of the hour (and when your friends ask you about your trip, you'll say, "What?"). The church, built upon the hill where the first monks founded the city in the 12th century, has a fine interior, with photos of the WWII bomb damage on a column near the entrance.

▲▲Residenz—For a long hike through rebuilt corridors of gilded imperial Bavarian grandeur, tour the family palace of the Wittelsbachs, who ruled Bavaria for more than 700 years (6 DM, Tuesday–Sunday 10:00–16:30, closed Monday, enter on Max-Joseph Platz, 3 blocks from Marienplatz). The Schatzkammer (treasury) shows off a thousand years of Wittelsbach crowns and knickknacks (same hours, another 6 DM from the same window). Vienna's palace and jewels are better, but this is Bavaria's best.

## Munich Center

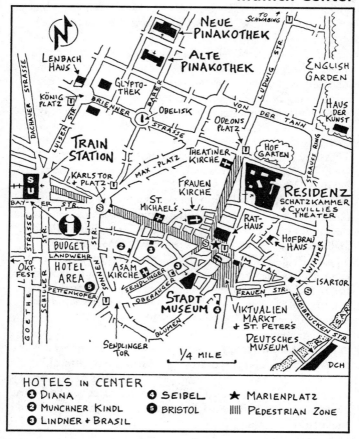

HOTELS IN CENTER
- ❶ DIANA
- ❷ MUNCHNER KINDL
- ❸ LINDNER + BRASIL
- ❹ SEIBEL
- ❺ BRISTOL
- ★ MARIENPLATZ
- ‖‖‖ PEDESTRIAN ZONE

▲**Cuvillies Theater**—Attached to the Residenz, this national theater designed by Cuvillies is dazzling enough to send you back to the days of divine monarchs (3 DM, Monday–Saturday 14:00–17:00, Sunday 10:00–17:00).

▲▲**Münchner Stadtmuseum**—This Munich city museum is a pleasant surprise. Exhibits include life in Munich through the centuries (including WWII) illustrated in paintings, photos, models, historic puppets, and carnival gadgets; a huge collection of musical instruments from around the world; old photography; and a medieval armory. No crowds, bored and

playful guards (5 DM, 7.50 DM for families, Tuesday–Sunday
10:00–17:00, Wednesday until 20:30, closed Monday; 3 blocks
off Marienplatz at St. Jakob's Platz 1, a fine children's playground faces the entry).

▲▲**Alte Pinakothek**—Bavaria's best collection of paintings is
slated to reopen in August of 1998. If it doesn't happen on
schedule, its top masterpieces will still be displayed in the
neighboring Neue Pinakothek. This is art concentrate, a
tourist's dream-come-true, with works by Fra Angelico, Botticelli, da Vinci, Raphael, Dürer, Rubens, Rembrandt, El Greco,
Goya, Monet, and Renoir all in a row (7 DM, Tuesday and
Thursday 10:00–20:00, Wednesday and Friday–Sunday
10:00–17:00, closed Monday, U-2 to Königsplatz or tram #27,
tel. 089/238-05195).

▲**Haus der Kunst**—Built by Hitler as a temple of Nazi art, this
bold and fascist building now houses modern art, much of which
the Führer censored. It's a fun collection—Kandinsky, Picasso,
Dalí, and much more from this century (6 DM, Tuesday–
Sunday 10:00–17:00, closed Monday, Prinzregentenstrasse 1).

**Bayerisches Nationalmuseum**—An interesting collection of
Riemenschneider carvings, manger scenes, traditional living
rooms, and old Bavarian houses (3 DM, Tuesday–Sunday
9:30–17:00, closed Monday; tram #20 or bus #53 or #55 to
Prinzregentenstrasse 3).

▲**Deutsches Museum**—Germany's answer to our Smithson-
ian Institution has everything of scientific and technical interest, from astronomy to zymurgy. With 10 miles of exhibits,
even those on roller skates will need to be selective. Technical
types enjoy lots of hands-on gadgetry, a state-of-the-art
planetarium, and an IMAX theater (10 DM, daily 9:00–17:00,
self-serve cafeteria, S-Bahn to Isartorplatz, tel. 089/217-9433).
Save this for a Monday, when virtually all of Munich's museums are closed.

**Schwabing**—Munich's artsy, bohemian university district, or
"Greenwich Village," has been called "not a place but a state of
mind." All I experienced was a mental lapse. The bohemians
run the boutiques. I think the most colorful thing about
Schwabing is the road leading back downtown. U-3 or U-6
will take you to the Münchener-Freiheit Center if you want to
wander. Most of the jazz and disco joints are near Occam-
strasse. The Haidhausen neighborhood (U-Bahn: Max Weber
Platz) is becoming the "new Schwabing."

▲**Englischer Garden**—Munich's "Central Park," the largest on the Continent, was laid out in 1789 by an American. There's a huge beer garden near the Chinese Pagoda. Caution: While a new local law requires sun-worshipers to wear clothes on the tram, this park is sprinkled with nude sunbathers. A rewarding respite from the city, it's especially fun on a bike under the summer sun (bike rental at train station).

**Asam Church**—Near the Stadtmuseum, this private church of the Asam brothers is a gooey, drippy masterpiece by Bavaria's top two Rococonuts, showing off their popular Baroque-concentrate style. A few blocks away, the small Damenstift Church has a sculptural rendition of the Last Supper so real you feel you're not alone (at intersection of Altheimer Ecke and Damenstiftstrasse, a block south of pedestrian street).

## Sights—Outer Munich

▲▲**Nymphenburg Palace**—This royal summer palace is impressive, but if you've already seen the Residenz, it's only mediocre. If you do tour it, don't miss King Ludwig's "Gallery of Beauties"—a room stacked with portraits of Bavaria's loveliest women, according to Ludwig (who had a thing about big noses). The palace park, good for a royal stroll, contains the tiny, more-impressive-than-the-palace Amalienburg hunting lodge, another Rococo jewel by Cuvillies. The sleigh and coach collection (Marstallmuseum) is especially interesting for "Mad" Ludwig fans (8 DM for everything, less for individual parts; Tuesday–Sunday 9:00–12:00 and 13:00–17:00, closed Monday, shorter hours October–March, use the little English guidebook; reasonable cafeteria; U-1 to Rotkreuzplatz, then tram or bus #12, tel. 089/179-080).

**BMW Museum**—The BMW headquarters, located in a striking building across the street from the Olympic Grounds, offers a good museum popular with car buffs (5.50 DM, daily 9:00–17:00, last ticket sold at 16:00, ask about their rare factory tours, closed much of August, U-3 to the last stop: Olympic, tel. 089/382-23-307).

▲**Olympic Grounds**—Munich's great 1972 Olympic stadium and sports complex is now a lush park offering a tower (5 DM, commanding but so high it's a boring view from 820 feet, 8:00–24:00, last trip 23:30), an excellent swimming pool (5 DM, 7:00–22:30, Monday from 10:00, Thursday closed at 18:00), a good look at its striking "cobweb" style of architecture, and plenty of sun, grass, and picnic potential. Take U-3 to Olympiazentrum direct from Marienplatz.

## Tours of Munich

**Walking Tours**—Original Munich Walks, run by the reputable people who started Berlin Walks, offers two tours: an introduction to the old town and "Infamous Third Reich Sites" (both tours are 15 DM, 2.5 hrs, tel. 0177-227-5901, e-mail: 106513.3461@compuserve.com). The old town tour starts daily at 10:00 (also at 15:00 May–October) and the Third Reich tour is offered at 10:00 Monday through Thursday and Saturday, June through October (less off-season). Both tours depart from the Euraide office (track 11) in the train station. There's no need to register; just show up. Bring along any type of Munich public transport ticket (like a Kurzstrecke) or buy one from your guide.

Radius-Turistik offers a wide variety of tours and guides (tel. 089/4366-0383, at train station). Renate Suerbaum is a good local guide (140 DM for two-hour walking tour, tel. 089/283-374).

**City Bus Tour**—Panorama Tours offers one-hour city orientation bus tours (17 DM; daily at 10:00, 11:30, 14:30, and 16:00; fewer off-season; near the train station, Arnulfstrasse 8, tel. 089/591-504).

## Oktoberfest

When King Ludwig I had a marriage party in 1810, it was such a success that they made it an annual bash. These days the Oktoberfest lasts 16 days (Sept. 19–Oct. 4 in 1998), ending with the first full weekend in October. It starts (usually on the third Saturday in September) with an opening parade of more than 6,000 participants and fills eight huge beer tents with about 6,000 people each. A million gallons of beer later, they roast the last ox.

It's crowded, but if you arrive in the morning (except Friday or Saturday) and haven't called ahead for a room, the TI can normally find you a place. The fairground, known as the Wies'n (a few blocks south of the train station), erupts in a frenzy of rides, dancing, and strangers strolling arm-in-arm down rows of picnic tables while the beer god stirs tons of beer, pretzels, and wurst in a bubbling caldron of fun. The three-loops roller coaster must be the wildest on earth (best before the beer-drinking).

During the fair, the city functions even better than normal, and it's a good time to sightsee even if beer-hall rowdiness isn't your cup of tea. The Fasching carnival time (early January–mid-February) is nearly as crazy. And the Oktoberfest grounds are set up for a mini-Oktoberfest to celebrate spring for the two weeks around May Day.

## Sights—Near Munich

**Castle Tours**—Two of King Ludwig's castles, Neuschwanstein and Linderhof, are an easy day trip by tour. Without a tour, only Neuschwanstein is easy (two hours by train to Füssen, ten-minute bus ride to Neuschwanstein). Panorama Tours offers all-day bus tours of the two castles (79 DM, castle admissions not included, near the train station, Arnulfstrasse 8, tel. 089/591-504). On Wednesdays in June and July, EurAide operates an all-day train/bus Neuschwanstein–Linderhof–Wies Church day tour (70 DM, 55 DM with a train pass, admissions not included, tel. 089/593-889), and also sells tickets for Panorama's castle tours (above) at a discount to railpass or ISIC holders. For info on Ludwig's castles, see the Bavaria and Tirol chapter.

**Berchtesgaden**—This resort, near Hitler's overrated "Eagle's Nest" getaway, is easier as a day trip from Salzburg (just 20 km away). See Salzburg chapter.

▲**Andechs**—Where can you find a fine Baroque church in a rural Bavarian setting at a monastery that serves hearty food and the best beer in Germany, in a carnival atmosphere full of partying locals? The Andechs Monastery, crouching quietly with a big smile between two lakes just south of Munich. Come ready to eat tender chunks of pork, huge and soft pretzels (best I've had), spiraled white radishes, savory sauerkraut, and Andecher monk-made beer that would almost make celibacy tolerable. Everything is served in medieval portions; two people can split a meal. Great picnic center offering first-class views and second-class prices (daily 9:00–21:00, TI tel. 08152/5227). To reach Andechs from Munich without a car, take the S-5 train to Herrsching and catch a "Rauner" shuttle bus (hourly) or walk 2 miles from there. Don't miss a stroll up to the church, where you can sit peacefully and ponder the striking contrasts a trip through Germany offers. . . .

▲▲**Dachau**—Dachau was the first Nazi concentration camp (1933). Today it's the most accessible camp to travelers and a

## Munich Area

very effective voice from our recent but grisly past, warning and pleading "Never Again," the memorial's theme. This is a valuable experience and, when approached thoughtfully, well worth the trouble. In fact, it may change your life. See it. Feel it. Read and think about it. After this most powerful sightseeing experience, many people gain more respect for history and the dangers of not keeping tabs on their government.

Upon arrival, pick up the mini-guide and note when the next documentary film in English will be shown (25 minutes, normally shown at 11:30 and 15:30). Both the museum and the movie are exceptional. Notice the Expressionist fascist-inspired art near the theater, where you'll also find English books, slides, and a WC. Outside, be sure to see the reconstructed barracks and the memorial shrines at the far end (Tuesday–Sunday 9:00–17:00, closed Monday). It's a 45-minute trip from downtown Munich: take S-2 (direction: Petershausen) to Dachau then, from the station, catch bus #724 or #726, Dachau-Ost, to Gedenkstätte (the camp). The two-zone 6.80-DM ticket covers the entire trip (one-way); with a train pass, just pay for the bus (1.80 DM one-way). If you're driving, follow Dachauerstrasse from downtown Munich to Dachau-

# Dachau

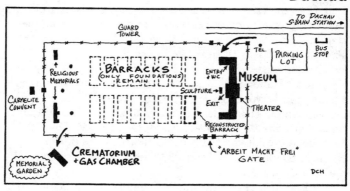

Ost. Then follow the KZ-Gedenkstätte signs. The town of Dachau (TI tel. 08131/84566) is more pleasant than its unfortunate image.

## Sleeping in Munich
**(1.7 DM = about $1, tel. code: 089)**
Sleep Code: **S**=Single, **D**=Double/Twin, **T**=Triple, **Q**=Quad, **b**=bathroom, **t**=toilet only, **s**=shower only, **CC**=Credit Card (**V**isa, **M**asterCard, **A**mex). English is nearly always spoken, unless otherwise noted. All prices include breakfast and increase with conventions and festivals. The cheapest rooms with no showers usually charge a few marks for one down the hall.

There are no cheap beds in Munich. Youth hostels strictly enforce their 26-year-old age limit, and side-tripping in is a bad value. But there are plenty of decent, moderately priced rooms. I've listed places in three areas: within a few blocks of the Hauptbahnhof (central train station), in the old center, and near the Deutsches Museum. Munich is packed during Oktoberfest (late September–early October) and room prices can triple. Call ahead and reserve one of my recommendations.

### Sleeping near the Train Station
Budget hotels (90-DM doubles, no elevator, shower down the hall) cluster in the area immediately south of the station. It's seedy after dark (erotic cinemas, barnacles with lingerie tongues, men with moustaches in the shadows) but dangerous only to those in search of trouble. Still, I've listed places in

more polite neighborhoods, generally a five- or ten-minute walk from the station and handy to the center. Places are listed in order of proximity to the station. Those farthest from the station are the most pleasant. The nearest Laundromat is at Paul-Heyse Strasse 21, near the intersection with Landswehrstrasse (daily 6:00–22:00, 8-DM wash and dry).

**Hotel Haberstock**, less than a block from the station, is homey, a little worn, old-fashioned, and relatively quiet. It's a classic example of an older European hotel (S-58–72 DM, Ss-82 DM, Sb-102 DM, D-110 DM, Ds-130 DM, Db-170 DM, good breakfast, CC:VMA, Schillerstrasse 4, 80336 Munich, tel. 089/557-855, fax 089/550-3634). Ask about week-end and winter discounts.

**4 You München**, my only listing north of the station, is a newly opened hotel and hostel for travelers of any age. The hotel rooms are frayed but comfortable, in an unrenovated part of the building (Sb-79 DM, Db-119 DM, extra bed-49 DM). In the hostel, people over 26 pay an elder tax of 15 percent (regular prices: a bed in ten-bed room-24 DM, in four- to eight-bed room-29 DM, in D-38 DM, in S-54 DM, sheets-5 DM, no membership card required). Breakfast, not included for hostel guests, costs 7.50 DM (elevator, handicapped facilities available, CC:V, 1 block north of station, Hirtenstrasse 18, 80335 Munich, tel. 089/552-1660, fax 089/5521-6666). Web site: www.the4you.de, e-mail: info@the4you.de).

**Hotel Europäischer Hof München** is a big hotel with fine rooms and cable TV (S-88 DM, Sb-122 DM, D-108 DM, Db-138 DM, Bayerstrasse 31, 80000 Munich, tel. 089/551-510, fax 089/5515-1222, e-mail: heh_munich@compuserve.com).

**Hotel Odeon** offers a combination of decent neighborhood, comfort, and price with a fine buffet breakfast and non-smoking rooms (Sb-95 DM, Db-130 DM, Tb-160 DM, 15-DM garage, elevator, CC:VMA, Goethestrasse 26, from the station walk 2 blocks down Goethestrasse, tel. 089/539-585, fax 089/550-4383).

**Jugendhotel Marienherberge** is a pleasant, friendly convent offering the best cheap beds in town to young women only (25-year age limit can flex upward a couple of years, S-40 DM, 35 DM per bed in D and T, 30 DM per bed in four- to seven-bed rooms, non-smoking, open 8:00–24:00, a block from the station down Goethestrasse at #9, tel. 089/555-805).

**YMCA (CVJM)**, open to people of all ages and sexes, has

clean, modern rooms (D-86 DM, T-120 DM, a bed in a shared triple-40 DM, those over 26 pay a 15 percent elder tax, free showers, elevator, Landwehrstrasse 13, 80336 Munich, tel. 089/552-1410, fax 089/550-4282, Web site: www.cvjm.org/ muenchen/hotel/, e-mail: muenchen@cvjm.org). Reservations are accepted up to six weeks in advance. The cafeteria offers 6-DM dinners (Tuesday–Friday 18:30–22:00). When the Y is full, they recommend these nearby hotels for cheap beds: **Hotel Pension Luna**, a dumpy building with cheery rooms (S-55 DM, Sb-65 DM, D/twin-80 DM, D-95 DM, Db-110 DM, T-125 DM, Tb-135 DM, lots of stairs, CC:V, Landwehr-strasse 5, tel. 089/597-833, fax 089/550-3761) and **Hotel Pen-sion Erika**, bright as dingy yellow can be (S-70 DM, Ss-80 DM, D-100 DM, Ds-110 DM, Db-130 DM, CC:VMA, Landwehrstrasse 8, tel. 089/554-327).

**Hotel Pension Utzelmann** has huge rooms, especially the curiously cheap room #6. Each lacy room is richly fur-nished. It's near a bakery, in an extremely decent neighbor-hood, a ten-minute walk from the station a block off Sendlinger Tor (S-50 DM, Ss-85 DM, Sb-125 DM, D-90 DM, Ds-110 DM, Db-145 DM, T-125 DM, Ts-150 DM, Tb-175 DM, hall showers-5 DM, Pettenkoferstrasse 6, enter through black iron gate, tel. 089/594-889, fax 089/596-228, Frau Earnst).

**Hotel Bristol**, nearly next door to Utzelmann, has reno-vated, comfortable rooms (Sb-89 DM, Db-129 DM, Tb-155 DM; to get these prices—which are 20–30 DM below the hotel's normal rates—ask for Johannes and mention this book if you call, or show this book if you walk in; non-smoking, hearty buffet breakfast on terrace, bike rental-20 DM/day, free parking, CC:VMA, Pettenkoferstrasse 2, 80336 Munich, one metro stop on U-1 or U-2 from station, tel. 089/595-151, fax 089/591-451). Johannes also has an apartment (45 DM per person, up to four people).

**Hotel Uhland**, a veritable mansion, is a worthwhile splurge (Sb-110 DM, Db-140 DM, Tb-180 DM, huge break-fast, elevator, Internet access, free parking, Uhlandstrasse 1, 80336 Munich, near the Theresienwiese Oktoberfest grounds, ten-minute walk from the station, tel. 089/543-350, fax 089/5433-5250, e-mail: Hotel_Uhland@compuserve.com, SE). Free use of computer, e-mail, and photocopier.

**Pension Westfalia** overlooks the Oktoberfest grounds

from the top floor of a quiet and elegant old building.
Well-run by Peter and Mary Deiritz, this is a great value if you
prefer sanity and personal touches to centrality (S-65 DM,
Sb-90 DM, D-90 DM, Db-110–125 DM, cheaper off-season,
extra bed 25 DM, hallway showers-3 DM, buffet breakfast, elevator, CC:VMA, Mozartstrasse 23, 80336 Munich, easy parking, U-3 or U-6 to Goetheplatz, tel. 089/530-377, fax
089/543-9120). Around the corner, **Pension Schubert** rents
four tidy and simple but elegant rooms (S-50 DM, D-85 DM,
Db-95 DM, Schubertstrasse 1, tel. 089/535-087.

### Sleeping in the Old Center

**Hotel Münchner Kindl** is the most comfortable of my
old-center listings (15 rooms, S-80 DM, Sb-110 DM, D-120
DM, Ds-140 DM, Db-160 DM, Tb-195 DM, Qs-200 DM, no
elevator, easy telephone reservations, CC:VM, 2 blocks off
main pedestrian drag from "Thomas" sign at Damenstiftstrasse
16, 80331 Munich, tel. 089/264-349, fax 089/264-526, run by
Gunter and English-speaking Renate Dittert).

**Pension Lindner** is clean, quiet, and modern, with
pastel-bouquet rooms (S-55 DM, D-95 DM, Ds-120 DM,
Db-135 DM, elevator, Dultstrasse 1, just off Sendlinger
Strasse, 80331 Munich, tel. 089/263-413, fax 089/268-760,
Marion Sinzinger). One floor below, the quirky **Pension
Brasil** isn't as homey, but will do just fine if the Lindner is full
(four Ds-120 DM, a tad smoky, Dulstrasse 1, tel. 089/263-417,
fax 089/267-548, some English spoken).

**Pension Seibel** has cozy rooms and a family atmosphere a
block off the Viktualienmarkt in a fun neighborhood (S-70 DM,
Sb-89 DM, D-99 DM, Db-129 DM, Tb-150 DM, family apartment for up to five people-45 DM each, soft prices, some non-
smoking rooms, big breakfast, no elevator, CC:VMA,
Reichenbachstrasse 8, 80469 Munich, tel. 089/264-043, fax 089/
267-803). You'll get these discounted prices if you call and ask
for Moe or Kirstin and mention this book, or show this book
when you drop in. (They also run the Hotel Siebel at 9 There-
sienhöhe, near the Oktoberfest grounds, tel. 089/540-1420).

### Sleeping near the Deutsches Museum

**Pension Beck** is well-worn and farther away but a good budget
bet (S from 60 DM, D from 90 DM, Db from 120 DM, rooms
for three to five people-42 DM each, free showers; family,

youth, and two-night deals; 50 spacious rooms on five floors with no elevator, east of Isartor near river and Marienplatz, Thierschstrasse 36, take streetcar #17 direct from station or any S-Bahn and get off at Isartor, tel. 089/220-708, fax 089/220-925).

American **Audrey Bauchinger** rents quiet, pleasant rooms (though some are cramped) and spacious apartments east of the Deutsches Museum in a quiet residential area (Ss-45 DM, D-75 DM, one D with private bath across hall-125 DM, Ds-80–105 DM, spacious Db/Tb with kitchenette-160 DM/200 DM, no breakfast included, CC:VMA accepted at 5 percent charge, Zeppelinstrasse 37, 81669 Munich, tel. 089/488-444, fax 089/489-1787, e-mail: 106437.3277@compuserve.com). From the station, take any S-bahn to Marienplatz, then bus #52 to Schweigerstrasse.

### Hostels and Cheap Beds

Munich's youth hostels charge 19 to 29 DM including breakfast (sheets-5 DM) and strictly limit admission to YH members who are under 27. **Burg Schwaneck Hostel** is a renovated castle (30 minutes from the center, S-7 to Pullach, then walk ten minutes to Burgweg 4, tel. 089/793-0643).

Munich's **International Youth Camp Kapuzinerhölzl** (a.k.a. "The Tent") offers 400 places on the wooden floor of a huge circus tent with a mattress, blankets, good showers, and free tea in the morning for 13 DM to anyone under 25 (flexible). Open late June through August, it's a fun experience—kind of a cross between a slumber party and Woodstock (if anyone under 25 knows what that was). Call 089/141-4300 (recorded message before 17:00) before heading out. No curfew. Cool ping-pong-and-frisbee atmosphere throughout the day. Take tram #17 from the train station to Botanischer Garden (direction: Amalienburgstrasse), and follow the youthful crowd down Franz-Schrankstrasse to the big tent. This is near the Nymphenburg Palace. There is a theft problem, so sleep with your backpack or bring a lock and use one of the lockers.

## Eating in Munich

Munich's most memorable budget food is in the beer halls. You have two basic choices: famous touristy places with music or mellower beer gardens with Germans.

The touristy ones have great beer, reasonable food, live music, and a central location. Germans go there for the entertainment—to sing "Country Roads," see how Texas girls party, and watch salarymen from Tokyo chug beer. The music-every-night atmosphere is thick; the fat and shiny-leather bands even get church mice to stand up and conduct three-quarter time with breadsticks. Meals are inexpensive (for a light 10-DM meal, I like the local favorite, *Schweinswurst mit Kraut*); huge, liter beers called *ein Mass* (or *"ein* pitcher" in English) are 10 DM; white radishes are salted and cut in delicate spirals; and surly beermaids pull mustard packets from their cleavages. You can order your beer *helles* (light, what you'll get if you say *"ein* beer"), *dunkel* (dark), or *Radler* (half lemonade, half light beer). Notice the vomitoriums in the WC.

The most famous beer hall, the **Hofbräuhaus**, is the most touristy (daily 9:30–24:00, Platzl 6, near Marienplatz, tel. 089/221-676, music for lunch and dinner). But check it out; it's fun to see 200 Japanese people drinking beer in a German beer hall. (They have a gimmicky folk evening upstairs in the *Festsaal* nightly at 19:00, 8 DM, tel. 089/290-13-610, food and drinks are sold from the same menu.) The tiny **Strudelstube**, less than a block south of the Hofbräuhaus, offers a rainbow array of strudel-to-go (daily 10:00–22:00, Orlandstrasse 4).

**Weisses Bräuhaus** is more local and features the region's fizzy "wheat beer" (daily 8:00–24:00, Tal 10, between Marienplatz and Isartor). Hitler met with fellow fascists here in 1920 when his Nazi party had yet to ferment. **Augustiner Beer Garden** is a sprawling haven for local beer-lovers on a balmy evening (10:00–23:00, across from the train tracks, three loooong blocks from the station, away from the center, on Arnulfstrasse 52). Upstairs in the tiny **Jodlerwirt** is a woodsy, smart-alecky, yodeling kind of pub (opens at 18:00, closed Sunday, Altenhofstrasse 4, between the Hofbräuhaus and Marienplatz). For a classier evening stewed in antlers and fiercely Bavarian, eat under a tree or inside at the **Nürnberger Bratwurst Glöckl am Dom** (daily 9:30–24:00, 20-DM dinners, Frauenplatz 9, at the rear of the twin-domed cathedral, tel. 089/220-385). Similarly stylish is the **Ratskeller Weinstuben**, with zither or *Akkordeon* music (daily 10:00–24:00, on Marienplatz, enter behind Rathaus and descend into the cellar, tel. 089/220-313). Locals enjoy the **Altes Hackerhaus** for traditional Bayerischer fare (Sendlingerstrasse 14, tel. 089/260-5026). On Marianplatz, the **Dom** has cheap 12-DM meals.

For outdoor atmosphere and a cheap meal, spend an evening at the Englischer Garden's **Chinesischer Turm** (Chinese Pagoda) **Biergarten.** You're welcome to BYO food and grab a table or buy from the picnic stall (*Brotzeit*) right there. Don't bother to phone ahead: they have 6,000 seats. For similar BYOF atmosphere right behind Marienplatz, eat at **Viktualien Markt's** beer garden. Lunch or dinner here taps you into about the best budget eating in town. Countless stalls surround the beer garden and sell wurst, sandwiches, produce, and so on. This BYOF tradition goes back to the days when monks were allowed to sell beer but not food. To picnic, choose a table without a tablecloth. This is a good place to grab the most typical meal in town: *Weisswurst* (white sausage) with *süss* (sweet) mustard, a salty pretzel, and *Weissbier.* **Suppenkuche** is fine for a small, cozy, sit-down lunch (soup kitchen, 6–9 DM soup meals, in Viktualien Markt near intersection of Frauenkirche and Reichenbachstrasse, everyone knows where it is).

For an easy (though not cheap) cafeteria meal, try **Marche** on Neuhauser pedestrian street, across from St. Michael's church (daily 8:00–23:00). Downstairs you get a card; as you load your tray, your card is stamped—pay after you eat.

The crown in its emblem indicates that the royal family assembled its picnics in the historic, and expensive **Alois Dallmayr** delicatessen at Dienerstrasse 14, behind the Rathaus (Monday–Friday 9:00–18:30, Saturday 9:00–16:00, closed Sunday). Explore this dieter's purgatory, put together a royal picnic, and eat it in the nearby Hofgarten. To save money, browse at Dallmayr's but buy in the basement supermarkets of the Kaufhof stores across Marienplatz or at Karlsplatz.

## Transportation Connections—Munich

Munich is a super transportation hub (one reason it was the target of so many WWII bombs).

**By train to: Füssen** (10/day, 2 hrs, the 8:53 departure is good for a Neuschwanstein castle day trip), **Berlin** (6/day, 8 hrs), **Würzburg** (hrly, 3 hrs), **Frankfurt** (14/day, 3.5 hrs), **Salzburg** (12/day, 2 hrs), **Vienna** (4/day, 5 hrs), **Venice** (2/day, 9 hrs), **Paris** (3/day, 9 hrs), **Prague** (3/day, 7–10 hrs), and just about every other point in western Europe. Munich is three hours from **Reutte** (hrly, 3 hrs, transfer in Garmish).

# BAVARIA
# AND TIROL

Two hours south of Munich, between Germany's Bavaria and Austria's Tirol, is a timeless land of fairy-tale castles, painted buildings shared by cows and farmers, and locals who still yodel when they're happy.

In Germany's Bavaria, tour "Mad" King Ludwig's ornate Neuschwanstein Castle, Europe's most spectacular. Stop by the Wies Church, a textbook example of Bavarian Rococo bursting with curly curlicues, and browse through Oberammergau, Germany's wood-carving capital and home of the famous *Passion Play*. In Austria's Tirol, hike to the Ehrenberg ruined castle, scream down a nearby ski slope on an oversized skateboard, then catch your breath for an evening of yodeling and slap-dancing.

In this chapter I'll cover Bavaria first, then Tirol. Austria's Tirol is easier and cheaper than touristy Bavaria. My favorite home base for exploring Bavaria's castles is actually in Austria, in the town of Reutte. Füssen, in Germany, is a handier home base for train travelers.

## Planning Your Time

While locals come here for a week or two, the typical speedy American traveler will find two days' worth of sightseeing. With a car and some time you could enjoy the more remote corners, but the basic visit ranges anywhere from a long day trip from Munich to a three-night, two-day visit. If the weather's good and you're not going to Switzerland, be sure to ride a lift to an Alpine peak.

A good schedule for a one-day circular drive from Reutte is: 7:30-breakfast; 8:15-depart; 8:45-arrive at Neuschwanstein, park and hike to the castle for a tour, possible visit to Hohenschwan-

## Highlights of Bavaria and Tirol

gau; 12:00-drive to the Wies Church (20-minute stop) and on to
Oberammergau for a stroll and lunch; 14:00-drive to Linderhof;
14:30-tour Linderhof; 16:30-drive along Plansee back into Austria; 17:30-back at hotel; 19:00-dinner at hotel and perhaps a
folk evening. In peak season you might arrive later at Linderhof
to avoid the crowds. The next morning you could stroll Reutte,
hike to the Ehrenberg ruins, and ride the luge on your way to
Innsbruck, Munich, Venice, Switzerland, or wherever.

## Getting Around Bavaria and Tirol

**By Car:** This region is ideal by car. All the sights are within an
easy 60-mile loop from Reutte or Füssen.

   **By Train and Bus:** It's frustrating by train. Local bus

service in the region is spotty for sightseeing. Without wheels, Reutte, the luge ride, and Wies Church are probably not worth the trouble. Füssen (with a two-hour train ride to and from Munich every hour, transfer in Buchloe) is 3 miles from Neuschwanstein Castle with easy bus and bike connections. Oberammergau (hourly two-hour trains from Munich with one change) has decent bus connections to nearby Linderhof Castle. Oberammergau to Füssen is a pain.

**By Tour:** If you're interested only in Bavarian castles, consider an all-day organized bus tour of the Bavarian biggies as a side trip from Munich (see Munich chapter).

**By Bike:** This is great biking country. Many train stations (including Reutte) and many hotels rent bikes for about 15 DM a day (tandems for 25 DM).

**By Thumb:** Hitchhiking, always risky, is a slow-but-possible way to connect the public transportation gaps.

## FÜSSEN, GERMANY

Füssen has been a strategic stop since ancient times. Its main street sits on the Via Claudia Augusta, which crossed the Alps (over Brenner Pass) in Roman times. The town was the southern terminus of the medieval trade route known among 20th-century tourists as the "Romantic Road." Dramatically situated under a renovated castle on the lively Lech River, Füssen just celebrated its 700th birthday.

Unfortunately, in the summer it's entirely overrun by tourists. Traffic can be exasperating, but by bike or on foot it's not bad. Off-season, the town is a jester's delight.

Apart from Füssen's cobbled and arcaded town center, there's little real sightseeing. The striking-from-a-distance castle houses a boring picture gallery. The mediocre city museum in the monastery below the castle exhibits lifestyles of 200 years ago and the story of the monastery, and offers displays on the development of the violin for which Füssen was famous (3 DM, Tuesday–Sunday 11:00–16:00, closed Monday, explanations in German only). Halfway between Füssen and the border (as you drive, or a woodsy walk from the town) is the Lechfall, a thunderous waterfall with a handy potty stop.

### Orientation (tel. code: 08362)

Füssen's train station is a few blocks from the TI, the town center (a cobbled shopping mall), and all my hotel listings.

**Tourist Information:** The TI has a free room-finding service (look for Kurverwaltung, Monday–Friday 8:00–12:00 and 14:00–18:00, weekends 10:00–12:00, shorter hours off-season and closed Sunday, tel. 08362/93850, fax 08362/938-520). After hours, try the little self-service info pavilion, near the front of the TI. It dispenses Füssen maps for 1 DM.

**Arrival in Füssen:** Exit left as you leave the train station and walk a few straight blocks to the center of town and the TI.

**Bike Rental:** Rad Zucherl, nearly next door to the train station, rents road bikes for 14 DM/day (passport number for deposit, Monday–Friday 9:00–12:00 and 14:00–18:00, Saturday 9:00–12:00, mountain bikes also available, Rupprechtstrasse 8).

## Sights—Bavaria, near Füssen

(These are listed in driving order from Füssen.)

▲▲▲**Neuschwanstein and Hohenschwangau Castles**—The fairy-tale castle Neuschwanstein looks medieval, but it's only about as old as the Eiffel Tower and feels like something you'd see at a home show for 19th-century royalty. It was built (1869–1886) to suit the whims of Bavaria's King Ludwig II and is a textbook example of the Romanticism that was popular in 19th-century Europe.

To beat the crowds, see Neuschwanstein, Germany's most popular castle, by 9:00 or late in the afternoon. The castle is open every morning at 8:30; by 11:00, it's packed. Rushed 35-minute English-language tours are less rushed early. Tours leave regularly, telling the sad story of Bavaria's "mad" king, who drowned under suspicious circumstances at age 41 after bankrupting Bavaria to build his castles. You'll go up and down more than 300 steps through lavish Wagnerian dream rooms, a royal state-of-the-19th-century-art kitchen, the king's gilded-lily bedroom, and his extravagant throne room. You'll see 15 rooms with their original furnishings and fanciful wall paintings. The rest of the castle is unfinished; the king lived here less than 200 days before he died.

After the tour, climb up to Mary's Bridge to marvel at Ludwig's castle, just as Ludwig did. This bridge was quite an engineering accomplishment 100 years ago. From the bridge, the frisky can hike even higher to the "Beware—Danger of Death" signs and an even more glorious castle view. For the most interesting (15-minutes longer and extremely slippery when wet) descent, follow signs to the Pöllat Gorge.

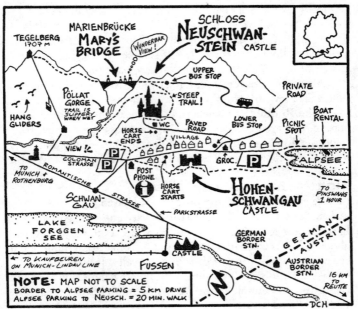

Neuschwanstein

Nearby, the big yellow **Hohenschwangau Castle** was Ludwig's boyhood home. It's more lived-in and historic, and actually gives a better glimpse of Ludwig's life. There are only three ways to get an English tour: Gather 21 people together; wait in line until 20 English speakers join you; or politely ask your German guide to say a few words in English after her German spiels. (Each castle costs 10 DM and is open daily April–September 8:30–17:30, October–March 9:30–16:00, no photography inside, guided tours mandatory.)

The "village" at the foot of the castles lives off the hungry, shopping tourists who come in droves to Europe's "Disney" castle. The big yellow Bräustüberl restaurant by the lakeside parking lot is cheapest, with food that tastes that way. Next door is a little family-run, open-daily souvenir/grocery store with the makings for a skimpy picnic and a microwave fast-food machine. Picnic in the lakeside park or in one of the old-fashioned rent-by-the-hour rowboats. The bus stop, the post/telephone office, and a helpful TI cluster around the main intersection (TI open daily 9:00–18:00; till 17:00 off-season, tel. 08362/819-840).

It's a steep 20- to 30-minute hike to the castle. If you arrive by bus, the quickest (and steepest) way to the castle starts in parking lot D. A more gradual ascent starts at the parking lot near the lake (Parkplatz am Alpsee, best for drivers, all lots cost 6 DM). To minimize hiking, you can take advantage of the shuttle buses (3.50 DM up, 5 DM round-trip; drops you off at Mary's Bridge, a steep ten minutes above the castle) or horse carriages (8 DM up, 4 DM down; slower than walking, stops five minutes short of the castle) that go constantly (watch your step). Signposts and books often refer to these castles in the German, *Königsschlösser.*

To give your castle experience a romantic twist, hike or bike over from Austria (trailhead is at the recommended Hotel Schluxen in Pinswang). When the dirt road forks at the top of the hill, go right (downhill), cross the Austrian-German border (marked by a sign and deserted hut), and follow the paved road to the castles. It's an hour's hike one way (can return by bus) or a great circular bike trip.

Buses run between the Füssen train station and Neuschwanstein (2/hr, ten minutes, 4.80 DM round-trip), and between Füssen and Reutte (5/day, 30 min, never on Sunday; get schedule at either TI).

▲**Tegelberg Gondola**—Just north of Neuschwanstein, hang gliders hover like vultures. They jumped from the top of the Tegelberg Gondola. For 26 DM, you can ride high to the 5,500-foot summit and back down (daily from 9:00, last lift at 17:00, closes earlier in winter, tel. 08362/98360). On a clear day, you get great views of the Alps and Bavaria and the vicarious thrill of watching hang gliders and parasailers leap into airborne ecstasy. From there, it's a steep 2.5-hour hike down to Ludwig's castle.

**Tegelberg Luge**—About 2 kilometers west of Neuschwanstein Castle is a new luge (like a bobsled on wheels; for details see "Sights—Near Reutte" below). The track, made of stainless steel, is often open when rainy weather shuts other luges. It's not as fast or scenic as Bichlbach and Biberweir (below), but it's close and cheap (3 DM per trip, 10 percent less when using six-trip cards, can be crowded on sunny summer weekends, tel. 08362/98360).

▲▲**Wies Church (Wieskirche)**—Germany's greatest Rococo-style church, Wieskirche ("the church in the meadow") is newly restored and looking as brilliant as the day it floated down from heaven. With flames of decoration, over-ripe but bright and bursting with beauty, this church is a divine droplet, a curly curlicue, the final flowering of the Baroque movement. The ceiling depicts the Last Judgment.

This is a pilgrimage church. In the early 1700s, a carving of Christ too graphic to be accepted by that generation's church was the focus of worship in a peasant's private chapel. Miraculously, it wept. And pilgrims came from all around. Bavaria's top Rococo architects, the Zimmerman brothers, were then commissioned to build the Wieskirche, which features the amazing carving above its altar and still attracts countless pilgrims. Take a commune-with-nature-and-smell-the-farm detour back through the meadow to the car park.

Wieskirche (donation requested, daily 8:00–20:00, less off-season) is 30 minutes north of Neuschwanstein. The northbound Romantic Road bus tour stops here for 15 minutes. Füssen-to-Wieskirche buses run several times a day. By car, head north from Füssen, turn right at Steingaden, and follow the signs. If you can't visit Wies, other churches that came out of the same heavenly spray can are Oberammergau's church, Munich's Asam Church, the Würzburg Residenz Chapel, or the splendid Ettal Monastery (free and near Oberammergau).

If you're driving from Wies Church to Oberammergau, you'll cross the Echelsbacher Bridge, arching 250 feet over the Pöllat Gorge. Drivers should let their passengers walk across and meet them at the other side. Any kayakers? Notice the painting of the traditional village woodcarver (who used to walk from town to town with his art on his back) on the first big house on the Oberammergau side, a shop called Almdorf Ammertal. It has a huge selection of overpriced carvings and commission-hungry tour guides.

▲Oberammergau—The Shirley Temple of Bavarian villages and exploited to the hilt by the tourist trade, Oberammergau wears way too much makeup. It's worth a wander only if you're passing through anyway. Browse through the woodcarvers' shops—small art galleries filled with very expensive whittled works—or see folk art at the local Heimat Museum (TI tel. 08822/1021; closed Saturday afternoon and Sunday off-season).

Visit the church, a poor cousin of the one at Wies. This church looks richer than it is. Put your hand on the "marble" columns. If they warm up, they're painted fakes. Wander through the graveyard. Ponder the deaths that two wars dealt

Germany. Behind the church are the photos of three Schneller brothers, all killed within two years in World War II.

Still making good on a deal the townspeople made with God if they were spared devastation by the Black Plague 350 years ago, once each decade Oberammergau performs the *Passion Play*. The next show is in the year 2000, when 5,000 people a day for 100 summer days will attend Oberammergau's all-day dramatic story of Christ's crucifixion. For the rest of this millennium, you'll have to settle for browsing through the theater's exhibition hall (4 DM, daily 9:30–12:00 and 13:30–16:00, closed Monday off-season, tel. 08822/32278), seeing Nicodemus tool around town in his VW, or reading the *Book*.

**Gasthaus zum Stern** is friendly, serves good food (closed Tuesday in low season), and for this tourist town is a fine value (Sb-45 DM, Db-90 DM, closed November and December, Dorfstrasse 33, 82487 Oberammergau, tel. 08822/867, fax 08822/7027). Oberammergau's modern youth hostel is on the river a short walk from the center (20 DM beds, open all year, tel. 08822/4114).

Driving into town from the north, cross the bridge, take the second left, follow "Polizei" signs, and park by the huge grey Passionsspielhaus. Leaving town, head out past the church and turn toward Ettal on Road 23. You're 20 miles from Reutte via the scenic Plansee.

▲▲**Linderhof Castle**—This was Mad Ludwig's "home," his most intimate castle. It's small and comfortably exquisite, good enough for a minor god. Set in the woods, 15 minutes by car or bus (three per day) from Oberammergau, surrounded by fountains and sculpted, Italian-style gardens, it's the only palace I've toured that actually had me feeling envious. Don't miss the grotto (9 DM, daily April–September 9:00–17:30, off-season 10:00–16:00 with lunch break, fountains often erupt on the hour, English tours constantly, tel. 08822/3512). Plan for lots of crowds, lots of walking, and a two-hour stop. From mid-July through August, you can take a bus from Reutte to Linderhof in the morning and return in the afternoon (one-hour trip).

▲▲**Zugspitze**—The tallest point in Germany is a border crossing. Lifts from Austria and Germany go to the 10,000-foot summit of the Zugspitze. Straddle two great nations while enjoying an incredible view. There are restaurants, shops, and telescopes at the summit. The 75-minute trip from Garmisch on the German side costs 74 DM round-trip, with family discounts available (by direct lift or a combo cog-wheel train and cable car ride, tel. 08821/7970). On the Austrian side, from the less crowded Talstation Obermoos, above the village of Erwald, the tram zips you to the top in ten minutes (420 AS or 61 DM round-trip, daily late May–October 8:30–16:30, tel. in Austria 05673/2309). The German ascent is easier for those without a car, but buses do connect the Erwald train station and the Austrian lift about hourly.

## Sleeping in Füssen, Germany
**(1.7 DM = about $1, tel. code: 08362, zip code: 87629)**
Sleep Code: **S**=Single, **D**=Double/Twin, **T**=Triple, **Q**=Quad, **b**=bathroom, **t**=toilet only, **s**=shower only, **CC**=Credit Card (**V**isa, **M**asterCard, **A**mex).

Unless otherwise noted, breakfast is included, hall showers are free, and English is spoken. Prices listed are for one-night stays. Some places give a discount for longer stays. Always ask. Competition is fierce, and off-season prices are soft.

Füssen, 2 miles from Ludwig's castles, is a cobbled, crenelated, riverside oompah treat, but very touristy (notice the sushi bar). It has just about as many rooms as tourists, though, and the TI has a free room-finding service. All places I've listed (except the hostel) are within 2 or 3 blocks of the train station and the town center. They are used to travelers getting in after the Romantic Road bus arrives (20:40) and will hold rooms for a telephone promise.

**Hotel Kurcafé** is deluxe, with spacious rooms and all the modern conveniences, including cable TV and double-paned windows. Prices vary wildly with the season (July and August are sky-high), but the hotel's bakery can enjoyably ruin your budget, even in the off-season (Sb-89–129 DM depending on season, Db from 119–189 DM, third or fourth person pays 30 DM extra, older rooms about 10 DM less, CC:VMA, on the tiny traffic circle a block in front of the train station at Bahnhofstrasse 4, tel. 08362/6369, fax 08362/39424, e-mail: hotel.kurcafe@t-online.de). The attached restaurant has good, reasonable daily specials.

**Hotel Gasthaus zum Hechten** offers all the modern comforts in a friendly, traditional shell right under the Füssen Castle in the old-town pedestrian zone (S-60 DM, Sb-75 DM, D-95 DM, Db-110–120 DM, Tb-150 DM, Qb-180 DM, prices promised with this book in 1998, cheaper off-season and for stays of more than one night, attached popular restaurant,

Ritterstrasse 6, tel. 08362/91600, fax 08362/916099). The sound of the nearby bell tower, ringing four times hourly through the night, is muffled by the hotel's double-paned windows. To get to the hotel from the TI, walk down the pedestrian street and take the second right.

**Gasthof Krone**, a rare bit of pre-glitz Füssen also in the pedestrian zone, has dumpy halls and stairs but bright, cheery, comfy rooms (S-53 DM, D-96 DM, extra bed-48 DM, prices drop 6 DM for two-night stays, CC:VMA, Schrannenplatz 17, tel. 08362/7824, fax 08362/37505). From the TI, head down the pedestrian street and take the first left.

**Hotel Bräustüberl** has clean, bright, newly renovated rooms in a musty old beer-hall-type place (Db-90–110 DM, depending on season, Rupprechtstrasse 5, a block from the station, tel. 08362/7843, fax 08362/38781).

**Haus Peters**, Füssen's best value, is a comfy, smoke-free home renting four rooms, 2 blocks from the station (toward town, second left). Herr and Frau Peters are friendly, speak English, and know what travelers like: a peaceful garden, self-serve kitchen, and good prices (Db-86 DM, Tb-120 DM, Augustenstrasse 5, tel. 08362/7171). The funky, old, ornately furnished **Pension Garni Elisabeth**, in a garden just across the street, exudes an Addams-family friendliness (S-45 DM, D-80–90 DM, Db-100–170 DM, T-120 DM, Tb-150–180 DM, showers-6 DM, Augustenstrasse 10, tel. 08362/6275). Floors creak, dust balls wander, and the piano is never played. Consider the handy American-run **Suzanne's B&B** (D-80 DM, large Ds with balcony and fridge—100 DM for two; 135 DM for three; 160 DM for four; non-smoking, bike rental, backtrack 2 blocks from station, Venetianerwinkel 3, tel. & fax 08362/38485, e-mail: svorbrugg@t-online.de).

**Füssen Youth Hostel**, a fine, Germanly run youth hostel, welcomes travelers under 27 (four- to six-bed rooms, 20 DM for bed and breakfast, 8 DM for dinner, 5.50 DM for sheets, laundry facilities—7 DM/load, non-smoking, Mariahilferstrasse 5, tel. 08362/7754, fax 08362/2770). From the station, backtrack ten minutes along the tracks.

## Sleeping near Neuschwanstein Castle
### (code: 87645 Hohenschwangau)
Inexpensive farmhouse Zimmer (B&Bs) abound in the Bavarian countryside around Neuschwanstein and are a good value.

Look for signs that say "Zimmer Frei" ("room free," or vacancy). The going rate is about 80 DM per double including breakfast. For a Zimmer in a classic Bavarian home within walking distance of Mad Ludwig's place, try **Haus Magdalena** (Ss-48 DM, D-76 DM, Db-87 DM, extra bed-30 DM, free parking; from the castle intersection, about 2 blocks down the road toward Schwangau at Schwangauerstrasse 11, tel. 08362/81126, run by Brumme Family) or **Pension Weiher,** with lots of balconies and a flood-lit Neuschwanstein view (S-35–38 DM, D-77 DM, Db-90 DM, Hofwiesenweg 11, tel. & fax 08362/81161).

For more of a hotel, try **Alpenhotel Meier.** Within walking distance of the castle, in a rural setting, with rooms that have new furnishings and porches, it's a joy (Sb-78 DM, Db-130 DM, extra person-40 DM, easy parking, Schwangauerstrasse 37, tel. 08362/81152, fax 08362/987-028).

## Eating in Füssen

**Infooday** is a clever, modern self-service eatery that sells its hot meals and salad bar by weight and offers English newspapers (Monday–Friday 10:30–18:30, Saturday till 14:30, closed Sunday, 8 DM/filling salad, 12-DM meals; under the Füssen castle in Hotel zum Hechten, Ritterstrasse 6). A couple of blocks away, **Pizza Blitz** offers good take-out or eat-at-counter pizzas and hearty salads for about 8 DM apiece (Monday–Saturday 11:00–23:00, Sunday 12:00–23:00, Luitpoldstrasse 4). For more traditional fare, **Hotel Bräustüberl** (see above) has famous home-brewed beer and a popular kitchen (11:30–14:00 and 16:00– 22:00, closed Sunday evening and all day Monday). For picnicking, try the **Plus** supermarket on the tiny traffic circle a block from the train station (Monday–Friday 8:30–18:30, Saturday 8:00–13:00, closed Sunday, basement level of shopping complex).

## Transportation Connections—Füssen

**To: Neuschwanstein** (2 buses/hr, 10 min, 4.8 DM round-trip; taxis cost 14 DM), **Reutte** (5 buses/day, 30 min, no service on Sunday; taxis cost 35 DM), **Munich** (hrly, 2 hrs, transfer in Buchloe).

**Romantic Road Buses:** The northbound Romantic Road bus departs Füssen at 8:00, and the southbound bus arrives at Füssen at 20:40 (bus stops at train station).

# REUTTE, AUSTRIA
## (12 AS=about $1)
Reutte (ROY-teh, rolled "r"), population 5,500, is a relaxed town, far from the international tourist crowd but popular with Germans and Austrians for its climate. Doctors recommend its "grade 1" air.

Reutte isn't in any other American guidebook. Its charms are subtle. It never was rich or important. Its castle is ruined, its buildings have paint-on "carvings," its churches are full, its men yodel for each other on birthdays, and lately its energy is spent soaking its Austrian and German guests in *gemütlichkeit*. Most guests stay for a week, so the town's attractions are more time-consuming than thrilling. If the weather's good, hike to the mysterious Ehrenberg ruins or ride the luge. For a slap-dancing bang, enjoy a Tirolean folk evening.

## Orientation (tel. code: 05672)
**Tourist Information:** Reutte's helpful TI is a block in front of the train station (Monday–Friday 8:00–12:00 and 13:00–17:00, Saturday 8:30–12:00, tel. 05672/62336 or, from Germany, 0043-5672/62336). Go over your sightseeing plans, ask about a folk evening, pick up a city map, and ask about discounts with the hotel guest cards.

**Arrival in Reutte:** Head straight out of the station 1 long block to the TI. At the TI, turn left to reach the center of town.

**Bike Rental:** The train station rents bikes for 100 AS, mountain bikes for 200 AS (50 AS discount if you have a rail-pass or train ticket).

**Laundry:** Don't ask the TI about a Laundromat. Unless you can infiltrate the local campground, Hotel Maximilian, or Gasthof zum Schluxen (see Sleeping, below), the town has none.

## Sights—Reutte
▲▲**Ehrenberg Ruins**—The brooding ruins of Ehrenberg Castle are a mile outside of Reutte on the road to Lermoos and Innsbruck. This 13th-century rock pile, a great contrast to King Ludwig's "modern" castles, is a super opportunity to let your imagination off its leash. Hike up from the parking lot at the base of the hill; it's a 25-minute walk to the castle for a great view from your own private ruins. (Facing the hill from the parking lot, the steeper trail is to the right, the easy

gravelly road is to the left.) Imagine how proud Count Meinrad II of Tirol (who built the castle in 1290) would be to know that his castle repelled 16,000 Swedish soldiers in the defense of Catholicism in 1632.

The easiest way down is via the small road leading from the gully. The car park, with a café/guest house (closed Wednesday, offers a German-language flyer about the castle), is just off the Lermoos/Reutte road. Reutte is a pleasant one-hour walk away. In Reutte, Café Valier has a wall painting of the intact castle.

**Folk Museum**—Reutte's Heimatmuseum, offering a quick look at the local folk culture and the story of the castle, is more cute than impressive (20 AS, Tuesday–Sunday 10:00–12:00 and 14:00–17:00, closed Monday and off-season, in the Green House on Untermarkt, around the corner from Hotel Goldener Hirsch).

**▲▲Tirolean Folk Evening**—Ask the TI or your hotel if there's a Tirolean folk evening scheduled. About once a week in the summer, Reutte or a nearby town puts on an evening of yodeling, slap-dancing, and Tirolean frolic—usually worth the 80 AS and short drive. Off-season, you'll have to do your own yodeling. There are also weekly folk concerts in the park (ask at TI).

**Swimming**—Plunge into Reutte's Olympic-sized swimming pool to cool off after your castle hikes (60 AS, daily 10:00–21:00, off-season 14:00–21:00 and closed Monday).

**Reuttener Bergbahn**—This mountain lift swoops you high above the tree line to a starting point for several hikes and an Alpine flower park with special paths leading you past countless local varieties.

**Flying and Gliding**—For a major thrill on a sunny day, drop by the tiny airport in Hofen across the river and fly. A small single-prop plane can buzz the Zugspitze and Ludwig's castles and give you a bird's-eye peek at Reutte's Ehrenberg ruins (two people for 30 minutes, 1,350 AS; one hour, 2,700 AS; tel. 05672/63207). Or, for something more angelic, how about *Segelfliegen*? For 500 AS, you get 30 minutes in a glider for two (you and the pilot). Just watching the tow-rope launch the graceful glider like a giant slow-motion rubber-band gun is thrilling (late May–October 11:00–19:00, in good weather only, tel. 05672/71550).

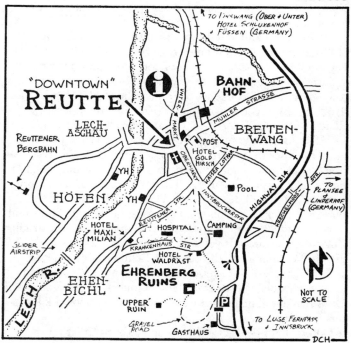

"DOWNTOWN"
REUTTE

BAHN-HOF

TO INNSWANG (OBER & UNTER)
HOTEL SCHLUXENHOF
& FÜSSEN (GERMANY)

LECH-ASCHAU

MUHLER STRASSE

BREITEN-WANG

Reuttener
Bergbahn

POST

YH

HOTEL
GOLD
HIRSCH

POOL

HIGHWAY 314

TO
PLANSEE
&
LINDERHOF
(GERMANY)

HÖFEN

YH

HOTEL
MAXI-
MILIAN

HOSPITAL

CAMPING

GLIDER
AIRSTRIP

KRANKENHAUS STR.

HOTEL
WALDRAST

LECH R.

EHEN-
BICHL

EHRENBERG
RUINS

NOT TO
SCALE

"UPPER"
RUIN

P

GRAVEL
ROAD

GASTHAUS

TO LUGE, FERNPASS
& INNSBRUCK

DCH

## Sights—Tirol, Near Reutte

▲▲**Sommerrodelbahn, the Luge**—Near Lermoos, on the Innsbruck–Lermoos–Reutte road, you'll find two rare and exciting luge courses or *Sommerrodelbahn*. To try one of Europe's great $5 thrills: take the lift up, grab a sled-like go-cart, and luge down. The concrete course banks on the corners, and even a novice can go very, very fast. Most are cautious on their first run and speed demons on their second. (A woman once showed me her journal illustrated with her husband's dried 5-inch-long luge scab. He disobeyed the only essential rule of luging: Keep both hands on your stick.) No one emerges from the course without a windblown hairdo and a smile-creased face. Both places charge a steep 70 AS per run, with five-trip or ten-trip discount cards, and are open weekends from late May and daily from about mid-June through

September or October, weather permitting, from 9:00 until about 17:00. They're closed in wet weather, so call before going out.

**The small and steep luge:** Bichlbach, the first course (100-meter drop over 800-meter course), is 6 kilometers beyond Reutte's castle ruins. Look for a chairlift on the right and exit on the tiny road at the yellow "Riesenrutschbahn" sign (call ahead, tel. 05674/5350, or contact the local TI at 05674/5354). If you're without wheels, catch the train from Reutte to Bichlbach (6/day, 20 min) and walk 1 km to the luge.

**The longest luge:** The Biberwier Sommerrodelbahn, 15 minutes closer to Innsbruck, just past Lermoos in Biberwier (the first exit after a long tunnel), is a better luge and, at 1,300 meters, the longest in Austria. The only drawback is its shorter season (9:00–16:30, tel. 05673/2111, local TI tel. 05673/2922). One or 2 blocks downhill from this luge, behind the Sport und Trachtenstüberl shop, is a wooden church dome with a striking Zugspitze backdrop. If you have sunshine and a camera, don't miss it. Without a car, the bus from Reutte to Biberwier is your best bet (8/day, fewer on Sunday, 45 min; bus stop and posted schedule near Reutte's Hotel Goldener Hirsch on Untermarket). The nearest train station is Lermoos, 4 kilometers from the luge.

▲**Fallerschein**—Easy for drivers and a special treat for those who may have been Kit Carson in a previous life, this extremely remote log-cabin village is a 4,000-foot-high, flower-speckled world of serene slopes and cowbells. Thunderstorms roll down the valley like it's God's bowling alley, but the pint-sized church on the high ground, blissfully simple in a land of Baroque, seems to promise that this huddle of houses will survive and the river and breeze will just keep flowing. The couples sitting on benches are mostly Austrian vacationers who've rented cabins here. Many of them, appreciating the remoteness of Fallerschein, are having affairs.

For a rugged chunk of local Alpine peace, spend a night in the local Matratzenlager Almwirtschaft Fallerschein, run by Kerle Erwin (120 AS per person with breakfast, open—weather permitting—mid-May–October, 27 cheap beds in a very simple loft dorm, meager plumbing, good, inexpensive meals, 6671 Weissenbach Pfarrweg 18, b/Reutte, tel. 05678/5142, rarely answered, and then not in English). It's crowded only on weekends. Fallerschein is at the end of a miserable 2-kilometer fit-for-jeep-or-rental-car-only paved road that looks more closed than it is, near Namlos on the Berwang Road southwest of Reutte.

## Sleeping in Reutte, Austria
### (12 AS = about $1, tel. code: 05672, zip code: 6600)

For fewer crowds, easygoing locals with a contagious love of life, and a good dose of Austrian ambience, those with a car should home-base in nearby Reutte. (To call Reutte from Germany, dial 0043-5672 and the local number.) You'll drive across the border but probably won't even have to stop.

### Hotels

Reutte is popular with Austrians and Germans who come here year after year for a one- or two-week vacation. The hotels are big and elegant, full of comfy, carved furnishings and creative ways to spend so much time in one spot. They take great pride in their restaurants, and the owners send their children away to hotel management schools.

**Hotel Goldener Hirsch**, a grand old hotel renovated with a mod Tirolean Jugendstil flair, has sliding automatic doors, mini-bars, TV with cable in the room, and one lonely set of antlers. The hotel is located right downtown (2 long blocks from the station). For those without a car, this is the most convenient hotel (Sb-540 AS, Db-860 AS, decent attached restaurant, CC:VMA, 6600 Reutte-Tirol, tel. 05672/62508 and ask for Monika or grumpy Helmut, fax 05672/625-087).

**Hotel Maximilian**, up the river a mile or so in the village of Ehenbichl, is a fine splurge that includes the use of bicycles, ping-pong, a children's playroom, and the friendly service of the Koch family. Daughter Gabi speaks fine English. There always seems to be a special event here, and the Kochs host many Tirolean folk evenings (Sb-450 AS, Db-840–880 AS, Tb-1260 AS, cheaper for families, laundry service, far from the train station in the next village, A-6600 Ehenbichl-Reutte, tel. 05672/62585, fax 05672/625-8554, e-mail: maxhotel@ping.at). You can use their laundry service even if you're not staying at the hotel.

**Gutshof zum Schluxen** gets the "remote-old-hotel-in-an-idyllic-setting" award. This working farm offers good food, modern rustic elegance draped in goose down and pastels, and a chance to pet the rabbit. Its picturesque meadow setting will turn you into a dandelion-picker (Sb-460–540 AS, Db-920–1,080 AS, extra person-220 AS, through 1998 only with this book, discounts for stays of at least two nights, excellent breakfast, self-service laundry, bikes free of charge for hotel guests, free parking, free e-mail service, no credit cards but traveler's checks accepted without commission, A-6600 Pinswang-Reutte, between Reutte and Füssen in the village of Unterpinswang, tel. 05677/8903, fax 05677/890-323, e-mail: schluxen@eunet.at). Schluxen is in the village of Pinswang, between Reutte and Füssen.

**Gasthof-Pension Waldrast**, separating a forest and a meadow, is warmly run by the Huter family. It has big rooms like living rooms, many with fine castle views, and it's a good coffee stop if you're hiking into town from the Ehrenberg ruins (640–700 AS per double, 6600 Ehenbichl, on Ehrenbergstrasse, a half-mile out of town toward Innsbruck, past the campground, just under the castle, tel. & fax 05672/62443).

## Zimmer

The tourist office has a list of over 50 private homes that rent out generally elegant rooms with facilities down the hall, pleasant communal living rooms, and breakfast. Most charge 200 AS per person per night, don't like to rent to people staying less than three nights, and speak little if any English. Reservations are nearly impossible for one- or two-night stays. But short stops are welcome if you just drop in and fill in available gaps. The TI can always find you a room when you arrive (free service).

The tiny village of Breitenwang is older and quieter than Reutte and has all the best Zimmer (a 20-minute walk from the Reutte train station: at the post office roundabout, follow Plannseestrasse past the onion dome to the pointy straight dome; unmarked Kaiser Lothar Strasse is the first right past this church). These four places are comfortable, quiet, and kid-friendly, have few stairs, speak some English, and are within 2 blocks of the Breitenwang church steeple: **Inge Hosp** (an old-fashioned place, S-200 AS, D-380 AS, one night OK, includes antlers over the breakfast table, Kaiser Lothar Strasse 36, tel. 05672/62401); her cousins **Walter and Emilie Hosp** across the street (D-380 AS for one night, D-350 AS for two or more, third or fourth person pays 150 AS, Kaiser Lothar Strasse 29, tel. 05672/65377); and **Maria Auer** (D-350 AS, minimum stay two nights, Kaiser Lothar Strasse 25, tel. 05672/67166); and **Helene Haissl** (fine rooms, S-180 AS, D-360 AS, 320 AS for a two-night stay, Planseestrasse 63, tel. 05672/67913). Zimmer charge 15 AS to 20 AS extra for heat in winter—worth it.

## Hostels

Reutte has two excellent little hostels. If you've never hosteled and are curious, try one of these. They accept non-members of any age. The downtown hostel is a minimal place: clean, rarely full, and lacking in personality. It serves no meals but has a members' kitchen (68 AS per bed, open mid-June–late August, a pleasant ten-minute walk from the town center, follow the Jugendherberge signs to the Kindergarten sign, 6600 Reutte, Prof. Dengelstrasse 20, Tirol, tel. 05672/72309).

The homey, newly renovated **Jugendgastehaus Graben** has two to six beds per room and includes breakfast and sheets (160 AS per bed, Db-400 AS, self-service laundry; from downtown Reutte, cross the bridge and follow the road left along the river, about 2 miles from station; A-6600 Reutte-Höfen, Graben 1, tel. 05672/62644, fax 05672/626-444). Frau Reyman keeps the place traditional, clean, and friendly and serves a great 80 AS dinner. No curfew, open all year, bus connection to Neuschwanstein. This is a super value.

## Eating in Reutte

Each of the hotels takes great pleasure in serving fine Austrian food at reasonable prices. Rather than go to a cheap restaurant, I'd order low on a hotel menu. For cheap food, the **Prima** self-serve cafeteria near the station (Monday–Friday 9:00–18:30, Mühler Strasse 20) and the **Metzgerei Storf Imbiss** (better but open only Monday–Friday 8:30–15:00), above the deli across from the Heimatmuseum on Untermarkt Street, are the best in town. For a late dinner, try **Zum Mohren** on the main street (serving until 22:30, across from #31, tel. 05672/2345). **Carina** in Breitenwang is a fine Italian restaurant with decent prices (near Zimmer, Bachweg 17).

## Transportation Connections—Reutte

**To: Füssen** (5 buses/day, 30 min; departures at 7:10, 8:30, 12:10, 13:45, 16:45; returning from Füssen to Reutte at 8:00, 13:10, 15:30, 17:10, 19:02, no service on Sunday, confirm schedule; taxis cost 35 DM), **Linderhof** (1 bus/day, 60 min, mid-July–August only), **Garmisch** (2 trains/hr, 60 min), **Munich** (hrly trains, 3 hrs; transfer in Garmisch).

# BADEN-BADEN AND THE BLACK FOREST

Combine Edenism and hedonism as you explore this most romantic of German forests and dip into its mineral spas.

The Black Forest, or *Schwarzwald* in German, is a range of hills stretching 100 miles north-south along the French border from Karlsruhe to Switzerland. Its highest peak is the 4,900-foot-tall Feldberg. Because of its thick forests, people called it black.

Until this century, the Schwarzwald had been cut off from the German mainstream. The poor farmland drove medieval locals to become foresters, glassblowers, and clock-makers. Strong traditions continue to be woven through the thick dialects and thatched roofs. On any Sunday, you will find *Volksmarches* (group hikes) and traditional costumes coloring the Black Forest.

Popular with German holiday-goers and patients whose doctors have prescribed some serious "R & R," the Black Forest offers clean air, cuckoo clocks, cherry cakes, cheery villages, and countless hiking possibilities.

The area's two biggest tourist traps are the tiny Titisee Lake (not quite as big as its tourist parking lot) and Triberg, a small town filled with cuckoo-clock shops.

In spite of the crowds, the drives are extremely scenic, hiking is *wunderbar*, and the attractions listed below are well worth a visit. The two major (and very different) towns are Baden-Baden in the north and Freiburg in the south. Freiburg may be the Black Forest's capital, but Baden-Baden is Germany's greatest 19th-century spa resort. Stroll through its elegant streets and casino. Grin and bare it for a *Kur* (sauna, massage, and utter restfulness).

# The Black Forest

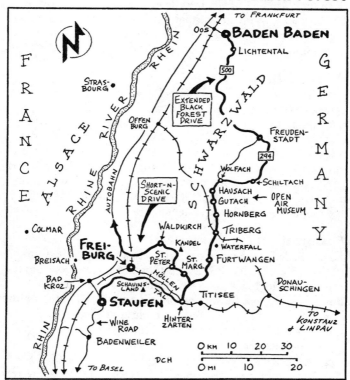

## Planning Your Time

Tour Freiburg, but spend the night in the charming and over-looked village of Staufen. By train Freiburg and Baden-Baden are easy, as is a short foray into the forest from either. With more time, do the small-town forest medley between the two. The region is best by car, with which I'd do the whole cuckoo thing: a night in Staufen, a busy day touring north, and two nights and a relaxing day in Baden-Baden.

A blitz day from Murten or Interlaken (Switzerland) would go like this: 8:30-depart, 11:00-Staufen (change money, buy picnic), 12:30-scenic drive to Furtwangen with a scenic picnic along the way, 2:30-tour clock museum, 15:30-drive to

Gütach, 16:30-tour open-air folk museum, 18:00-drive from
Schwarzwald Hochstrasse into Baden-Baden, 20:00-arrive in
Baden-Baden. With an overnight in Staufen, you could spend
the morning in Freiburg and have a more reasonable schedule
throughout.

# BADEN-BADEN
Of all the high-class resort towns I've seen, Baden-Baden is the
easiest to enjoy in blue jeans and with a picnic. This was the
playground of Europe's high-rolling elite 150 years ago. Royalty and aristocracy would come from all corners to take the
*Kur*—a soak in the curative (or at least they feel that way) mineral waters—and enjoy the world's top casino. Today this town
of 55,000 attracts a more middle-class crowd, both tourists in
search of a lower pulse and Germans enjoying the fruits of
their generous healthcare system.

## Orientation (tel. code: 07221)
Baden-Baden is made for strolling with a poodle. The train
station, in a suburb called Baden-Oos, is 5 kilometers from the
center, but city bus #201 easily connects the station with
downtown. Except for the station and a couple of hotels on the
opposite side of town, everything is clustered within a ten-
minute walk between the baths and the casino.

**Tourist Information:** The TI is behind the fountain on
Augustaplatz 8 (daily 9:30–18:00, less in winter, tel. 07221/
275-200; additional office on B-500 autobahn exit at Schwartz-
waldstrasse 52, longer hours). It has enough recommended
walks and organized excursions to keep even the most energetic vacationers happy.

**Getting Around Baden-Baden:** Only one bus matters.
Bus #201 runs straight through Baden-Baden, connecting its
Oos train station, town center, and the far end of town (runs
every ten minutes; buy 3-DM per person one-ride tickets or
the 8-DM 24-hour pass, good for two people, from the driver).
Tickets are valid for two hours but only in one direction. With
bus #201 you don't need to mess with downtown parking.

## Sights-Sights—Baden-Baden
▲▲**Strolling Lichtentaler Allee**—Bestow a royal title on
yourself and promenade down the famous Lichtentaler Allee, a
pleasant 1.5-mile lane through a park along the babbling Oos

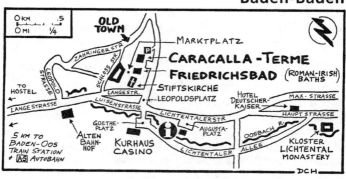

River and past old mansions, hearty oaks, and exotic trees (lit until 22:00). At the mini-golf and tennis courts, cross the bridge into the free Art Nouveau rose garden (*Gönneranlage*, more than 100 labeled kinds of roses, great lounge chairs). Either walk the whole length and all the way back (try the riverside path), or take city bus #201 one way (runs between downtown and Klosterplatz, near the monastery). Many bridges cross the river, making it easy to shortcut to bus #201 any time.

For a longer walk, consider riding the cogwheel Merkur Bergbahn (take bus #204 or #205 from Leopoldsplatz to the end of the line and catch 4-DM train up, tel. 07221/277-614) to the 2,000-foot summit of Merkur and following the trails to the monastery and then along Lichtentaler Allee into town.

▲▲**Casino and Kurhaus**—The impressive building called the Kurhaus is wrapped around a grand casino. Built in the 1850s in wannabe-French style, this is—according to Marlene Dietrich—the most beautiful casino anywhere. Inspired by the Palace of Versailles, filled with rooms honoring French royalty who never set foot in the place, and paying the state 90 percent of its $75-million-a-year earnings, this is the toast of Baden-Baden, or at least its bread and butter. Even if you don't gamble, tour the place. It's open for gambling from 14:00 to 2:00, baccarat until 6:00 (5-DM entry, 5-DM minimum bet, no jeans or tennis shoes, tie and coat required and rentable, 20 DM). A third of those who go in just observe; you don't need to gamble.

The casino gives 30-minute German-language tours of its Versailles-rivaling interior every morning from 9:30 to 12:00

(5 DM, two per hour, last one at 11:30, tel. 07221/21060, call to see if there's a freeloadable English tour scheduled, pick up the paltry English brochure). Even peasants in T-shirts, shorts, and thongs are welcome on tours.

The Baden-Baden orchestra plays most days in the Kurhaus garden in front of the casino (free, usually at 16:00).

The other casino in town, Alter Bahnhof, is a dreary roomful of one-armed bandits—not worth the 2-DM admission. It will move in 1998 when the building is converted into a theater.

▲**Trinkhalle**—More aristocratic Old World elegance surrounds the casino and Kurhaus. Drop by the Trinkhalle next door for its 300-foot-long entrance hall decorated with springwater nymphs and romantic legends. Walk under the Corinthian pillars and grab a free glass of the mineral water. Enjoy the latest *Herald Tribune* in the reading room on the side of the hall nearest the casino.

▲▲▲**Roman-Irish Bath (Friedrichsbad)**—The highlight of most Baden-Baden visits is a sober two-hour ritual called the Roman-Irish Bath. Friedrichsbad, on Römerplatz 1, pampered the rich and famous in its elegant surroundings when it opened 120 years ago. Today this steamy world of marble, brass columns, tropical tiles, herons, lily pads, and graceful nudity welcomes gawky tourists as well as locals.

For 48 DM you get up to three hours and the works (36 DM without the eight-minute massage; at some hotels, you can buy a reduced-admission ticket). The routine seems complex. Pick up and read the blue English brochure when you enter, then simply follow the numbers and arrows from room to room. The routine is written on the walls with recommended time and a description in English: take a shower; grab a towel and put on plastic slippers before hitting the warm-air bath for 15 minutes and the hot-air bath for five minutes; shower; soap-brush massage—rough, slippery, and finished with a spank; play Gumby in the shower; lounge under sunbeams and caryatids in one of several different thermal steam baths; glide like a swan under a divine dome in a royal pool (the one "mixed" area); cold plunge; dry in warmed towels; and, thus cocooned, lay clean and thinking prenatal thoughts on a bed for 30 minutes in the mellow, yellow, silent room. You don't appreciate how really clean you are after this experience until you put your dirty socks back on. (Bring clean ones.)

All you need is money. You'll get a key, locker, and towel (Monday–Saturday 9:00–22:00, Sunday 12:00–20:00, men and women together Wednesday, Saturday, Sunday, and from 16:00–22:00 on Tuesday and Friday, last admission at 19:00 if you'll get a massage, at 19:30 otherwise, tel. 07221/275-920). When you pay, you receive a ticket that gets you in, releases your locker key, and gets you out (if you didn't overstay your allotted three hours). The dress code is always nude. During separate times, men and women use parallel and nearly identical facilities. "Mixed" is still mostly separate, with men and women sharing only the royal pool. Couples will do most of the regimen separated (though women sometimes accompany their partners throughout). Being your average American, I'm not used to nude. But naked, bewildered, and surrounded by beautiful people with no tan lines is a feeling Woody Allen could write a movie about. Sitting in the men's sauna while a lost, naked, and nearly-blind-without-her-glasses female tourist wanders by is just plain funny.

Afterward, before going downstairs, browse through the Roman artifacts in the Renaissance Hall, sip just a little terrible but "magic" hot water (*Thermalwasser*) from the elegant fountain with wistful older ladies, and stroll down the broad royal stairway feeling, as they say, five years younger—or at least no older.

▲▲**Caracalla Therme**—For more of a glorified swimming-pool experience, spend a few hours at the Baths of Caracalla (daily 8:00–22:00, last entry at 20:00), a huge palace of water, steam, and relaxed people, next to the Friedrichsbad. (Drivers can park under the Thermen for free for two hours if they validate your ticket at the Caracalla turnstile.) At Caracalla you'll find more singles and more activities than at Friedrichsbad, which has more couples and an established routine.

Bring a towel and swimsuit (shorts are OK for men). Buy a card (19 DM for three hours, 25 DM for four hours, pricier in shoulder season and winter), put the card in the locker to get a key, change, strap the key around your wrist, and go play. Your key gets you into another poolside locker if you want money for a tan or a drink. The Caracalla Therme is an indoor/outdoor wonderland of steamy pools, waterfalls, neck showers, Jacuzzis, hot springs, cold pools, lounge chairs, exercise instructors, saunas, a cafeteria, and a bar. After taking a few laps around the fake river, you can join the kinky gang for water spankings (you may have to wait a few minutes to grab a vacant waterfall). The steamy "inhalation" room seems like purgatory's waiting room, with 6 misty inches of visibility, filled with strange, silently aging bodies.

Climb the spiral staircase into a naked world of saunas, tanning lights, cold plunges, and sunbathing. There are three eucalyptus-smelling saunas of varying temperatures: 80, 90, and 95 degrees. Read and follow the instructions on the wall. Towels are required, not for modesty but to separate your body from the wood that every other body sits on. The highlight for me was the Arctic bucket in the shower room. Pull the chain. Only rarely will you feel so good. And you can do this over and over.

As you leave, take a look at the old Roman bath that Emperor Caracalla himself soaked in to conquer his rheumatism nearly 2,000 years ago.

## Sleeping in Baden-Baden
**(1.7 DM = about $1, tel. code: 07221, zip code: 76530)**
Sleep Code: **S**=Single, **D**=Double/Twin, **T**=Triple, **Q**=Quad, **b**=bathroom, **t**=toilet only, **s**=shower only, **CC**=Credit Card (**V**isa, **M**asterCard, **A**mex), **SE**=Speaks English, **NSE**=No English.

Except for its hostel, rooms in Baden-Baden are expensive. The TI can nearly always find you a room, but don't use them for places listed here or you'll pay more. Go direct! The only tight times are during the horse races (May 16–24 and August 28–September 6 in 1998). If you arrive at Baden-Baden's Oos station, either stay near the station (see below) or hop on the wonderful bus line #201, which takes you to the center of town (Augustaplatz, TI, baths, casino, hotels) and continues to budget hotels on the east end of town. Hotel am Markt and Hotel Deutsche Kaiser, clearly the best values, are worth calling in advance.

Unless otherwise noted, assume that breakfast is included. All hotels and pensions are required to extract an additional 4 DM per-person per-night "spa tax."

### Sleeping in the Center
There are several affordable hotels right in the almost traffic-free old town, five minutes from the TI, baths, and casino.

**Hotel am Markt** is the best deal for a warm, small, family-run hotel with all the comforts a commoner could want in a peaceful, central location, two cobbled blocks from the baths (S-55 DM, Sb-75–90 DM, Dt-92–100 DM, Db-128–140 DM, Tb-155 DM, extra person-30 DM, CC:VMA, Marktplatz 18, tel. 07221/27040, fax 07221/270-444, Herr und Frau Bogner and Frau Jung SE). The church bells blast charmingly through each room every quarter hour from 6:30 until 22:00. Otherwise, quiet rules. The ambience and the clientele make killing time on their small terrace a joy. The daily menu offers a good dinner deal (orders 18:00–19:30, limited to guests only). The hotel is a few minutes' walk from central Leopoldsplatz uphill to Marktplatz. A popular restaurant nearby is La Provence, with an ecletic menu and good food and prices (daily 12:00–1:00, CC:VMA, from Marktplatz hike up Schloss Strasse to #20, tel. 07221/25550).

Around the corner from Hotel am Markt, **Bratwurst-glöckel** is a 16th-century guest house with eight cozy rooms, several with views—ask for "*mit Ausblick*" (Sb-100 DM, Db-135–150 DM, cable TV, good meals at attached restaurant, CC:VMA, tel. 07221/90610, fax 07221/906-161, NSE).

**Gästehaus Löhr** has soft prices and is worthwhile as a last resort (one tiny S-35 DM, several S-55–65 DM, Db-90–110 DM, CC:VMA, office at Café Löhr at 19 Lichtentaler Strasse, on the main drag—rooms 2 blocks away, tel. 07221/26204 or 07221/306-125, SE).

**Hotel Beeg** is a splurge, with attractive rooms and all the comforts. It's centrally located on a little square in a pedestrian zone, a minute from the baths and above a delectable pastry shop with a sidewalk café (Sb-120 DM, Db-160 DM, extra person-45 DM, balcony-10 DM extra, CC:VMA, on Romer-platz, Gernsbacher Strasse 44, tel. 07221/36760, fax 07221/367-610, SE).

## Sleeping on Lichtentaler Allee ·

Good budget beds and easy parking are down Lichtentaler Allee on the east side of town. **Deutscher Kaiser** offers some of the best rooms in town for the money. This big, traditional guest house enjoys taking care of my readers. Mr. Peter cooks good local-style 14-DM to 30-DM meals in the hotel restaurant. It's in a down-to-earth suburb, right on the bus #201 line (across the street from the Eckerlestrasse stop, 30–45 minutes from the train station, depending on traffic) or a 20-minute stroll down polite Lichtentaler Allee (S-55–60 DM, Sb-75–80 DM, D-80–90 DM, Db-110–120 DM, hall showers-3 DM, CC:VMA, Hauptstrasse 35, 76534 Baden-Baden-Lichtental, tel. 07221/72152, fax 07221/72154, Mrs. Peter SE). **Gasthof Cäcilienberg** is comfortable and beautifully situated even farther out in a quiet area at the end of Lichtentaler Allee (S-58 DM, Sb-68 DM, D-88 DM, Db-98 DM, take bus #201 and get off at Brahmsplatz, Geroldsauer Strasse 2, tel. 07221/ 72297, fax 07221/70459, NSE). Drivers entering town from the autobahn can skip the town center by following signs to "Congress" into Michaelstunnel. Take the first exit in the tunnel (Lichtental) and you'll come out near Hotel Deutscher-Kaiser.

### Sleeping near the Oos Train Station
The train takes you only as close as the suburb of Oos. Those driving in from the autobahn hit Oos first. These places on Ooser Hauptstrasse, with easy parking, are a short walk from the station (Adler is three minutes away, Goldener Stern is eight minutes away).

**Gasthof Adler** is clean, comfortable, and friendly (S-60 DM, Ss-65 DM, Sb-85 DM, D-100 DM, Ds-110 DM, Db-120– 145 DM, CC:VM, veer right from station, walk past post office to stoplight, hotel is on corner, Ooser Hauptstrasse 1, 76532 Baden-Baden Oos, tel. 07221/61858 or 07221/61811, fax 07221/17145, some English spoken). **Hotel Goldener Stern** has big, bright rooms (Ss-60 DM, D-110 DM, Db-120 DM, CC:VMA, follow above directions, at stoplight, turn left and walk five minutes to Ooser Hauptstrasse 16, tel. 07221/61509, fax 07221/54323, NSE).

### Hostel
Baden-Baden's **Werner Dietz Hostel**, while not cheap, is your budget ace in the hole (beds in six-bed rooms, sheets, and breakfast for 27.50 DM, 32.50 DM if you're 27 or older, add 6 DM if you have no hostel card, Hardbergstrasse 34, bus #201 from the station or downtown to Grosse Dollenstrasse— announced as "Jugendherberge stop," tel. 07221/52223, SE). They save 25 beds to be doled out at 17:00, have an overflow hall when all beds are taken, give 4.60-DM discount coupons for both city baths, and serve cheap meals. (Drivers, turn left at the first light after the freeway into Baden-Baden ends, and

follow the signs, winding uphill to the big, modern hostel next to a public swimming pool.)

## Transportation Connections—Baden-Baden

**By train to: Freiburg** (hrly, 60 min), **Triberg** (8/day, 60 min), **Heidelberg** (hrly, 60 min, catch Castle Road bus to Rothenburg), **Munich** (hrly, 4 hrs, with two changes), **Frankfurt** (2/hr, 1.5 hrs with a change), **Koblenz** (2/hr, 2.5 hrs with a change), **Mainz on the Rhine** (hrly, 90 min), **Strasbourg** (5/day, 45 min), **Bern** (hrly, 3.5 hrs, transfer in Basel).

## FREIBURG

Freiburg (FRY-burg) is worth a quick look. The "sunniest town in Germany" feels like the university town it is, with 30,000 students. Freiburg, nearly bombed flat in 1944, skillfully put itself back together. And it feels cozy, almost Austrian; it was Habsburg territory for 500 years. It's the "capital" of the Schwarzwald, surrounded by lush forests and filled with environmentally sensitive people. Enjoy the pedestrian-only old center. Freiburg's trademark is its system of *Bächle*, tiny streams running down each street. These go back to the Middle Ages (fire protection, cattle refreshment, constantly flushing disposal system). A sunny day turns any kid into a puddle-stomper. Enjoy the ice cream and street-singing ambience of the cathedral square, which has a great produce and craft market (Monday–Saturday 8:00–14:30).

### Orientation (tel. code: 0761)

**Tourist Information:** Freiburg's busy TI offers a good 6-DM city guidebook, room-finding service, a city map, a 1-DM brochure with a self-guided walking tour, 10-DM German-English guided walks (several days a week at 10:30 or 14:30), information on the Black Forest region, and an American Express booth (Monday–Saturday 9:30–20:00, Sunday 10:00–12:00, less off-season, tel. 0761/388-1881). Free public WC sans TP around the corner.

**Arrival in Freiburg:** As you leave the train station, head straight ahead down Eisenbahnstrasse, the tree-lined boulevard (passing the post office). Within 3 blocks you'll take an underpass under a busy road; as you emerge, the TI is on your left and the town center is dead ahead.

## Sights—Freiburg

▲Church (Münster)—This impressive church, completed in 1513, took more than three centuries to build, and ranges in style from late Romanesque to lighter, brighter Gothic. Though it was virtually the only building in town to survive WWII bombs, its tower is still not worth the 329-step ascent. From this lofty perch, watchmen used to scan the town for fires. Look for the 123 representations of Mary throughout the church; the less sublime can find the "mooning" gargoyle and wait for rain. Enjoy the market in the square. The ornate Historisches Kaufhaus, across from the church, was a trading center in the 16th century.

Augustiner Museum—This offers a good look at the local culture and medieval art, including (downstairs) a close-up look at some of the Münster's medieval stained glass (4 DM, Tuesday–Sunday 10:00–17:00, closed Monday).

Schauinsland—Freiburg's own mountain, while little more than an oversized hill, offers the handiest quick look at the Schwarzwald for those without wheels. A gondola system, one of Germany's oldest, was designed for Freiburgers relying on public transportation. At the 4,000-foot summit are a panorama restaurant, pleasant circular walks, and the Schniederli Hof, a 1592 farmhouse museum. A tower on a nearby peak offers a commanding Black Forest view. About 20 DM gets you up and back (ride tram #4 from the town center to the end of the line, then take bus #21 seven stops to the lift). This excursion will not thrill Americans from Colorado.

## Sleeping in Freiburg
(1.7 DM = about $1, tel. code: 0761, zip code: 79098)
I prefer to sleep in Staufen (see below), a pleasant, cheaper, small-town alternative to Freiburg. The first two Freiburg listings are a 15-minute walk or easy bus ride from the station. Prices include breakfast and English is spoken.

Hotel Alleehaus is tops. Located on a quiet, leafy street in a big house that feels like home, it's thoughtfully decorated and warmly run (S-75 DM, Ss-80 DM, Sb-98 DM, D-105 DM, one small Db-120 DM, Db-140 DM, CC:VM, take cable car #4 from the station to Holzmarkt, Marienstrasse 7, at intersection with Wallstrasse, tel. 0761/387-600, fax 0761/387-6099, phone answered 7:00–18:30).

Hotel am Stadtgarten is also a couple of blocks from the

old town, with comfortable rooms heavy on beige (S-87 DM, Ss-92 DM, Sb-97 DM, Db-129 DM, Tb-186 DM, Q with kitchenette-228 DM, rooms with fridge available, take tram #5 two stops from the station to Bernhardstrasse 5, at intersection with Karlstrasse, tel. 0761/282-9002, fax 0761/282-9022).

If you're willing to pay dearly for proximity to the train station, dump your bags at **Hotel Barbara**. Its rooms are much brighter than its dark lobby (Sb-125 DM, Db-160–170 DM, some non-smoking rooms, CC:VM, on quiet street two minutes from station, head towards TI but turn left to reach Poststrasse 4, tel. 0761/26060, fax 0761/26688).

**City Hotel** is corporate clean with modern rooms, near the station, the main shopping street, and the old town (Db-160–185 DM, Weberstrasse 3, tel. 0761/388-070, fax 0761/388-0765).

The big, modern **Freiburg Youth Hostel** is on the east edge of Freiburg on the scenic road into the Black Forest (27.50 DM per bed with sheets and breakfast, "seniors" over 26 pay 32.50 DM, hostel card required, Kartuserstrasse 151, tram #1 to Römerhof, tel. 0761/67656).

## Eating in Freiburg

Because Freiburg is a university town, you'll find plenty of cheap eateries, such as **Brennessel** on Escholzstrasse and **Egon 54** on Egonstrasse, both behind the train station.

## Transportation Connections—Freiburg

**By train to: Staufen** (hrly, 30 min, 3/day are direct, others require easy change in Bad Krozingen), **Baden-Baden** (6/day, 60 min), **Munich** (hrly, 4.5 hrs, transfer in Mannheim), **Mainz on the Rhine** (6/day, 2.5 hrs), **Basel** (hrly, 60 min), **Bern** (hrly, 2.5 hrs, transfer in Basel).

## Route Tips for Drivers

**Murten to Staufen/Freiburg (130 miles):** From Murten (French Switzerland), follow signs to Bern, then to Basel/Zürich. Before Basel you'll go through a tunnel and come to Raststätte Pratteln Nord, a strange orange shopping mall that looks like a swollen sea cucumber laying eggs on the freeway. Take a break here for a look around one of Europe's greatest freeway stops. You'll find a bakery and grocery store for picnickers, a restaurant, showers, and a change desk open daily until 21:00, with rates about 2 percent higher than banks.

At Basel, follow the signs to Karlsruhe (Deutschland). Once in Germany (reasonable bank at the border station, open daily 7:00–20:00), the autobahn zips along the French border which, for now, is the Rhine River. For Staufen, take the Bad Krozingen exit. For Freiburg, exit at Freiburg mitte. Park near TI and cathedral (single, tall, see-through spire).

## STAUFEN

Staufen makes a delightful home base for your exploration of Freiburg and the southern trunk of the Black Forest. A mini-Freiburg, it's a perfect combination of smallness and off-the-beaten-pathness with a quiet pedestrian zone of colorful old buildings bounded by a happy creek that actually babbles. There's nothing to do here but enjoy the marketplace atmosphere. Hike through the vineyards to the ruined castle overlooking the town and savor a good dinner with local wine. A pub at the base of the castle hill offers *Winzergnossenshaft* (wine tasting).

### Orientation (tel. code: 07633)

**Tourist Information:** Staufen's TI, on the main square in the Rathaus, can help you find a room (Monday–Friday 8:00–16:30, closed Saturday afternoon and Sunday, tel. 07633/80536).

**Arrival in Staufen:** At the train station, as you face the Gasthaus Bahnhof (see Sleeping, below), angle right up Bahnhofstrasse. Turn right at the post office on Hauptstrasse, which takes you to the town center, hotels, and TI in a couple of minutes.

### Sights—Near Staufen

**Wine Road (Badische Weinstrasse)**—The wine road of this part of Germany staggers from Staufen through the tiny towns of Grunern, Dottingen, Sulzburg, and Britzingen, before sitting down in Badenweiler. If you're in the mood for some tasting, look for "Winzergnossenshaft" signs, which invite visitors in to taste and buy the wines, and often to tour the winery.

▲**Badenweiler**—If ever a town was a park, Badenweiler is it; an idyllic, poodle-elegant, and finicky-clean spa town known only to the wealthy Germans who soak there. Its *Markgrafenbad* (bath) is next to the ruins of a Roman mineral bath in a park of imported and exotic trees (including a California redwood). This prize-winning piece of architecture perfectly mixes trees and peace with an elegant indoor/outdoor swimming pool (daily 8:00–18:00, Monday, Wednesday, and Friday until 20:00). The locker procedure, combined with the language barrier, makes getting to the pool more memorable than you'd expect (three hours for 14 DM; towels, required caps, and suits are rentable). Badenweiler is a 20-minute drive south of Staufen.

## Sleeping in Staufen
**(1.7 DM = about $1, tel. code: 07633, zip code: 79219)**
The TI has a list of private Zimmer (posted on the window after hours), but most don't like one-nighters. Prices listed are for one night. You'll usually get a 10-DM discount for stays of three nights or more. Some English is spoken.

**Gasthaus Bahnhof** is the cheapest place in town, with a castle out back, self-service kitchen, and 12-DM to 14-DM dinners (S-30 DM, D-70 DM, no breakfast, across from the train station, tel. 07633/6190). It can seem a little depressing during the day, but at night, master of ceremonies Lotte makes it the squeeze-box of Staufen. People come from miles around to party with Lotte. If you want to eat red meat in a wine barrel under a tree, this is the place. For longer stays, ask her about the rooms next door (Sb-50 DM, Db-80 DM, minimum three-night stay).

**Hotel Krone** gilds the lily but is still the best value in this price range (Sb-90 DM, Db-130 DM, Tb-170 DM, CC:VMA, Hauptstrasse 30, on the main pedestrian street, tel. 07633/5840, fax 07633/82903). Its restaurant appreciates vegetables and offers good splurge meals (closed Saturday).

**Gasthaus Hirschen**, which has a storybook location in the old pedestrian center and a characteristic restaurant (closed Monday and Tuesday), is family-run with all the comforts (Sb-80 DM, Db-120 DM, Tb-170 DM, Haupstrasse 19 on the main pedestrian street, tel. 07633/5297, fax 07633/5295). They have a penthouse apartment for four (220 DM).

**Hotel Sonne**, with eight comfortable rooms, is at the edge of the pedestrian center (Sb-80 DM, Db-110 DM, continue straight past the Hotel Krone, turn right at T-intersection, and take second left on Muhlegasse to reach Albert-Hugard Strasse 1, tel. 07633/95100).

## Sights—Black Forest

**▲▲Short and Scenic Black Forest Joyride**—This pleasant loop from Staufen (or Freiburg) takes you through the most representative chunk of the area, avoiding the touristy and overcrowded Titisee. Leave Staufen on Schwarzwaldstrasse (signs to Donaueschingen), which becomes scenic road 31 down the dark and fertile-with-fairy tales Höllental (Hell's Valley) toward Titisee. Turn left at Hinterzarten onto Road 500, follow signs to St. Margen, then to St. Peter—one of the healthy, go-take-a-walk-in-the-clean-air places that doctors actually prescribe for people from all over Germany. There is a fine 7-kilometer walk between these two towns, with regular buses to bring you back. St. Peter's TI, just next to the Benedictine Abbey (closed to the public), can recommend a walk (Monday–Friday 8:00–12:00 and 14:00–17:00, Saturday 11:00–13:00, tel. 07660/910-224). If you want to stay the night, the traditional old Gasthof Hirschen is on the main square (Db-130 DM, St. Peter/Hochschwarzwald, tel. 07660/204, fax 07660/920-070) and Pension Kandelblick offers the best budget beds (D-60 DM, Db-70 DM, Schweighofweg, tel. 07660/349). Several morning and late-afternoon buses connect Freiburg and St. Peter.

From St. Peter, wind through idyllic Black Forest scenery up to Kandelhof. At the summit is the Berghotel Kandel. You can park here and take a short walk to the 4,000-foot peak for a great view. Then the road winds steeply through a dense forest to Waldkirch, where a fast road takes you to the Freiburg Nord autobahn entrance. With a good car and no stops, you'll get from Staufen/Freiburg to Baden-Baden in three hours.

**▲▲Extended Black Forest Drive**—Of course, you could spend much more time in the land of cuckoo clocks and healthy hikes. For a more thorough visit, still connecting with Baden-Baden, try this drive: As described above, drive from Staufen or Freiburg down Höllental. After a short stop in St. Peter, wind up in Furtwangen, with the impressive Deutsches Uhrenmuseum (German clock museum, 4 DM, daily April–October 9:00–17:00, less off-season, tel. 07723/920-117). More than a chorus of cuckoo clocks, this museum traces (with interesting English descriptions) the development of timekeeping devices from the Dark Ages to the space age. It has an upbeat combo of mechanical musical instruments as well.

**Triberg**—Deep in the Black Forest, Triberg's famous for its

Gutach Waterfall (a 500-foot fall in several bounces, 3 DM to see it, drivers can drop passengers at top and meet them at the 2-DM putt-putt golf course in town, a 15-minute downhill walk) and, more important, the Heimat Museum, which gives a fine look at the costumes, carvings, and traditions of the local culture (4 DM, daily 8:00–18:00, fewer hours off-season). Touristy as Triberg is, it offers an easy way for travelers without cars to enjoy the Black Forest (TI tel. 07722/953-230).
▲**Black Forest Open-Air Museum (Schwarzwälder Freilichtermuseum)**—This offers the best look at this region's traditional folk life. Built around one grand old farmhouse, the museum is a collection of several old farms filled with exhibits on the local dress and lifestyles (7 DM, free guides with small groups but call first, daily April–October 8:30–18:00, last entry 17:00, north of Triberg, through Hornberg to Hausach/Gutach, tel. 07831/230). The surrounding shops and restaurants are awfully touristy. Try your *Schwarzwald Kirschetorte* (Black Forest cherry cake) elsewhere.

Continue north, through Freudenstadt, the capital of the northern Black Forest, and onto the Schwarzwald-Hochstrasse, which takes you along a ridge through 30 miles of pine forests before dumping you right on Baden-Baden's back porch.

# ROTHENBURG AND THE ROMANTIC ROAD

From Munich or Füssen to Frankfurt, the Romantic Road takes you through Bavaria's medieval heartland, a route strewn with picturesque villages, farmhouses, onion-domed churches, Baroque palaces, and walled cities.

Dive into the Middle Ages via Rothenburg (ROE-ten-burg), Germany's best-preserved walled town. Countless renowned travelers have searched for the elusive "untouristy Rothenburg." There are many contenders (such as Michelstadt, Miltenberg, Bamberg, Bad Windsheim, and Dinkelsbühl), but none holds a candle to the king of medieval German cuteness. Even with crowds, overpriced souvenirs, Japanese-speaking night watchmen, and yes, even with *Schneeballs*, Rothenburg is best. Save time and mileage, and be satisfied with the winner.

## Planning Your Time

The best one-day look at the heartland of Germany is the Romantic Road bus tour. Eurail travelers pay only a 10-DM registration fee for a ride (daily, Frankfurt to Munich or Füssen, and vice versa). Drivers can follow the route laid out in the tourist brochures (available at any TI). The only stop worth more than a few minutes is Rothenburg. Twenty-four hours is ideal for this town. Two nights and a day is a bit much, unless you're actually relaxing on this trip.

Rothenburg in a day is easy, with four essential experiences: the Medieval Crime and Punishment Museum, the Riemenschneider wood carving in St. Jacob's Church, the city walking tour, and a walk along the wall. With more time there are several mediocre but entertaining museums, walking and biking in the nearby countryside, and lots of cafés and shops.

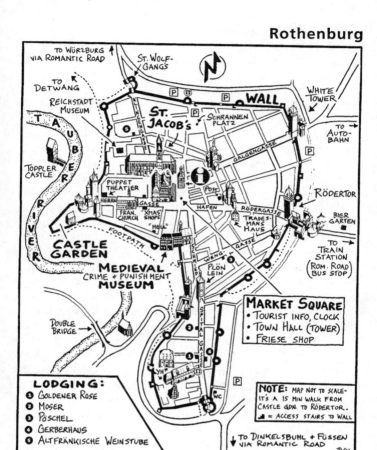

Make a point to spend at least one night. The town is yours after dark, when the groups vacate, and the town's floodlit cobbles wring some romance out of any travel partner.

# ROTHENBURG

In the Middle Ages, when Frankfurt and Munich were just wide spots on the road, Rothenburg was Germany's second-largest free imperial city, with a whopping population of 6,000. Today it's her best-preserved medieval walled town, enjoying tremendous tourist popularity without losing its charm. Get medievaled in Rothenburg.

## Orientation (tel. code: 09861)

To orient yourself in Rothenburg, think of the town map as a human head. Its nose—the castle garden—sticks out to the left, and the neck is the skinny lower part, with the hostel and my favorite hotels in the Adam's apple. The town is a joy on foot. No sight or hotel is more than a 15-minute walk from the train station or each other.

During Rothenburg's heyday, from 1150 to 1400, it was the crossing point of two major trade routes: Tashkent–Paris and Hamburg–Venice. Most of the buildings you'll see were built by 1400. The city was born around its long-gone castle, which was built in 1142, destroyed in 1356, and is now the site of the castle garden. You can see the shadow of the first town wall, which defines the oldest part of Rothenburg, in its contemporary street plan. A few gates from this wall survive. The richest and therefore biggest houses were in this central part. The commoners built higgledy-piggledy (read: picturesquely) farther from the center near the present walls. Today the great trade is tourism; two-thirds of the townspeople are employed to serve you. Too often Rothenburg brings out the shopper in visitors before they've had a chance to appreciate the historic city. True, this is a great place to do your German shopping, but first see the town. While 2.5 million people visit each year, a mere 500,000 spend the night. Rothenburg is most enjoyable early and late, when the tour groups are gone.

**Tourist Information:** The TI is on the market square (Monday–Friday 9:00–12:30 and 14:00–18:00, Saturday 9:00–12:00 and 14:00–16:00, closed Sunday; off-season closed Saturday afternoon, tel. 09861/40492, after-hours board lists rooms still available). Pick up a map and the "Sights Worth Seeing and Knowing" brochure (a virtual walking guide to the town; read it all). The free "Hotels and Pensions of Rothenburg" map has the greatest detail and names all streets. Confirm sightseeing plans and ask about the daily 14:00 walking tour (April–December) and evening entertainment. The best town map is available free at the Friese shop, two doors toward Rothenburg's "nose."

**Arrival in Rothenburg:** Exit left from the train station, and turn right on the first busy street (Ansbacher Strasse). It'll take you to Rothenburg's market square within ten minutes. Day-trippers can leave luggage in lockers at the station (2 DM). The travel agency in the station is the place to arrange train and *couchette* (sleeper) reservations.

## Tours of Rothenburg

The TI on the market square offers 90-minute guided **walking tours** in English (6 DM, daily April–October at 14:00 from the market square). The equally informative but more dramatic **Night Watchman's Tour** leaves each evening at 20:00 (6 DM, April–December, in English). Or you can hire a private guide. For 85 DM, a local historian—who's usually an intriguing character as well—will bring the ramparts alive. Eight hundred years of history are packed between Rothenburg's cobbles. (Manfred Baumann, tel. 09861/4146, and Anita Weinzierl, tel. 09868/7993, are good guides.) If you prefer riding to walking, **horse-and-buggy rides** last 30 minutes and cost 10 DM per person for a minimum of three people.

## Sights—Rothenburg

▲▲**Walk the Wall**—Just over a mile around, providing great views and a good orientation, this walk can be done by those under 6 feet tall without a camera in less than an hour, and requires no special sense of balance. Photographers go through lots of film, especially before breakfast or at sunset, when the lighting is best and the crowds are fewest. The best fortifications are in the Spitaltor (south end). Walk from there counterclockwise to the "forehead." Climb the Rödertor en route. The names you see along the way are people who donated money to repair the wall after WWII.

▲**Rödertor**—The wall tower nearest the train station is the only one you can climb. It's worth the hike up for the view and a fascinating rundown on the bombing of Rothenburg in the last weeks of World War II—the northeast corner of the city was destroyed (2 DM, daily 9:00–17:00, closed off-season, photos, English translation).

▲▲**Town Hall Tower**—The best view of Rothenburg and the surrounding countryside, and a close-up look at an old tiled roof from the inside are yours for 1 DM and a rigorous (214 steps, 180 feet) but interesting climb (daily 9:30–12:30 and 13:00–17:00; off-season Saturday and Sunday 12:00–15:00 only). Entrance is on the market square. Women, beware: Some men find the view best from the bottom of the ladder just before the top.

▲▲**Medieval Crime and Punishment Museum**—It's the best of its kind, full of fascinating old legal bits and *Kriminal* pieces, instruments of punishment and torture, even a special cage—complete with a metal gag—for nags. Exhibits are in English (5 DM, daily 9:30–17:30, shorter hours in winter, fun cards, and posters).

▲▲St. Jacob's Church—Here you'll find a glorious 500-year-old wooden altarpiece by Tilman Riemenschneider, located up the stairs and behind the organ. Riemenschneider was the Michelangelo of German woodcarvers. This is the one required art treasure in town (2.50 DM, Monday–Saturday 9:00–17:30, Sunday 10:45–17:30, off-season 10:00–12:00 and 14:00–16:00, free helpful English info sheet).

Meistertrunk Show—Be on the market square at 11:00, 12:00, 13:00, 14:00, 15:00, 20:00, 21:00, or 22:00 for the ritual gathering of the tourists to see the less-than-breathtaking reenactment of the Meistertrunk story. In 1631, the Catholic army took the Protestant town and was about to do its rape, pillage, and plunder thing when, as the story goes, the mayor said, "Hey, if I can drink this entire 3-liter tankard of wine in one gulp, will you leave us alone?" The invading commander, sensing he was dealing with an unbalanced people, said, "Sure." Mayor Nusch drank the whole thing, the town was saved, and the mayor slept for three days. Hint: for the best show, don't watch the clock; watch the open-mouthed tourists gasp as the old windows flip open. At the late shows, the square flickers with flash attachments.

▲Toy Museum—Two floors of historic *kinder* cuteness is a hit with many (5 DM, 12 DM per family, daily 9:30–18:00, just off the market square, downhill from the fountain, Hofbronneng 13).

▲Historical Vaults—Under the town hall tower is a city history museum that gives a waxy but good look at medieval Rothenburg and a good-enough replica of the famous Meistertrunk tankard (3 DM, 9:00–18:00, closed in winter, well-described in English).

Museum of the Imperial City (Reichsstadt Museum)—This stuffier, less sensational museum, housed in the former Dominican Convent, gives a more scholarly look at old Rothenburg, with some fine art and the supposed Meistertrunk tankard, labeled "Kürfurstenhumpen" (4 DM, daily 9:30–17:30, in winter 13:00–16:00).

St. Wolfgang's Church—This fortified Gothic church is built into the medieval wall at Klingentor (near the "forehead"). Explore its dungeon-like passages below and check out the shepherd's dance exhibit to see where they hot-oiled the enemy back in the good old days (2 DM, daily 10:00–13:00 and 14:00–17:00, closed in winter).

**Alt Rothenburger Handwerkerhaus**—This tradesman's house, 700 years old, shows the typical living situation of Rothenburg in its heyday (3 DM, daily 9:00–18:00, closed in winter, Alter Stadtgraben 26, near the Markus Tower).

▲▲**Herrngasse and the Castle Garden**—Any town's *Herrngasse*, where the richest patricians and merchants (the *Herren*) lived, is your chance to see its finest old mansions. Wander from the market square down Herrngasse (past the old Rothenburg official measurement rods on the City Hall wall) and drop into the lavish front rooms of a ritzy hotel or two. Pop into the Franciscan Church (free, daily 10:00–12:00 and 14:00–16:00, built in 1285—the oldest in town, with a Riemenschneider altarpiece), continue on down past the old-fashioned puppet theater, through the old gate (notice the tiny after-curfew door in the big door and the frightening mask mouth from which hot Nutella was poured onto attackers) and into the garden that used to be the castle (great picnic spots and Tauber Riviera views at sunset).

▲**Walk in the Countryside**—Just below the *Burggarten* (castle garden) in the Tauber Valley is the cute, skinny, 600-year-old castle/summer home of Mayor Toppler (2 DM, 13:00–16:00 on Friday, Saturday, and Sunday). On the top floor, notice the photo of bombed-out 1945 Rothenburg. Then walk on past the covered bridge and huge trout to the peaceful village of Detwang. Detwang (from 968, the second-oldest village in Franconia) is actually older than Rothenburg, and also has a Riemenschneider altarpiece in its church. For a scenic return, loop back to Rothenburg through the valley along the river, past a café with outdoor tables, great desserts, and a town view to match.

**Festivals**—Rothenburgers dress up in medieval costumes and beer gardens spill out into the street to celebrate Mayor Nusch's Meistertrunk victory (Whitsun, six weeks after Easter) and 700 years of history in the Imperial City Festival (second weekend in September, with fireworks).

**Swimming**—Rothenburg has a fine modern recreation center, with an indoor/outdoor pool and sauna. It's just a few minutes' walk down Dinkelsbühl Road (Friday–Wednesday 8:00–20:00, opens at 10:00 on Thursday, tel. 09861/4565).

## Sights—Near Rothenburg

**A Franconian Bike Ride**—For a fun, breezy look at the countryside around Rothenburg, rent a bike from Rad & Tat (25 DM/day, Monday–Friday 9:00–18:00, Saturday 9:00–14:00, closed Sunday, Bensenstrasse 17, outside of town behind the "neck," near corner of Bensenstrasse and Erlbacherstrasse, no deposit except passport number, tel. 09861/87984). Return the bike the next morning before 10:00. For a pleasant half-day pedal, bike south down to Detwang via Topplerschlosschen. Go north along the level bike path to Tauberscheckenbach, then huff and puff uphill about 20 minutes to Adelshofen and south back to Rothenburg.

**Franconian Open-Air Museum**—A 20-minute drive from Rothenburg in the undiscovered "Rothenburgy" town of Bad Windsheim is a small, open-air folk museum that, compared with others in Europe, isn't much. But it's trying very hard and gives you the best look around at traditional rural Franconia (6 DM, Tuesday–Sunday 9:00–18:00, closed Monday, shorter hours off-season).

## Shopping

Be careful . . . Rothenburg is one of Germany's best shopping towns. Do it here, mail it home, and be done with it. Lovely prints, carvings, wineglasses, Christmas-tree ornaments, and beer steins are popular.

The Kathe Wohlfahrt Christmas trinkets phenomenon is spreading across the half-timbered reaches of Europe. In Rothenburg tourists flock to two Kathe Wohlfahrt Christmas Villages (on either side of Herrngasse, just off the market square). This Christmas wonderland is filled with enough twinkling lights to require a special electric hookup, instant Christmas spirit mood music (best appreciated on a hot day in July), and American and Japanese tourists hungrily filling little woven shopping baskets with 5-DM to 10-DM goodies to hang on their trees. (OK, I admit it, my Christmas tree sports a few KW ornaments.) Note: prices have hefty tour-guide kickbacks built into them.

The Friese shop (just off the market square, west of the tourist office on the corner across from the public WC) offers a charming contrast. Cuckoo with friendliness, it gives shoppers with this book tremendous service: a 10 percent discount, 14 percent tax deducted if you have it mailed, and a free

Rothenburg map. Anneliese, who runs the place with her sons, Frankie and Berni, charges only her cost for shipping, changes money at the best rates in town with no extra charge, and lets tired travelers leave their bags in her back room for free. Her pricing is good, but to comparison shop, go here last.

For prints, etchings, and paintings, 10 percent off marked prices with this book, and a free shot of German brandy, visit the Ernst Geissendörfer print shop, where the market square hits Schmiedgasse. For characteristic wineglasses and oinkology gear, drop by the Weinladen am Plonlein (Plonlein 27).

Shoppers who mail their goodies home can get handy boxes at the post office (Monday–Friday 9:00–12:30 and 14:00–17:00, Saturday 9:00–12:00, Milchmarkt 5).

Those who prefer to eat their souvenirs shop the *Bäckerei* (bakeries). Their succulent pastries, pies, and cakes are pleasantly distracting. Skip the good-looking but bad-tasting Rothenburger Schneeballs.

## Sleeping in Rothenburg
**(1.7 DM = about $1, tel. code: 09861, zip code: 91541)**
Sleep Code: **S**=Single, **D**=Double/Twin, **T**=Triple, **Q**=Quad, **b**=bathroom, **t**=toilet only, **s**=shower only, **CC**=Credit Card (**V**isa, **M**asterCard, **A**mex), **SE**=Speaks English, **NSE**=No English. Unless otherwise indicated, room prices include breakfast.

Rothenburg is crowded with visitors, including probably Europe's greatest single concentration of Japanese tourists. But when the sun sets, most retreat to the predictable plumbing of their big-city high-rise hotels. Except for the rare Saturday night, room-finding is easy throughout the year.

Many hotels and guest houses will pick up desperate heavy packers at the station. You may be greeted at the station by the Zimmer skimmer trying to waylay those on their way to a reserved room. If you arrive without a reservation, try talking yourself into one of these more desperate bed-and-breakfast rooms for a youth-hostel price. Be warned: Some take you to distant hotels and then charge you for a ride back if you decline a room.

### Hotels
I stay in **Hotel Goldene Rose**, where scurrying Karin serves breakfast and stately Henni keeps everything in good order. The hotel has only one shower for two floors of rooms, and

the streetside rooms can be noisy, but the rooms are clean and airy and you're surrounded by cobbles, flowers, and red-tiled roofs (one small S-25 DM, S-35 DM, D-65 DM, Ds-82 DM, Db-87 DM in classy annex behind the garden, some triples, and a spacious family apartment: for four-190 DM, for five-225 DM; closed in January and February, kid-friendly, ground-floor rooms in annex, CC:VMA, Spitalgasse 28, tel. 09861/4638, fax 09861/86417, Henni SE). The Favetta family also serves good, reasonably priced meals. Remember to keep your key to get in after they close (at the side gate in the alley). The hotel is a 15-minute walk from the station or a seven-minute (without shopping) walk downhill from the market square (walk downhill on Schmiedgasse, which becomes Plonlein, which becomes Spitalgasse).

**Gasthof Greifen** is a big, traditional 600-year-old place with all the comforts. It's family-run and creaks just the way you want it to (Sb-64–80 DM, one D-74 DM, Db-115–135 DM, Tb-180 DM, CC:VMA; half a block downhill from the market square at Obere Schmiedgasse 5, tel. 09861/2281, fax 09861/86374, SE).

Right on the market square, Herr Rosner's **Gasthof Marktplatz** has simple rooms and a cozy atmosphere (S-40 DM, D-69 DM, Ds-80 DM, Db-87 DM, T-89 DM, Ts-102 DM, Tb-115 DM, Grüner Markt 10, tel. & fax 09861/6722, some English spoken).

**Gastehaus Raidel**, a 500-year-old house packed with antiques, offers large rooms with cramped facilities down the hall. Run by grim people who make me want to sing the *Addams Family* theme song, it works in a pinch (S-35 DM, D-69 DM, Db-89 DM, Wenggasse 3, tel. 09861/3115, some English spoken).

In the modern world, a block from the train station, you'll find just-the-basics rooms at **Pension Willi und Helen Then,** run by a cool guy who played the sax in a jazz band for seven years after the war and is a regular at the English Conversation Club (D-70 DM, Db-80 DM, on a quiet street across from a handy Laundromat, Johannitergasse 8, tel. 09861/5177, fax 09861/86014).

### Splurges

**Hotel Gerberhaus**, a classy new hotel in a 500-year-old build-ing, is warmly run by Inge and Kurt, who mix modern comforts into bright and airy rooms while maintaining the half-timbered elegance. Great buffet breakfasts, a guests' washer and dryer, and pleasant garden in back (Sb-80 DM, Db-100–140 DM, Tb-165 DM, family room for five-185 DM, all with TV and telephones; CC:VM but prefer cash, Spitalgasse 25, tel. 09861/ 94900, fax 09861/86555, e-mail: Gerberhaus@t-online.de, SE). Claudia's café, downstairs, serves huge sandwiches.

Even classier than the Gerberhaus and my best Rothenburg splurge, **Hotel Klosterstuble** is deep in the old town near the castle garden. Jutta greets her guests while husband Rudolf does the cooking (Sb-90 DM, Db-120–150 DM, some luxurious family rooms, discounts for families, buffet breakfast, 10-DM parking garage, CC:V, Heringsbronnengasse 5, tel. 09861/6774, fax 09861/6474, some English spoken).

Bohemians with bucks enjoy the **Hotel Altfränkische Weinstube am Klosterhof**. Mario and Hanne run this dark and smoky pub in a 600-year-old building. Upstairs they rent *gemütliche* rooms with upscale Monty Python atmosphere, TVs, modern showers, open-beam ceilings, and "*himmel*" beds—canopied four-poster "heaven" beds (Sb-79 DM, Db-89 DM, Tb-109–119 DM, kid-friendly, CC:VM, walk under St. Jacob's church, take second left off Klingengasse at Klosterhof 7, tel. 09861/6404, fax 09861/6410, SE). Their pub is a candlelit classic, serving hot food until 22:30, closing at 1:00. You're welcome to drop by on Wednesday evening (18:30– 24:00) for the English Conversation Club.

### Pensions

**Pension Pöschel** is friendly with seven cozy rooms (S-35 DM, D-60 DM, T-90 DM, small kids free, Wenggasse 22, tel. 09861/3430, NSE).

**Pension Kittlitz** has six pleasant, ground-floor rooms with views of parked cars on a quiet street (Sb-40 DM, Db-80 DM, will pick up at the station, Millergasse 6, tel. 09861/1880; at tel. & fax 09861/3424, Christiana SE).

**Erich Endress** offers five airy, comfy rooms with woody decor above his grocery store (S-45 DM, D-70–90 DM, cheaper for three-night stays, non-smoking, Rodergasse 6, tel. 09861/2331, some English spoken). Coming from the station, look for the Endress grocery on your left, a few blocks within the town walls.

The recommended **Zum Schmolzer** restaurant (see

Eating, below) rents 14 well-maintained but drab-colored rooms, ideal if you like olive green (Sb-55 DM, Db-90 DM, Stollengasse 29, tel. 09861/3371, fax 09861/7204, SE).

**Cafe Uhl** offers several fine, slightly frayed rooms over a bakery (Sb-55–65 DM, Db-95–100 DM, CC:VA, Plonlein 8, tel. 09861/4895, fax 09861/92820, some English spoken).

### Private Rooms

For the best real, with-a-local-family, comfortable, and homey experience, stay with **Herr und Frau Moser** (D-65 DM, T-95 DM, back room has view—ask for *mit Ausblick*, Spitalgasse 12, tel. 09861/5971). This charming retired couple speak little English but try very hard. Speak slowly, in clear, simple English. They ask that readers honor their reservations.

**Frau Guldemeister** rents two simple ground-floor rooms (Ss-40 DM, Ds-60 DM, Db-70 DM, breakfast in room, minimum two-night stay, off the market square behind the Christmas shop, Pfaffleinsgasschen 10, tel. 09861/8988, NSE).

### Hostel

The fine **Rossmühle Youth Hostel** has two buildings. The droopy-eyed building (the old town horse-mill, used when the town was under siege and the river-powered mill was inaccessible) houses groups and the office. The adjacent and newly renovated hostel with smaller rooms is for families and individuals (22-DM bed and breakfast, Db-54 DM, 5.50-DM sheets, 9-DM dinners, Muhlacker 1, tel. 09861/ 94160, fax 09861/941-620, e-mail: JHRothen@aol.com, SE). The reception (open 7:00–19:00, 20:30–22:00), will hold rooms until 18:00 if you call. This popular place takes reservations (even more than a year in advance). Here in Bavaria, hosteling is limited to those under 27, except for families traveling with children under 18.

### Sleeping in nearby Detwang and Bettwar

The town of Detwang, a 15-minute walk below Rothenburg, is loaded with quiet Zimmer. The clean, quiet, and comfortable old **Gasthof zum Schwarzen Lamm** in Detwang (D-85 DM, Db-110 DM, tel. 09861/6727, fax 09861/86899) serves good food, as does the popular and very local-style Eulenstube next door. **Gastehaus Alte Schreinerei** offers good food and quiet, comfy, reasonable rooms a little farther down the road in Bettwar (Db-70 DM, 8801 Bettwar, tel. 09861/1541).

## Eating in Rothenburg

Most places serve meals only from 11:30 to 13:30 and 18:00 to 20:00. At **Goldene Rose** (see Sleeping, above), Reno cooks up traditional German fare at good prices (11:30–14:00, 17:30–21:00, closed Tuesday evening and all day Wednesday, in sunny weather the garden terrace is open in the back, Spitalgasse 28).

Galgengasse (Gallows Lane) has two cheap and popular standbys: **Pizzeria Roma** (11:30–24:00, 10-DM pizzas and normal schnitzel fare, Galgengasse 19) and **Gasthof zum Ochsen** (Friday–Wednesday 11:30–13:30 and 18:00–20:00, closed Thursday, uneven service but decent 10-DM meals, Galgengasse 26). **Landsknechtstuben**, at Galgengasse 21, is pricey but friendly, with some cheaper schnitzel choices. The smoky **Zum Schmolzer** is a local favorite for its cheap beer and good food (Rosengasse 21, at intersection with Stollengasse, a block south of Galgengasse, closed Wednesday).

**Gasthaus Siebersturm** serves up tasty, reasonable meals in a bright, airy dining room (Spitalgasse). For a break from schnitzel, the **Lotus China** serves good Chinese food daily (2 blocks behind TI near the church, Eckele 2, tel. 09861/86886).

There are two **supermarkets** near the wall at Rödertor (the one outside the wall to the left is cheaper).

## Evening Fun and Beer Drinking

The best beer garden for balmy summer evenings is at Gasthof Rödertor, just outside the wall at the Rödertor (red gate). Two popular discos are a few doors farther out near the Sparkasse bank (T.G.I. Friday's at Ansbacher 15, in the alley next to the bank, open Wednesday, Friday, and Saturday; the other is Check Point, around the corner from the bank, open Wednesday and Friday–Sunday). A more central and touristy beer garden is behind Hotel Eisenhut (open nightly until 22:00 but may be closed in '98, access from Burggasse or through the hotel off Herrngasse). Next door (a block past the Criminal Museum on Burggasse, with the devil hanging out front) is the dark and foreboding Trinkstube Höll (Hell).

For a rare chance to mix it up with locals who aren't selling anything, bring your favorite slang and tongue-twisters to the English Conversation Club at Mario's Altfränkische Weinstube (Wednesday 18:30–24:00, Anneliese from the Friese shop is a regular). This dark and smoky pub is an atmospheric hangout any night but Tuesday, when it's closed (Klosterhof 7, off Klingengasse, behind St. Jacob's church, tel. 09861/6404).

For mellow ambience, try the beautifully restored Alte Keller's Weinstube under walls festooned with old pots and jugs (closed Tuesday, Alter Keller 8). Wine lovers enjoy the Glocke Hotel's stube (Plonlein 1).

## Transportation Connections—Rothenburg

The Romantic Road bus tour takes you in and out of Rothenburg each afternoon (April–October) heading to Munich, Frankfurt, or Füssen (your choice). See the Romantic Road bus schedule on page 94.

A tiny train line runs between Rothenburg and Steinach (almost hourly, 15 min). **Steinach by train to: Würzburg** (hrly, 30 min), **Munich** (hrly, 2 hrs), **Frankfurt** (hrly, 2 hrs, change in Würzburg). Rothenburg train info: tel. 079511/19419.

## Route Tips for Drivers

**Rothenburg to Füssen or Reutte, Austria:** Get an early start to enjoy the quaint hills and rolling villages of what was Germany's major medieval trade route. The views of Rothenburg from the west, across the Tauber Valley, are magnificent.

After a quick stop in the center of Dinkelsbühl, cross the baby Danube River (Donau) and continue south along the Romantic Road to Füssen. Drive by Neuschwanstein Castle just to sweeten your dreams before crossing into Austria to get set up at Reutte.

If detouring past Oberammergau, you can drive through Garmisch, past Germany's highest mountain (the Zugspitze), into Austria via Lermoos, and on to Reutte. Or you can take the small scenic shortcut to Reutte past Ludwig's Linderhof and along the windsurfer-strewn Plansee.

## ROMANTIC ROAD

The Romantic Road (Romantische Strasse) winds you past the most beautiful towns and scenery of Germany's medieval heartland. Once Germany's medieval trade route, now it's the best way to connect the dots between Füssen, Munich, and Frankfurt.

Wander through quaint hills and rolling villages, and stop wherever the cows look friendly or a town fountain beckons. My favorite sections are from Füssen to Landsberg and

Rothenburg to Weikersheim. (If you're driving with limited time, you can connect Rothenburg and Munich by autobahn, but don't miss these two best sections.)

Throughout Bavaria, you'll see colorfully ornamented Maypoles decorating town squares year-round. Many are painted in Bavaria's colors, blue and white. The decorations that line each side of the pole symbolize the crafts or businesses to be found in that town or community. Each May Day they are festively replaced. Traditionally, rival communities try to steal each other's Maypole. Locals will guard their new pole night and day as May Day approaches. Stolen poles are ransomed only with lots of beer for the clever thieves.

## Getting Around the Romantic Road

**By Bus:** The Europa Bus Company runs buses daily between Frankfurt and Munich in each direction (April–October). A second route goes between Dinkelsbühl and Füssen daily. Buses leave from train stations in towns served by a train. The 11-hour ride costs 120 DM but is only 10 DM with a Eurailpass (uses up a day of a flexipass). Each bus stops in Rothenburg (1.5–2 hours) and Dinkelsbühl (about an hour) and briefly at a few other attractions, and has a guide who hands out brochures and narrates the journey in English. While many claim Eva Braun survives as a Romantic Road bus-tour guide, there is no quicker or easier way to travel across Germany and get such a hearty dose of its countryside. Bus reservations are free, easy, and smart—without one you can lose your seat down the road to someone who does (especially on summer weekends; call 069/79030 one day in advance and leave your name). You can start, stop, and switch over where you like. If you plan to break your journey, you'll be guaranteed a seat only if you reserve each segment.

**By Car:** Follow the brown "Romantische Strasse" signs.

## Sights—Along the Romantic Road

(These sights are south to north.)

**Füssen**—This town, the southern terminus of the Romantic Road, is 2 miles from the startlingly beautiful Neuschwanstein Castle, worthy of a stop on any sightseeing agenda. See the Bavaria and Tirol chapter for description and accommodations.

▲▲**Wieskirche**—Germany's most glorious Baroque-Rococo church. It's in a sweet meadow and is newly restored.

## Romantic Road

Heavenly! Northbound Romantic Road buses stop here for 15 minutes. See the Bavaria and Tirol chapter.

**Rottenbuch**—Nondescript village with an impressive church in a lovely setting.

▲**Dinkelsbühl**—Rothenburg's little sister is cute enough to merit a short stop. A moat, towers, gates, and a beautifully preserved medieval wall surround this town and its interesting local museum. The Kinderzeche children's festival turns Dinkelsbühl wonderfully on end in mid-July (TI tel. 09851/90240). On Neustädtlein, you'll find 80-DM doubles with bath and TV at friendly Haus Küffner (tel. 09851/1247) and Zur Linde (tel. 09851/3465).

▲▲▲**Rothenburg**—See opening of this chapter for information on Germany's best medieval town.

▲**Herrgottskapelle**—This peaceful church, graced with

## 1998 Romantic Road Bus Schedule (Daily, April–October)

| | | |
|---|---|---|
| Frankfurt | 8:00 | — |
| Würzburg | 9:45 | — |
| Arrive Rothenburg | 12:45 | — |
| Depart Rothenburg | 14:30 | — |
| Arrive Dinkelsbühl | 15:25 | — |
| Depart Dinkelsbühl | 16:15 | 16:15 |
| Munich | 19:50 | — |
| Füssen | — | 20:40 |
| | | |
| Füssen | 8:00 | — |
| Arrive Wieskirche | 8:35 | — |
| Depart Wieskirche | 8:55 | — |
| Munich | — | 9:00 |
| Arrive Dinkelsbühl | 12:00 | 12:45 |
| Depart Dinkelsbühl | — | 14:00 |
| Arrive Rothenburg | — | 14:40 |
| Depart Rothenburg | — | 16:15 |
| Würzburg | — | 18:30 |
| Frankfurt | — | 20:30 |

Tilman Riemenschneider's greatest carved altarpiece (2 DM, daily 9:15–17:30), is 1 mile from Creglingen and across the street from the Fingerhut thimble museum (2 DM, daily 9:00–18:00). The south-bound Romantic Road bus stops here for 15 minutes, long enough to see one or the other.
**Weikersheim**—This untouristy town has a palace with fine Baroque gardens (luxurious picnic spot), a folk museum, and a picturesque town square.

## WÜRZBURG
A historic city, though freshly rebuilt since World War II, Würzburg is worth a stop to see its impressive Prince Bishop's Residenz, the bubbly Baroque chapel (Hofkirche) next door, and the palace's sculpted gardens.

## Orientation (tel. code: 0931)

**Tourist Information:** Würzburg has a helpful TI just outside the train station (Monday–Saturday 10:00–18:00) and another TI on Marktplatz (Monday–Friday 10:00–18:00, weekends 10:00–14:00, closed Sunday off-season, tel. 0931/373-335). The produce market near the Marktplatz TI bustles daily except Sunday.

## Sights—Würzburg

▲▲▲**Residenz**—This Franconian Versailles with grand rooms, 3-D art, and a tennis-court-sized fresco by Tiepolo, is worth a tour. English tours are scheduled on weekends at 11:00 and 15:00 from April through October (confirm at TI or call ahead). During the week, the best strategy is to take the TI's walking tour at 11:00, which includes a tour of the Residenz along with a walk through the "old" city (13 DM, Tuesday–Saturday April–October, two hours, all in English, includes admission to Residenz; meet at the TI on Marktplatz). Or buy the 5-DM guide at the Residenz; it's dry and lengthy, but you can use the pictures to figure out what room you're in. No English labels or descriptions are provided. The top sights are the grand staircase with the Tiepolo ceiling, the reconstructed Room of Mirrors (destroyed during WW II), and the grandly Tiepoloed Imperial Hall (5 DM, Tuesday–Sunday April–October 9:00–17:00, November–March 10:00–16:00, closed Monday, last entry a half-hour before closing). The elaborate Hofkirche chapel is next door (as you exit the palace, go left) and the entrance to the picnic-worthy garden is just beyond. Easy parking is available. Don't confuse the Residenz (a 15-minute walk from the train station) with the fortress on the hilltop.

**Fortress**—Along with a city history museum, the fortress contains the Mainfränkisches Museum, highlighting the work of Riemenschneider, Germany's top woodcarver and past mayor of Würzburg (3.50 DM, Tuesday–Sunday 10:00–17:00, less off-season). Riemenschneider fans will find his work throughout Würzburg's many churches (which look closed but are likely open; the sign on the door, *"Bitte Türe schliessen,"* simply means "Please close the door").

**Veitshöchheim**—Consider a cruise to Veitshöchheim, 5 kilometers away, to see the fanciful Baroque gardens and the Summer Residenz (gardens free, open daily 7:00 till dusk; 3 DM for palace, Tuesday–Sunday 9:00–12:00 and 13:00–17:00, closed Monday). Catch the boat at the Würzburg dock (13 DM round-trip, leaves hourly, daily April–October 10:00–17:00) or bus #11 from the Würzburg station (3.2 DM, hourly, ten min).

## Sleeping in Würzburg
**(1.7 DM = about $1, tel. code: 0931, zip code: 97070)**
All listings include breakfast, and prices are soft off-season.

For budget hotels near the train station, try **Pension Siegel** (S-46 DM, D-89 DM, from station, go straight on Kaiserstrasse and turn left at Muller store, Reisbrubengasse 7, tel. 0931/52941, NSE). The fresher **Hotel-Pension Spehnfuch** is on a busy street but has double-paned windows (S-50 DM, D-90 DM, T-130 DM, two minutes' walk from station, exit station and take a right on Rontgenring, at #7, tel. 0931/54752, fax 0931/54760, SE).

Three fine hotels cluster within a block on Theaterstrasse. Quieter rooms are in back; front rooms have street noise. **Hotel Barbarossa**, tucked away on the fourth floor, has 17 comfortable rooms (Ss-75 DM, Sb-95 DM, one Ds-110 DM, Db-140 DM, Tb-170 DM, elevator, CC:VMA, Theaterstrasse 2, tel. 0931/321-370, fax 0931/321-3737, e-mail: marchiorello@ t-online.de, SE). **Hotel Schönleber** is a cheery vision of pastel yellow (S-70–100 DM, Sb-95–110 DM, D-100 DM, Ds-110 DM, Db-150 DM, hall showers-4 DM, elevator, CC:VMA, Theaterstrasse 5, tel. 0931/12068, fax 0931/16012), and the **Altstadt Hotel** is a slight cut above, with a wonderfully fragrant Italian restaurant below (Ss-85 DM, Sb-95 DM, Ds-110 DM, Db-140 DM, CC:VMA, Theaterstrasse 7, tel. 0931/321-640, fax 0931/321-6464, e-mail: marchiorello@t-online.de, SE).

**Sankt Josef Hotel** has a more Franconian feel, with a woody restaurant on a quieter street (Sb-90 DM, Db-145–165 DM, CC:VMA, Semmelstrasse 28, coming from station, take left off Theaterstrasse, tel. 0931/308-680, fax 0931/308-6860, NSE). Across the street is the elaborately painted **Hotel zur Stadt Mainz**, dating from 1430. You'll pay 40 to 50 DM more for the privilege of sleeping here (CC:VA, Semmelstrasse 39, tel. 0931/53155, fax 0931/58510).

# FRANKFURT
Frankfurt, the northern terminus of the Romantic Road, is actually pleasant for a big city and offers a good look at today's

no-nonsense urban Germany. You know you're in Germany when you can buy raw meat at the train station.

## Orientation (tel. code: 069)

**Tourist Information:** For a quick look at the city, pick up a 1-DM map at the TI in the train station (Monday–Friday 8:00–21:00, weekends 9:00–18:00, tel. 069/212-38-849). It's a 20-minute walk from the station down Kaiserstrasse past Goethe's house (great man, mediocre sight, Grosser Hirschgraben 23) to Römerberg, Frankfurt's lively market square (or you can take subway U-4 from the station to Römer). The TI's brochure "Frankfurt Day & Night" describes a self-guided walking tour you can take from this square. A string of museums is just across the river along Schaumainkai (Tuesday–Sunday 10:00–17:00, Wednesday until 20:00, closed Monday). The TI also has info on bus tours of the city (44 DM, 2.5 hrs). Near the train station, a browse through Frankfurt's red-light district offers a fascinating way to kill time between trains. ("Annabella Eros Centers," with two five-floor towers of prostitutes, is at Tannusstrasse 26.)

**Romantic Road Bus:** If you're taking the bus out of Frankfurt, you can buy your ticket either in the Deutsches Touring office at the train station (Monday–Friday 7:30–18:00, Saturday 7:30–15:00, Sunday 7:30–14:00, CC:VMA, entrance at Mannheimer Strasse 4, tel. 069/230-735) or pay cash when you board the bus. Eurail and Europass holders pay only 10 DM (7-DM registration fee, including 3 DM for one piece of luggage).

## Sleeping in Frankfurt
### (1.7 DM = about $1, tel. code: 069, zip code: 60329)

Avoid driving or sleeping in Frankfurt, especially during Frankfurt's numerous trade fairs (about five days a month), which send hotel prices skyrocketing. Pleasant Rhine or Romantic Road towns are just a quick train ride or drive away. But if you must spend the night in Frankfurt, here are some places within a block of the train station (and its handy train to the airport). This isn't the safest neighborhood; stay off the streets after dark (or try one of the last two listings). Get a map at the TI, but for a rough idea of directions to hotels, stand with your back to the main entrance of the station: Using a 12-hour clock, Hotel Manhattan is down the street at 10:00, Hotel Wiesbaden and Hotel Europa at 4:00, and the Goldner Stern at 5:00. Breakfast is included in all listings and English is spoken.

**Hotel Manhattan,** with newly remodeled, sleek, arty rooms, is expensive—best for a splurge on a first or last night in Europe, but more than I'd want to spend for a room (Sb-135 DM, Db-165 DM, show this book to get a break during non-convention times, elevator, CC:VMA, Dusseldorfer Strasse 10, tel. 069/234-748, fax 069/234-532).

**Hotel Wiesbaden** has worn rooms and a kind manager (Sb-95 DM, Db-110–135 DM, Tb-150 DM, elevator, CC:VMA, Baseler Strasse 52, tel. 069/232-347, fax 252-845). **Hotel Europa,** with well-maintained rooms, is the better value (Sb-90 DM, Db-130 DM, Tb-150 DM, some non-smoking rooms, garage, CC:VMA, aseler Strasse 17, tel. 069/236-013, fax 069/236-203).

**Hotel Goldner Stern,** a vintage hotel with dim rooms and hallways, is sleepable (S-43–50 DM, D-65–75DM, hall showers-4 DM, Karlsruherstrasse 8, tel. 069/233-309). It may close in 1998.

Farther from the station, you'll find **Pension Backer** (S-50 DM, D-60 DM, showers-3 DM, near the botanical gardens, Mendelssohnstrasse 92, tel. 069/747992). It's a 20-minute walk from the station, or take the S-Bahn two stops to Hauptwache, then transfer to U-6 or U-7 for two stops to Westend.

The **hostel** is open to members of any age (eight-bed rooms, 29 DM per bed with sheets and breakfast, bus #46 from station to Frankenstein Place, or S-2, S-3, S-4, S-5, or S-6 to Lokelbahnhof, Deutschherrnufer 12, tel. 069/619-058).

## Transportation Connections—Frankfurt
**By train to: Rothenburg** (hrly, 3 hrs, changes in Würzburg and Steinach; the tiny Steinach–Rothenburg train often leaves from the "B" section of track, away from the middle of the station, shortly after the Würzburg train arrives; don't miss it; Steinach has no tourism—for good reason), **Würzburg** (hrly, 90 min.), **Munich** (hrly, 3.5 hrs), **Baden-Baden** (hrly, 90 min.), **Freiburg** (hrly, 2 hrs, change in Mannheim), **Bonn** (hrly, 2 hrs), **Koblenz** (hrly, 90 min.), **Köln** (hrly, 2 hrs), **Berlin** (hrly, 5 hrs), **Amsterdam** (8/day, 5 hrs), **Bern** (14/day, 4.5 hrs, changes in Mannheim and Basel), **Brussels** (6/day, 5 hrs), **Copenhagen** (3/day, 10 hrs), **London** (5/day, 9.5 hrs), **Milan** (6/day, 9 hrs), **Paris** (4/day, 6.5 hrs), **Vienna** (7/day, 7.5 hrs).

## Frankfurt's Airport

The airport (*Flughafen*) is just a 12-minute train ride from downtown (4/hr, 5.5 DM, ride included in Frankfurt's 8.5-DM all-day city transit pass or the 13-DM two-day city pass). The airport is user-friendly, offering showers; baggage check; fair-rate banks with long hours; grocery store; train station; lounge where you can sleep overnight; easy rental-car pickup; plenty of parking; big green meeting-point sign; an information booth; and even McBeer. McWelcome to Germany. Airport English-speaking info: tel. 069/6901 (will transfer you to any of the airlines for booking or confirmation). Lufthansa—069/255-255, American Airlines—069/271-130, Delta—069/664-1212, Northwest—0180/525-4650.

**To Rothenburg:** Train travelers can validate railpasses or buy tickets at the airport station and catch a train to Würzburg, connecting to Rothenburg via Steinach (hrly, 3 hrs). If driving to Rothenburg, follow autobahn signs to Würzburg.

**Flying Home from Frankfurt:** The airport has its own train station, and many of the trains from the Rhine stop there on their way into Frankfurt (e.g., hrly 90-min rides direct from Bonn; hrly 2-hr rides from Bacharach with a change in Mainz, earliest train from Bacharach to Frankfurt leaves just before 6:00). By car, head toward Frankfurt on the autobahn and follow the little airplane signs to the airport ("Flughafen").

## Route Tips for Drivers

**Frankfurt to Rothenburg:** The three-hour drive from the airport to Rothenburg is something even a jetlagged zombie can handle. It's a 75-mile straight shot to Würzburg; just follow the blue autobahn signs. Leave the freeway at the Heidingsfeld-Würzburg exit. If going directly to Rothenburg, follow signs south to Stuttgart/Ulm/Road 19, then to Rothenburg via a scenic slice of the Romantic Road. If stopping at Würzburg, follow "Stadtmitte" then "Residenz" signs from the same freeway exit. From Würzburg, follow Ulm/Road 19 signs to Bad Mergentheim/Rothenburg.

# RHINE AND MOSEL VALLEYS

These valleys are storybook Germany, a fairy-tale world of Rhine legends and robber-baron castles. Cruise the most castle-studded stretch of the romantic Rhine as you listen for the song of the treacherous Loreley. For hands-on castle thrills, climb through the Rhineland's greatest castle, Rheinfels, above the town of St. Goar. Then, for a sleepy and laid-back alternative, mosey through the neighboring Mosel Valley.

In the north you'll find the powerhouse cities of Köln (Cologne) and Bonn on an industrial stretch of the unromantic Rhine. Bonn is Germany's easygoing capital (until Berlin takes over in 1999), and Köln has Germany's greatest Gothic cathedral, best collection of Roman artifacts, a world-class art museum, and a good dose of German urban playfulness. These bustling cities merit a visit, but spend your nights in a castle-crowned village. On the Rhine, stay in St. Goar or Bacharach. On the Mosel, choose Zell.

## Planning Your Time

The Rhineland does not take much time. The blitziest tour is one hour on the train. For a better look, cruise in, tour a castle, sleep in a medieval town, and train out. With limited time, cruise less and be sure to get into a castle. Ideally, spend two nights here, sleep in Bacharach, cruise the best hour of the river (from Bacharach to St. Goar), and tour the Rheinfels Castle. Those with more time could bike the riverside bike path. With two days, split your time between the Rhine and Mosel, seeing Berg Eltz and Cochem. With three days, add Bonn and/or Köln, and for four days include Trier and a sleepy night in the Mosel River Valley.

## Rhine and Mosel Valleys

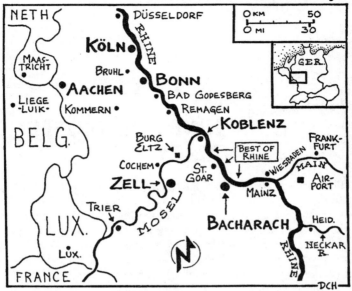

## THE RHINE

Ever since Roman times, when this was the Empire's northern boundary, the Rhine has been one of the world's busiest shipping rivers. You'll see a steady flow of barges with 1,000- to 2,000-ton loads. Tourist-packed buses, hot train tracks, and highways line both banks.

Many of the castles were "robber baron" castles, put there by petty rulers (there were 300 independent little countries in medieval Germany) to levy tolls on passing river traffic. A robber baron would put his castle on, or even in, the river. Then, often with the help of chains and a tower on the opposite bank, he'd stop each ship and get his toll. There were ten customs stops between Mainz and Koblenz alone (no wonder merchants were early proponents of the creation of larger nation-states).

Some castles were built to control and protect settlements, and others were the residences of kings. As times changed, so did the lifestyles of the rich and feudal. Many castles were abandoned for more comfortable mansions in the towns.

Most of the Rhine castles date from the 11th, 12th, and

13th centuries. When the pope successfully asserted his power over the German emperor in 1076, local princes ran wild over the rule of their emperor. The castles saw military action in the 1300s and 1400s, as emperors began reasserting their control over Germany's many silly kingdoms.

The castles were also involved in the Reformation wars in which Europe's Catholic and "protesting" dynasties fought it out using a fragmented Germany as their battleground. The Thirty Years' War (1618–1648) devastated Germany. The outcome: Each ruler got the freedom to decide if his people would be Catholic or Protestant, and one-third of Germany was dead. Production of Gummi Bears ceased entirely.

The French destroyed most of the castles prophylactically (Louis XIV in the 1680s, the revolutionary army in the 1790s, and Napoleon in 1806). They were often rebuilt in neo-Gothic style in the Romantic Age—the late 1800s—and today are enjoyed as restaurants, hotels, hostels, and museums. Check out the Rhine Web site at www.loreleytal.com.

## Getting Around the Rhine

While the Rhine flows from Switzerland to Holland, the stretch from Mainz to Koblenz hoards all the touristic charm. Studded with the crenelated cream of Germany's castles, it bustles with boats, trains, and highway traffic. Have fun exploring with a mix of big steamers, tiny ferries, bikes, and trains.

**By Boat:** While many travelers do the whole trip by boat, the most scenic hour is from St. Goar to Bacharach. Sit on the top deck with your handy Rhine map-guide (or the kilometer-keyed tour in this book) and enjoy the parade of castles, towns, boats, and vineyards. Rhine boats cruise only from Easter through October. Off-season is so quiet that many hotels close.

There are several boat companies, but most travelers sail on the bigger, more expensive, and romantic Köln–Düsseldorf (K-D) line (free with Eurail, otherwise about 15 DM for the first hour, then progressively cheaper per hour, tel. 06741/ 1634 in St. Goar). Boats run daily in both directions (no express boat on Monday) from April through October, with fewer boats off-season. Complete, up-to-date, and more complicated schedules are posted in any station, Rhineland hotel, TI, or current Thomas Cook Timetable. Purchase tickets at the dock five minutes before departure. The boat is never full. (Confirm times at your hotel the night before.)

## Best of the Rhine

The smaller Bingen–Rüdesheimer line is 25 percent cheaper than K-D (Eurail not valid, buy tickets on the boat, tel. 06721/14140), with three two-hour round-trip St. Goar–Bacharach trips daily in summer (12 DM one way, 16 DM round-trip; departing St. Goar at 11:00, 14:10, and 16:10; departing Bacharach at 10:10, 12:30, 15:00).

Drivers have these options: (1) skip the boat; (2) take a round-trip cruise from St. Goar or Bacharach on the Bingen–Rüdesheimer line; (3) draw pretzels and let the loser drive, prepare the picnic, and meet the boat; (4) rent a bike, bring it on the boat for free, and bike back; or (5) take the boat one way and return by train.

**By Train:** Hourly milk-run trains down the Rhine hit every town: St. Goar–Bacharach, 12 min; Bacharach–Mainz, 60 min; Mainz–Frankfurt, 45 min. (Some train schedules list St. Goar but not Bacharach as a stop, but any schedule listing St. Goar also stops at Bacharach.)

## 1998 Rhine Cruise Schedule

| Koblenz | Boppard | St. Goar | Bacharach |
|---------|---------|----------|-----------|
| — | 9:00 | 10:15 | 11:20 |
| 9:00 | 10:50 | 12:05 | 13:05 |
| 11:00 | 12:50 | 14:05 | 15:05 |
| 14:00 | 15:50 | 17:05 | 18:05 |
| 11:05 | 11:30 | 11:50 | 12:10* |
| 13:00 | 11:45 | 10:50 | 9:05 |
| 14:15 | 13:10 | 12:15 | 11:30 |
| — | 14:00 | 13:15 | 12:30 |
| 17:55 | 16:45 | 15:50 | 15:05 |
| 20:00 | 18:50 | 18:00 | 17:20 |

* *Hydrofoil, Koblenz-Bacharach, 8 DM with Eurail, 22.40 DM without.*
*Note: Schedule applies to summer; fewer boats run in spring and fall.*

**By Bike:** In St. Goar you can rent bikes at the Golf Pavilion along the Rhine (13 DM/day, 10 DM/4 hrs, 50 DM or passport as deposit, open April–October 10:00–21:00, tel. 06741/1360). In Bacharach try Pension Lettie (15 DM/day, 10 DM/4 hrs, no deposit for guests, otherwise passport or credit-card imprint, tel. 06743/2115), Hotel Gelberhof (20 DM/day for ten-speeds, 25 DM for "trekking" bikes, 5 DM for child's seat, tel. 06743/1017, ring bell when closed), Hotel Hillen (15 DM/day, 10 DM/half-day, cheaper for guests, lots of bikes), or Frau Feldhege (free if you rent a room from her, see Sleeping, below). The best riverside bike path is from Bacharach to Bingen. The path is also good from St. Goar to Bacharach, but it's closer to the highway. Consider sailing to Bingen and biking back, visiting Rheinstein Castle (you're on your own to wander the well-furnished castle) and Reichenstein Castle (admittance with groups), and maybe even taking a ferry across the river to Kaub (where a tiny boat shuttles sightseers to the better-from-a-distance castle on the island). While there are no bridges between Koblenz and Mainz, several small ferries do their job constantly and cheaply.

## Sights—The Romantic Rhine

(These sights are south to north, from Bingen to Koblenz.)

▲▲▲**Der Romantische Rhine Blitz Zug Fahrt**—One of Europe's great train thrills is zipping along the Rhine in this fast train tour. Here's a quick and easy, from-the-train-window tour (also works for car, boat, or bike) that skips the syrupy myths and the life story of Dieter von Katzenelnbogen that fill normal Rhine guides.

For more information than necessary, buy the handy *Rhine Guide from Mainz to Cologne* (7-DM book with foldout map, at most shops). Sit on the right (river) side of the train going north from Bingen. While nearly all the castles listed are viewed from this side, clear a path to the left window for the times I yell, "Crossover."

You'll notice large black-and-white kilometer markers along the riverbank. I put those up years ago to make this tour easier to follow. They tell the distance from the Rhinefalls where the Rhine leaves Switzerland and becomes navigable. Now the river-barge pilots have accepted these as navigational aids as well. We're tackling just 36 miles of the 820-mile-long Rhine. Your Blitz Rhine Tour starts near Mainz, Rüdesheim, and Bingen. If you're going the other direction, it still works. Just follow the kilometer markings.

**Km 528: Niederwald Monument**—Across from the Bingen station on a hilltop is the 120-foot-high Niederwald monument, a memorial built with 32 tons of bronze in 1877 to commemorate "the re-establishment of the German Empire." A lift takes tourists to this statue from the famous and extremely touristy wine town of Rüdesheim.

**Km 530: Ehrenfels Castle**—Opposite Bingerbrück and the Bingen station, you'll see the ghostly Ehrenfels Castle (clobbered by the Swedes in 1636 and by the French in 1689). Since it had no view of the river traffic to the north, it built the cute little *Mäuseturm* (Mouse Tower) on an island (the yellow tower you'll see near the train station today). Rebuilt in the 1800s in neo-Gothic style, today it's used as a Rhine navigation signal station.

**Km 533: Burg Rheinstein, and Km 534: Burg Reichenstein**—Cross to the other side of the train to see some of the first castles to be rebuilt in the Romantic era (both are privately owned, tourable, and connected by a pleasant trail; info at TI).

**Km 538: Castle Sooneck**—Cross to the other side of the

train. Built in the 11th century, this castle was twice destroyed by people sick and tired of robber barons.

**Km 540: Lorch**—This pathetic stub of a castle is barely visible from the road. Notice the small car ferry, one of several between Mainz and Koblenz, where there are no bridges.

**Km 543: Bacharach and Burg Stahleck**—Cross to the other side of the train. Bacharach is a great stop (see details and accommodations below). Some of the Rhine's best wine is from this town, whose name means "altar to Bacchus." (The local vintners brag that the medieval Pope Pius II ordered it by the cartload.) Perched above the town, the 13th-century Burg Stahleck is now a hostel.

**Km 546: Burg Gutenfels and Pfalz Castle**—Burg Gutenfels (see the white painted "Hotel" sign) and the ship-shape Pfalz Castle (built in the river in the 1300s, notice the overhanging his-and-hers "outhouses") worked very effectively to tax medieval river traffic. The town of Kaub grew rich as Pfalz raised its chains when boats came and lowered them only when the merchants had paid their duty. Those who didn't pay spent time touring its fascinating prison, on a raft at the bottom of its well. In 1504, a pope called for the destruction of Pfalz, but a six-week siege failed. Pfalz is tourable but bare and dull (3-DM ferry from Kaub, 4 DM, Tuesday–Sunday 9:00–13:00 and 14:00–18:00, closed Monday, tel. 06774/570).

**Km 550: Oberwesel**—Cross to the other side of the train. Oberwesel was a Celtic town in 400 B.C., then a Roman military station. It now boasts some of the best Roman wall-and-tower remains on the Rhine. Notice how many of the train tunnels have entrances designed like medieval turrets built in the Romantic 19th century. OK, back to the riverside.

**Km 554: The Loreley**—Steep a big slate rock in centuries of legend and it becomes a tourist attraction, the ultimate Rhinestone. The Loreley (two flags on top, name painted near shoreline) rises 450 feet over the narrowest and deepest point of the Rhine. (In the old days, the fine echoes here were thought to be ghostly voices, fertilizing the legendary soil.)

Because of the killer reefs just upstream (at km 552, called the "Seven Maidens"), many ships never made it to St. Goar. Sailors (after days on the river) blamed their misfortune on a *wunderbar Fräulein* whose long blond hair almost covered her body. (You can see her statue at about km 555.) Heinrich Heine's *Song of Loreley* (the *Cliffs Notes* version is on local postcards) tells the story of a count who sent his men to kill or capture this siren after his son was killed because of her. When the soldiers cornered the nymph in her cave, she called her father (Father Rhine) for help. Huge waves, the likes of which you'll never see today, rose from the river and carried her to safety. And she has never been seen since.

But alas, when the moon shines brightly and the tour buses are parked, a soft, playful Rhine whine can still be heard from the Loreley. As you pass, listen carefully ("Sailors . . . sailors . . . over my bounding mane").

**Km 556: Burg Katz**—From the town of St. Goar, you'll see Burg Katz (Katzenelnbogen) across the river. Look back on your side of the river to see the mighty Rheinfels Castle over St. Goar.

Together, Burg Katz (b. 1371) and Rheinfels had a clear view up and down the river and effectively controlled traffic. There was absolutely no duty-free shopping on the medieval Rhine. Katz got Napoleoned in 1806 and rebuilt around 1900; today it's a convalescent home.

**Km 557: St. Goar and Rheinfels Castle**—The pleasant town of St. Goar (gwahr) was named for a sixth-century home-town monk. It originated in Celtic times (really old) as a place where sailors would stop, catch their breath, send home a post-card, and give thanks after surviving the seductive and treach-erous Loreley crossing. St. Goar is worth a stop (see Sleeping below) to explore its Rheinfels Castle. Sitting like a dead pit bull above St. Goar, this mightiest of Rhine castles rumbles with ghosts from its hard-fought past. Burg Rheinfels (built in 1245) withstood a siege of 28,000 French troops in 1692, but was creamed by the same team in 1797. It was huge, the biggest on the Rhine, then used as a quarry. Today this hollow but interesting shell offers your best single hands-on castle experience on the river. Follow the castle map with English instructions (.30 DM from the ticket window, English brochure-3.5 DM, tiny flashlight-5 DM). Follow the castle's perimeter, circling counterclockwise and downward, to find an easy-to-explore chunk of the several miles of spooky tunnels. Bring your flashlight (and bayonet). These tunnels were used to lure and entomb enemy troops. You'll be walking over the remains (from 1626) of 300 unfortunate Spanish soldiers. The reconstruction of the castle in the museum shows how much bigger it was before Louis XIV destroyed it. The museum's

## St. Goar

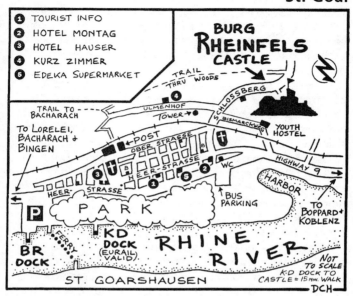

fine exhibits are well-explained in English. Climb to the top for the Rhine view (5 DM, daily 9:00–18:00, last entry at 17:00; Saturday and Sunday only in winter; gather ten English-speaking tourists to get a cheaper ticket and a free English tour, tel. 06741/383). It's a 15-minute steep hike up from St. Goar or you can call a taxi (7-DM lift from the boat dock to the castle, 11 DM for a mini-bus, tel. 06741/93100).

The St. Goar TI offers free left-luggage service (Monday–Friday 8:00–12:30 and 14:00–17:00, Saturday 9:30–12:00 May–October; closed Sunday and earlier in winter, tel. 06741/383). You can rent a bike at the Golf Pavilion near the river (13 DM/day).

St. Goar's waterfront park is hungry for a picnic. The small EDEKA supermarket on main street is fine for picnic fixings (Monday–Friday 8:30–19:00, Saturday 8:00–16:00, closed Sunday).

The friendly and helpful Montag family in the shop under Hotel Montag has Rhine guidebooks (Koblenz–Mainz), fine steins, and copies of this guidebook.

For a good two-hour hike from St. Goar, catch the ferry across to St. Goarshausen, hike to the Katz castle, and traverse along the hillside from there to the top of the Loreley. From the Loreley, the trail winds down to the river and then takes you back to the St. Goarshausen to St. Goar ferry (4/hr, 3-DM round-trip).

**Km 559: Burg Maus**—The Maus got its name because the next castle was owned by the Katzenelnbogen family. In the 1300s, it was considered a state-of-the-art fortification . . . until Napoleon had it blown up in 1806 with state-of-the-art explosives. It was rebuilt true to its original plans around 1900.

**Km 567: Burg Sterrenberg and Burg Liebenstein**—These are the "Hostile Brothers" castles (with the white square tower). Take the wall between the castles (actually designed to improve the defenses of both castles), add two greedy and jealous brothers and a fair maiden, and create your own legend. The castles are restaurants today.

**Km 570: Boppard**—Once a Roman town, Boppard has some impressive remains of fourth-century walls. Notice the Roman tower just after the Boppard train station and the substantial chunk of Roman wall just before. Boppard is worth a stop. Just above the market square are the remains of the Roman wall. Below the square is a fascinating church. Notice the carved Romanesque crazies at the doorway. Inside, to the right of the entrance, you'll see Christian symbols from Roman times. Also notice the painted arches and vaults. Originally most Romanesque churches were painted this way. Down by the river, look for the high water (*Hochwasser*) marks on the arches from various flood years. (Throughout the Rhine and Mosel Valleys you'll see these flood marks.)

**Km 580: Marksburg**—This castle (with the three modern chimneys behind it) is the best-looking of all the Rhine castles and the only surviving medieval castle on the Rhine. Because of its commanding position, it was never attacked. It's now open as a museum with a medieval interior second only to the Mosel's Burg Eltz (7 DM, daily 10:00–17:00, tour required—in German, worth a visit only if you can tag along with a rare English tour, call ahead, tel. 02627/206).

**Km 585: Burg Lahneck**—Above the modern autobahn bridge over the Lahn River, this castle was built in 1240 to defend local silver mines, ruined by the French in 1688 and rebuilt in the 1850s in neo-Gothic style. Burg Lahneck faces the yellow Schloss Stolzenfels (out of view above the train, a ten-minute climb from the tiny car park, open for touring, closed Monday).

**Km 590: Koblenz**—The Romantic Rhine thrills and the Blitz Rhine Tour ends at Koblenz. It's not a nice city (it was really hit hard in World War II), but its place as the historic *Deutsches-Eck* (German corner)—the tip of land where the Mosel joins the Rhine—gives it a certain magnetism. Koblenz, Latin for "confluence," has Roman origins. Walk through the park, noticing the reconstructed memorial to the Kaiser. Across the river, the yellow Ehrenbreitstein Castle now houses a hostel. It's a 30-minute hike from the station to the Koblenz boat dock.

## BACHARACH

Bacharach, once prosperous from the wine and wood trade, is now just a pleasant medieval village that misses most of the tourist glitz. Among its 14th-century fortifications is a tower that holds my favorite Rhine hotel—the Hotel Kranenturm—5 screaming yards from the train tracks.

The TI is on the main street a block from the train station; you'll get a town history and blurry photocopied map. Look for the "i" sign (Monday–Friday 9:00–12:30 and 13:30–17:00, Saturday 10:00–12:00, tel. 06743/1297; the TI might move closer "downtown" on Oberstrasse to the Posthof, just before the church and the intersection with Blücherstrasse).

The huge Jost beer stein "factory outlet" carries everything a shopper could want. It has one shop across from the church in the main square and a slightly cheaper shop a block away on Rosenstrasse 16 (Monday–Friday 8:30–18:00, Saturday 8:30–17:00, Sunday 10:00–17:00, ships overseas, 10 percent discount with this book on non-sale items, CC:VM, tel. 06743/1224).

Get acquainted with Bacharach by taking a walking tour. Herr Rolf Jung, retired headmaster of the Bacharach school, gives excellent guided tours in English with plenty of history and photos (50 DM, 1.5 hrs, tel. 06743/1519). Or try this self-guided walk:

## Introductory Tour of Bacharach

Start at the Köln–Dusseldorf ferry dock (next to a fine picnic park). View the town from the parking lot—a modern landfill.

**Bacharach**

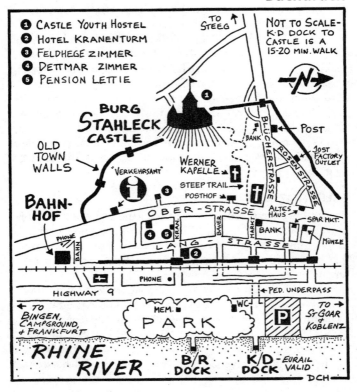

1 CASTLE YOUTH HOSTEL
2 HOTEL KRANENTURM
3 FELDHEGE ZIMMER
4 DETTMAR ZIMMER
5 PENSION LETTIE

TO STEEG

NOT TO SCALE—
K·D DOCK TO
CASTLE IS A
15–20 MIN. WALK

N

BURG STAHLECK CASTLE

OLD TOWN WALLS

BANK

POST

BLÜCHERSTRASSE

ROSENSTRASSE

JOST FACTORY OUTLET

"Verkehrsamt"

WERNER KAPELLE

STEEP TRAIL

POSTHOF

BAHN-HOF

OBER - STRASSE

ALTES HAUS

SPAR MKT.

BANK

MÜNZE

PHONE

KRAN.

BAUER

MARKT

LANG - STRASSE

PHONE

HIGHWAY 9

PED. UNDERPASS

TO BINGEN, CAMPGROUND, & FRANKFURT

WC

MEM. PARK

P

TO ST GOAR & KOBLENZ

RHINE RIVER

B/R DOCK

K/D DOCK — EURAIL VALID

DCH

The Rhine used to lap against Bacharach's town wall. Two of its original 16 towers are visible from here (up to five if you look real hard). The huge roadside wine keg declares this town was built on the wine trade. Reefs up the river forced boats to unload upriver and reload here. As a result, Bacharach became the biggest wine trader on the Rhine. A riverfront crane hoisted huge kegs of prestigious "Bacharach" wine (which in practice was from anywhere in the region). The tour buses next to the dock remind you today's economy is basically tourism.

At the big town map and public WC, take the underpass, ascend on the right, and walk under the train tracks through the medieval gate (one out of an original six 14th-century gates) and to the two-tone Protestant church which marks the town center. From this intersection, Bacharach's main street (Ober-strasse) goes right to the half-timbered Altes Haus (from 1368, the oldest house in town) and left to the TI and train station. To the left (or south) of the church, duck into old Posthof. Notice the fascist eagle—on the left doorstep as you enter—and the fine view of a chapel and church. This post station dates from 1724, when stagecoaches ran from Köln to Frankfurt.

Two hundred years ago this was the only road along the Rhine. Napolean widened it to fit his cannon wagons. The steps alongside the church lead to the castle.

Inside the church you'll find grotesque and brightly painted capitals and a mix of round Romanesque and pointed Gothic arches. In the upper left corner some medieval frescos survive where an older Romanesque arch was cut by a pointed Gothic one.

Walk past Bacharach's main intersection and past the Altes Haus to the old mint (Münze) marked by a crude coin in its sign. Across from the mint, the wine garden of Fritz Bastian is the liveliest place in town after dark. Above you in the vine-yards stands a ghostly black and gray tower—your destination. Wander 30 meters up Rosenstrasse to the well. Notice the sun-dial and the wall painting of 1632 Bacharach with its walls intact. Climb the tiny stepped lane behind the well up into the vineyard and to the tower. The slate steps deposit you at a viewpoint atop the stubby remains of the old town wall just above the tower's base.

A grand medieval town spreads before you. When Frank-furt had 15,000 residents, medieval Bacharach had 6,000. For 300 years (1300–1600) Bacharach was big, rich, and politically powerful.

From this perch you can see the chapel ruins and six of the nine surviving city towers. Visually trace the wall to the castle, home of one of seven electors who voted in the Holy Roman Emperor in 1275. To protect their own power, these elector princes did their best to choose the weakest guy on the ballot. The elector from Bacharach helped select a two-bit prince named Rudolf von Habsburg (from a two-bit castle in Switzer-land). The underestimated Rudolf brutally silenced the robber barons along the Rhine and established the mightiest dynasty in European history. His family line, the Habsburgs, ruled the Austro-Hungarian empire until 1918.

Plagues, fires, and the Thirty Years War (1618–1648)

finally did Bacharach in. The town has slumbered for several centuries, with a population of about a thousand.

In the mid-19th century, artists and writers such as Victor Hugo were charmed by the Rhineland's romantic mix of past glory, present poverty, and rich legend. They put this part of the Rhine on the old "grand tour" map as the "Romantic Rhine." Victor Hugo pondered the ruined 15th-century chapel which you can see under the castle. In his 1842 travel book, *Rhein Reise*, (Rhine Travels) he wrote, "No doors, no roof or windows, a magnificent-skeleton puts its sillouette against the sky. Above it, the ivy-covered castle ruins provide a fitting crown. This is Bacharach, land of fairy tales, covered with legends and sagas."

A path leads along the wall up the valley to the next tower and down onto the street. The road leads under the gate and back into the center. If you're enjoying the Romantic Rhine, thank Victor Hugo and company.

## Sleeping on the Rhine
### (1.7 DM = about $1)

Sleep Code: **S**=Single, **D**=Double/Twin, **T**=Triple, **Q**=Quad, **b**=bathroom, **t**=toilet only, **s**=shower only, **CC**=Credit Card (Visa, MasterCard, Amex), **SE**=Speaks English, **NSE**=No English. All hotels speak some English. Most Zimmer do not. Breakfast is included unless otherwise noted.

The Rhine is an easy place for cheap sleeps. Zimmer and Gasthäuser with 35-DM beds abound (and Zimmer normally discount their prices for longer stays). Several exceptional Rhine-area hostels offer even cheaper beds (for travelers of any age). Each town's helpful TI is eager to set you up, and finding a room should be easy any time of year (except for wine-festy weekends in September and October). Bacharach and St. Goar, the best towns for an overnight stop, are about 10 miles apart, connected by milk-run trains, river boats, and a riverside bike path. Bacharach is less touristy, St. Goar has the famous castle.

### Sleeping in Bacharach
**(tel. code: 06743, zip code: 55422)**

### Hotels

**Hotel Kranenturm** gives you the feeling of a castle without the climb. This is my choice for the best combination of comfort and hotel privacy with Zimmer warmth, central location, and medieval atmosphere. Owned and run by hardworking Kurt Engel and his intense but friendly wife, Fatima, this hotel is actually part of the medieval fortification. Its former *Kranen* (crane) towers are now round rooms. When the riverbank was higher, cranes on this tower loaded barrels of wine onto Rhine boats. Hotel Kranenturm is 5 yards from the train tracks (just under the medieval gate at the Frankfurt end of town), but a combination of medieval sturdiness, triple-paned windows, and included ear plugs makes the riverside rooms sleepable (Sb-60–65 DM, Db-90–95 DM, Tb-125–130 DM, Qb-160–165 DM with this book, cheaper price is for stays of at least two days, kid-friendly, Rhine views come with train noise, the back rooms—some with castle views—are quieter, laundry service, CC:VMA but prefer cash, reservations easiest by phone with CC, Langstrasse 30, tel. 06743/1308, fax 06743/1021, Fatima SE). Kurt, a great cook, serves fine 15–20 DM dinners. His big-enough-for-three Kranenturm ice-cream special may ruin you (10.20 DM). For a quick trip to Fiji in a medieval German cellar, check out his tropical bar. From the train station, take the main street (Oberstrasse), then turn right on Kranenstrasse.

**Hotel Altkölnischer Hof**, on the main square, rents attractive rooms, some with balconies overlooking the quaint square (Sb-90–95 DM, Db-110–130 DM, Db with terrace-140 DM, with balcony-150–160 DM, TV and phones in rooms, elevator, attached restaurant, CC:VA, tel. 06743/1339 or 06743/2186, fax 06743/2793, some English spoken).

**Hotel Gelberhof** has bright, comfortable rooms worthy of a splurge (S-55 DM, Sb-75–85 DM, one small Db-110 DM, Db-120–140 DM, popular with groups, attached restaurant, elevator, bike rental, CC:M, Blucherstrasse 26, tel. 06743/910-100, fax 06743/910-1050, e-mail: gelberhof@fh-bingen.de). Coming from the train station, turn left at the main square on Blucherstrasse.

**Hotel Hillen**, a block south of the Hotel Kranenturm, has less charm and as much train noise, with friendly owners and lots of rental bikes (S-45 DM, Sb-60 DM, D-80 DM, Db-90 DM, Tb-126 DM, CC:VMA, Langstrasse 18, tel. 06743/1287, fax 06743/1037, some English spoken).

### Pensions and Private Rooms
Friendly **Pension Lettie** offers four cheery, newly remodeled rooms (Sb-55–60 DM, Db-80–90 DM, Tb-115–120 DM with

this book, cheaper price is for longer stays, non-smoking, CC:VMA but prefers cash, a few doors down from Hotel Kranenturm, Kranenstrasse 6, tel. & fax 06743/2115, SE). Lettie also does laundry (16 DM per load, guests only) and rents bikes (15 DM/day, no deposit for guests, non-guests need to leave a passport or credit-card imprint).

**Frau Feldhege** rents two rooms in her quiet, homey, traditional place (Db-55 DM, no breakfast, Oberstrasse 13, in the old center on a small lane a few yards off the main street, tel. 06743/1271). Guests get a cushy living room, a self-serve kitchen, and free use of bikes.

Entreprenurial **Annelie und Hans Dettmar** rent four smoke-free rooms in a modern house on the main drag in the center (Db-50–70 DM, Tb-75 DM, Qb-100 DM, free use of bikes for guests, laundry-17 DM, Oberstrasse 8, tel. 06743/2661, fax 06743/2979, SE). One room is huge, easily fits a family of four, and has a kitchenette that costs 20 DM if you use it. Skip their other building up the hill; it's a long, steep walk away. Readers give this couple mixed reviews, but their place is handy for those who need a smoke-free option.

**Ursula Orth** offers four small, bright rooms in her home around the corner from the Dettmars' in the town center (Sb-30 DM, Db-55–60 DM, Tb-75 DM for one night and less for two, Spurgasse 3, tel. 06743/1557, some English spoken). Coming from the station, her place is about a block past the TI; turn right on alley.

The home of **Herr und Frau Theilacker** is a German-feeling Zimmer with comfortable rooms and no outside sign, and is likely to have a room when others don't (S-30 DM, D-60 DM, in the town center behind the Altes Haus at Oberstrasse 57, tel. 06743/1248, NSE).

### Hostel

Bacharach's hostel, **Jugendherberge Stahleck**, is a 12th-century castle on the hilltop, 500 steps above Bacharach, with a royal Rhine view. Open to travelers of any age, this is a newly redone gem with eight beds and a private modern shower and WC in each room. A 15-minute climb on the trail from the town church, the hostel is warmly and energetically run by Evelyn and Bernhard Falke (FALL-kay), who serve hearty, 9-DM buffet all-you-can-eat dinners. The hostel pub serves cheap local wine until midnight (23.50-DM dorm beds with breakfast; 6 DM extra if over 26, without a card, or in a double; groups are welcome for 32 DM per bed with breakfast and dinner; accepts traveler's checks, no smoking in rooms, easy parking, beds normally available but call and leave your name, they'll hold a bed until 18:00, can help you find a place if full, tel. 06743/1266, SE).

## Sleeping in St. Goar
### (tel. code 06741, zip code: 56329)

**Hotel Montag** is just across the street from the world's largest free-hanging cuckoo clock. Manfred Montag, his wife, Maria, and son Mike speak New Yorkish. Even though Montag gets a lot of bus tours, it's friendly, laid-back, and comfortable (Sb-70 DM, Db-130 DM, price can drop if you arrive late or it's a slow time, CC:VMA, Heerstrasse 128, tel. 06741/1629, fax 06741/2086). Check out their adjacent crafts shop (heavy on beer steins).

**Hotel Hauser**, very central and newly redone, is warmly run by Frau Velich (S-42 DM, D-88 DM, Db-98 DM, Db with Rhine-view balconies-110 DM, show this book to get these prices, cheaper in off-season, CC:VMA, Heerstrasse 77, telephone reservations easy, tel. 06741/333, fax 06741/1464, SE).

**Hotel am Markt**, well-run by Herr and Frau Velich, is rustic with all the modern comforts, featuring a hint of antler with a pastel flair and bright rooms in the center of town (18 rooms, Ss-65 DM, Sb-80 DM, Db-100 DM, Tb-140 DM, Qb-160 DM, cheaper off-season, open March–November, CC:VMA, Am Markt 1, tel. 06741/1689, fax 06741/1721, SE).

**Hotel Silberne Rose** has comfortable rooms with older decor, some with Rhine views (Sb-65 DM, Db-100 DM, Tb-120–140 DM, cheaper price for longer stays, across street from dock, Heerstrasse 63, tel. 06741/7040, fax 06741/2865).

St. Goar's best Zimmer deal is the home of **Frau Kurz**, with a breakfast terrace, fine view, easy parking, and all the comforts of a hotel (S-34 DM, D-60 DM, Db-70 DM, showers-5 DM, one-night stays cost extra, confirm prices, Ulmenhof 11, tel. & fax 06741/459, some English spoken). From the train station, it's a steep three-minute hike (memorable with luggage). Exit left from the station, take an immediate left at the post office and go under the tracks to the paved path. Take a right partway up the stairs, then climb just a few more stairs to a road where you'll find the Zimmer.

The Germanly run **St. Goar Hostel**, the big beige building under the castle, is a good value, with two to 12 beds per room, a 22:00 curfew, and hearty 9-DM dinners (19.50-DM beds with breakfast, 5-DM sleep sacks, open all day, Bismarckweg 17, tel. 06741/388, SE).

## Eating in Bacharach

For inexpensive and atmospheric dining in Bacharach, try **Hotel Kranenturm** (see above) or **Altes Haus** (the oldest building in town, on main square, 20-DM dinners, closed Wednesday). **Bastian Weingut** offers delicious cold lunches and the **Posthof** beer garden has good, cheap pub grub, served outside in the courtyard.

**Wine Tasting:** Drop in on entertaining Fritz Bastian's **Weingut zum Gruner Baum** wine bar (just past the Altes Haus, tel. 06743/1208, evenings only, closed Thursday). He's the president of the local vintner's club and his calling is giving travelers an understanding of the subtle differences among the Rhine wines. Groups of two to ten people pay 26 DM for a "carousel" of 15 glasses of 14 different white wines and one lonely red. Spin the lazy Susan, share a common cup, and discuss the taste.

## Transportation Connections—Rhine

Milk-run trains stop at all Rhine towns each hour starting around 6:00. Koblenz, Boppard, St. Goar, Bacharach, Bingen, and Mainz are each about 15 minutes apart. From Koblenz to Mainz takes 75 minutes. To get a faster big train, go to Mainz or Koblenz.

**From Mainz by train to: Bacharach/St. Goar** (hrly, 1 hr), **Cochem** (hrly, 2.5 hrs, changing in Koblenz), **Köln** (3/hr, 90 min), **Baden-Baden** (hrly, 2.5 hrs), **Munich** (hrly, 4 hrs), **Frankfurt** (3/hr, 45 min), **Frankfurt Airport** (3/hr, 25 min).

**From Frankfurt by train to: Koblenz** (hrly, 90 min), **Rothenburg** (hrly, 3 hrs, transfers in Würzburg and Steinach), **Würzburg** (hrly, 90 min), **Munich** (hrly, 3.5 hrs), **Amsterdam** (8/day, 5 hrs), **Paris** (4/day, 6.5 hrs).

## MOSEL VALLEY

The misty Mosel is what many visitors hoped the Rhine would be—peaceful, sleepy, romantic villages slipped between the steep vineyards and the river, fine wine, a sprinkling of castles, and lots of friendly Zimmer. Boat, train, and car traffic here is a trickle compared to the roaring Rhine. While the swan-speckled Mosel moseys 300 miles from France's Vosges Mountains to Koblenz, where it dumps into the Rhine, the most scenic piece of the valley lies between the towns of Bernkastel-Kues and Cochem. I'd savor only this section.

Throughout the region on summer weekends and during the fall harvest time, wine festivals with oompah bands, dancing, and colorful costumes are powered by good food and wine.

## Getting Around the Mosel Valley

The train gets you to Cochem or Trier in a snap. Regular buses connect the smallest train stations with Mosel villages. The Beilstein–Cochem bus takes 15 minutes (7/day, fewer on weekends, 4 DM). Consider a boat ride from Cochem to Zell (2/day, 3 hrs, 23 DM one-way, 33 DM round-trip) or Beilstein (5/day, 60 min, 12 DM one-way, 17 DM round-trip, tel. 02673/1515). The K-D (Köln–Düsseldorf) line sails once a day in each direction (May–mid-October, Koblenz to Cochem 10:00–14:30, or Cochem to Koblenz 15:50–20:10, free with Eurail). You can also rent bikes at some stations and leave them at others, or rent a bike in Cochem from the K-D line kiosk at the dock (summers only) or year-round from Kreutz at the Shell station on Ravenestrasse 7 (7 DM/4 hrs, 14 DM/day, no deposit required, just your passport number). If you find yourself stranded, hitching isn't bad.

## Sights—Mosel Valley

**Cochem**—With a majestic castle and picturesque medieval streets, Cochem is the very touristic hub of this part of the river. The Cochem TI has a free town history and a walking tour brochure. The pointy Cochem Castle is the work of overly imaginative 19th-century restorers (6 DM, daily mid-March–October 9:00–17:00, 15-minute walk from Cochem, tel. 02761/255). German-language tours, with written English explanation, are given frequently. Try to gather a group of ten to 12 English speakers to get part of the tour in English.

The Cochem TI books rooms (same day only), keeps a thorough 24-hour listing in its window, and offers lots of brochures and concert info (Monday–Friday 10:00–13:00 and 14:00–17:00, summer Saturday 10:00–15:00 and Sunday

## Mosel Valley

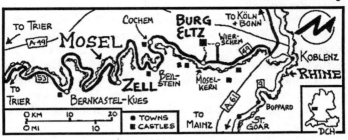

10:00–12:00, off-season closed weekends, tel. 02671/3971). The "Moselle Wine Road" flyer is perfect for wine-lovers. Day-trippers can check luggage at the station. Many train travelers end up sleeping in Cochem (see Sleeping, below). Stroll along the pleasant paths that line the river. Cochem is right on the train line (to Koblenz, hrly, 60 min; to Trier, hrly, 60 min). ▲▲▲**Burg Eltz**—My favorite castle in all of Europe lurks in a mysterious forest, has been left intact for 700 years, and is furnished throughout as it was 500 years ago. Thanks to smart diplomacy and clever marriages, Burg Eltz was never destroyed. (It survived one five-year siege.) It's been in the Eltz family for 820 years. The countess arranges for new flowers in each room weekly. The only way to see the castle is with a one-hour tour (included in admission ticket). German tours (with pathetic English fact sheets) go constantly. Organize an English tour. (Corral 20 English-speakers in the inner courtyard—they'll thank you for it. Push the red button on the white porch and politely beg for an English guide. This is well worth a short wait. You can also telephone ahead to see if there's an English-language group scheduled that you could tag along with.)

Reaching Burg Eltz by train, walk one steep hour from Moselkern station (midway between Cochem and Koblenz; trail is slippery when wet) through a pine forest where sparrows carry crossbows, and maidens, disguised as falling leaves, whisper "watch out." Driving to Burg Eltz, leave the river at Moselkern (shortest drive) or Hatzenport (but not Muden), following the white "Burg Eltz P&R" signs to the castle car park, a ten-minute walk from the castle. There are three "Burg Eltz" parking lots; only this one is close enough for an easy

walk (8 DM, daily April–October 9:30–17:30, constant
1.50-DM shuttle bus service from car park, tel. 02672/1300).
▲**Beilstein**—Farther upstream is the quaintest of all Mosel
towns (see Sleeping, below). Beilstein is Cinderella land. Check
out the narrow lanes, ancient wine cellar, resident (and very
territorial) swans, and ruined castle. The small 1.50-DM ferry
goes constantly back and forth. Two shops rent bikes for the
pleasant riverside roll (toward Zell is best). The TI is in a café
(summer Tuesday–Sunday 9:00–18:00, closed Monday, tel.
02673/1417).
▲**Zell**—This is the best Mosel town for an overnight stop (see
Sleeping, below). It's peaceful, with a fine riverside promenade,
a pedestrian bridge over the water, plenty of Zimmer, and a
long pedestrian zone filled with colorful shops, restaurants,
*Weinstubes*, and a fun oompah folk band on weekend evenings
on the main square. Walk up to the medieval wall's gatehouse
and through the cemetery to the old munitions tower for a village view. The fine little Wein und Heimat Museum features
Mosel history (Wednesday and Saturday 15:00–17:00). Locals
know the town for its Schwarze Katz (Black Cat) wine. (TI
open Monday–Friday 8:00–12:30 and 13:30–17:00, Saturday
9:00–14:00, off-season closed on Saturday, tel. 06542/4031.)

## Sleeping on the Mosel
**(1.7 DM = about $1)**

### Sleeping in Cochem
**(tel. code: 02671, zip code: 56812)**
All places include breakfast. The little town is strung along the
river. Exit right from the station onto Ravenestrasse. A
seven-minute walk brings you to the TI (on your left, past the
bus lanes). To get to the main square (Markt), continue under
the bridge, then angle right and follow Bernstrasse.
   **Gästezimmer Hüsgen** is a good and handy value that
welcomes one-night stays (Ss-40–45 DM, D-64 DM, Ds-68
DM, Db-82 DM, family deals, ground-floor rooms, small view
terrace, Ravenestrasse 34, near the station, tel. 02671/5817,
Andrea SE). Across the street, the **Ravene** offers six rooms
varying in size and quality from odd to comfortable (Sb-60
DM, Db-80–100 DM, Tb-132 DM, add 5 DM per person for
one-night stay, Ravenestrasse 43, tel. 02671/980-177, fax
02671/91119, some English spoken).

The rustic **Hotel Lohspeicher**, just off the main square, is for those who want a real hotel (and much higher prices). The best values are the bigger #4 and small view room #8 (Sb-75–95 DM, Db-170 DM, elevator, CC:VMA, Obergasse 1, on tiny-stepped street off main square, tel. 02671/3976, fax 02671/1772, Ingo SE). Farther up the quiet street, you'll find the **Stolz Zimmer** at 20 Obergasse, with big rooms that look like they were decorated by an elderly aunt (Ss-30 DM, Sb-30 DM, Ds-60 DM, Db-60 DM, less for stays of two nights or more, tel. 02671/1509, friendly Mrs. Stolz NSE).

**Haus Andreas** has small but modern rooms (S-25 DM, Sb-40 DM, Db-60 DM, Schlosstrasse 16, tel. 02671/1370 or 02671/5155, fax 02671/1370). From the main square, take Herrenstrasse; after 1 block, angle right uphill on Schlosstrasse.

### Sleeping in Zell
**(tel. code: 06542, zip code: 56856)**
If the Mosel charms you into spending the night, do it in Zell. By car, this is a natural. By train, you'll need to go to Bullay (from Cochem or Trier), where the bus takes you to little Zell (2.60 DM, 2/hr, 10 min; bus stop is across street from Bullay train station; check yellow MB schedule for times). Its hotels are a disappointment, but its private homes are great. The owners speak almost no English and discount their rates if you stay more than one night. They can't take reservations long in advance for one-night stays; just call a day ahead. They ask that you honor your reservations. My favorites are on the south end of town, a two-minute walk from the town hall square and the bus stop. Breakfast is included.

**Gästhaus Gertrud Thiesen** is classy, with a TV-living-breakfast room and a river view. The Thiesen house has big, bright rooms and is on the town's first corner overlooking the Mosel from a great terrace (S or D-70 DM, Balduinstrasse 1, tel. 06542/4453, SE).

Friendly **Natalie Huhn**, your German grandmother, has the cheapest beds in town in her simple but comfortable house (S-30 DM, D-60 DM, cheaper for two-night stays, near the pedestrian bridge behind the church at Jakobstrasse 32, tel. 06542/41048).

**Weinhaus Zum Fröhlichen Weinberg** offers cheap, basic rooms (D-60 DM, family Zimmer, Mittelstrasse 6, tel. 06542/4308) above a *Weinstube* disco (noisy on Friday and

Saturday nights). **Gästehaus Am Römerbad** is also central and a decent value (Db-80 DM, Am Römerbad, tel. 06542/41602, Elizabeth Münster).

The comfortable and modern home of **Fritz Mesenich** is quiet, friendly, clean, central, and across from a good wine bar (D-60 DM, 50 DM if you stay two nights, Oberstrasse 3, tel. 06542/4753, NSE). Herr Mesenich can take you into his cellar for a look at the *haus* wine. Notice the flood (*Hochwasser*) marks on the wall across the street.

If you're looking for room service, a sauna, pool, and elevator, sleep at **Hotel Grüner Kranz** (Db-160 DM with Mosel views, 140 DM without, elevator, CC:VMA, tel. 06542/98610, fax 06542/986-180). **Weinhaus Mayer**, a classy—if stressed out—old pension next door, is perfectly central with Mosel-view rooms (13 rooms, Db-120 DM, Balduinstrasse 15, tel. 06542/4530, fax 06542/61160).

### Sleeping in Beilstein
### (tel. code: 02673, zip code: 56814)

Cozier and farther north, Beilstein (BILE-shtine) is very small and quiet (no train; 7 buses/day to nearby Cochem, fewer buses on weekends; 15-minute trip). Breakfast is included.

**Hotel Haus Lipmann** is your chance to live in a medieval mansion with hot showers and TVs. A prize-winner for atmosphere, it's been in the Lipmann family for 200 years. The creaky wooden staircase and the elegant dining hall, with long wooden tables surrounded by antlers, chandeliers, and feudal weapons will get you in the mood for your castle sightseeing, but the riverside terrace may mace your momentum (five rooms, Db-120–150 DM, tel. 02673/1573, fax 02673/1521).

**Gasthaus Winzerschenke an der Klostertreppe** is comfortable and a great value, right in the tiny heart of town (Db-75 DM, bigger Db-95 DM, discount for two-night stays, tel. 02673/1354, Frau Sausen).

The half-timbered, riverfront **Altes Zollhaus Gästzimmer** has crammed all the comforts into tight, bright (if a bit musty), and modern rooms (Db-95 DM, deluxe Db-135 DM, 15 DM more on Friday and Saturday, open March–October, tel. 02673/1574 or 02673/1850, fax 02673/1287).

# TRIER

Germany's oldest city lies at the head of the scenic Mosel Valley, near the Luxembourg border. An ancient Roman capital,

Trier brags that it was inhabited for 1,300 years before the Romans came. A short stop here offers you a look at Germany's oldest Christian church, one of its most enjoyable market squares, and its best Roman ruins.

Founded by Augustus in 15 B.C., Trier was the Roman "Augusta Treverorum" for 500 years. When Emperor Diocletian divided his overextended Roman empire into four sectors in A.D. 285, he made Trier the capital of the West (Germany, France, Spain, and Britain). For most of the fourth century, this city of 80,000 with a 4-mile-long wall, four great gates, and 47 round towers was the favored residence of Roman emperors. Emperor Constantine used the town as the capital of his fading western Roman Empire. Much of the building was built under Constantine before he left for Constantinople. In 480, Trier fell to the Franks. Today Trier's Roman sights include the huge city gate (Porta Nigra), basilica, baths, and amphitheater.

## Orientation (tel. code: 0651)

**Tourist Information:** Trier's TI, next to the Porta Nigra, organizes two-hour, 10-DM town walks in English daily at 13:30 (Monday–Saturday 9:00–18:30, Sunday 9:00–15:30, less off-season, tel. 0651/978-080).

**Arrival in Trier:** From the train station, walk 4 boring blocks up Theodor-Heuss Allee to the big black Roman gate, where you'll find the TI. From here the main pedestrian mall leads into the town's charm: the market square, cathedral, and basilica—all within a five-minute walk. Drivers stay on the autobahn until it ends and follow signs to Zentrum. There is parking near the gate and TI.

## Sights—Trier

▲**Porta Nigra**—Roman Trier was built as a capital. Its architecture mirrored the grandeur of the Empire. Of the 4-mile wall's four huge gates, only this north gate survives. This most impressive Roman fortification in Germany was built without mortar—only iron pegs hold the sandstone blocks together. While the other three gates were destroyed by medieval metal and stone scavengers, this "black gate" survived because it became a church. Saint Simeon—a pious Greek recluse—lived inside the gate for seven years. After his death in 1035, the Simeon monastery was established and the gate was made into a 2-story church—lay church on the bottom, monastery church on top. While Napoleon had the church destroyed in 1803, the 12th-century Romanesque apse—the round part which you can see at the east end—survived. (For a small entrance fee, you can climb around the gate.)

Trier's main pedestrian drag, which leads away from the gate, is named for Saint Simeon. The arcaded courtyard and buildings of the monastery of Saint Simeon survive. They now house the (skippable) city museum and TI.

▲▲**Market Place**—Trier's Hauptmarkt square is a people-filled swirl of fruit stands, flowers, painted facades, and fountains—with a handy public WC. One of Germany's most in-love-with-life marketplaces, its centerpiece, a market cross from 958 (with an ancient Roman pedestal), celebrates the trading rights given to the town by King Otto the Great. The adjacent Renaissance St. Peter's Fountain (1595) symbolizes thoughtful city government with allegorical statues of justice (sword and scale), fortitude (broken column), temperance (wine and water), and prudence (snake and mirror). From this square you can survey a textbook of architectural styles. Overlooking it all (as its fire watchman did in medieval times) is the Gothic tower of the church of St. Gangolf.

▲▲**Cathedral**—This church, the oldest in Germany, goes back to Roman times. St. Helena, the mother of Emperor Constantine (who legalized Christianity in the Roman Empire in A.D. 312) and an important figure in early Christian history, let part of her palace be used as the first church on this spot. (A fine Roman-painted ceiling survives under today's altar.) In 326, to celebrate the 20th anniversary of his reign, Constantine began the construction of St. Peter's in Rome and a huge cathedral (*Dom*) in Trier. The cathedral's most important relic is the "Holy Robe" of Christ (rarely on display, found by St. Helena on a pilgrimage to Jerusalem). The Leibfrau Church, connected to the Dom, dates from 1235 and claims to be the oldest Gothic church in Germany (8:00–12:00 and 14:00–18:00).

▲▲**Basilica**—At two hundred feet long and one hundred feet high, this is the largest intact Roman building outside of Rome. Picture this hall of justice in ancient times, decorated with golden mosaics, rich marble, colorful stucco, and busts of Constantine and his family filling the niches. The emperor sat in majesty under a canopy on his altarlike throne. The last emperor moved out in 395, and petty kings set up camp in the basilica throughout the Middle Ages. The building became a church in 1856.

Long after its Roman days, Trier was important enough to have a prince "elector" who helped elect the legal successors of the "Holy Roman Emperor." A Rococo wing, the Elector's Palace, was added to the basilica in the 18th century. This faces a fragrant garden which leads to the remains of a Roman bath and a 25,000-seat amphitheater.

**Karl Marx's House**—Last but not least, Communists can lick their wounds at Karl Marx's house. Early manuscripts, letters, and photographs of the influential economist/philosopher fill several rooms of his birth house. Sliding out of a shrinking middle class, people still sneer (3 DM, Tuesday–Sunday 10:00–18:00, Monday 13:00–18:00, lunch breaks in winter, 15-minute film at 20 minutes after each hour, a reasonable amount of English descriptions; from the Market Square walk down Fleischstrasse to Brückenstrasse 10).

## Sleeping in Trier
### (tel. code: 0651, zip code: 5500)

The best value in town is the Catholic Church–run **Kolping-haus Warsberger Hof**. This place is super-clean, well run, and serves inexpensive meals in its open-to-anyone restaurant (27 DM per bed with sheets and breakfast in two- to six-bed dorm rooms, or 39 DM per person in the S, D, or T hotel rooms, no private showers, 1 block off the market square, Dietrichstrasse 42, tel. 0651/975-250, fax 0651/975-2540, e-mail: v-hof@t-online.de). On the same street, **Hotel Frankenturm** is plain, comfortable, and simple, above a classy saloon (S-70 DM, Sb-110 DM, D-90 DM, Db-140 DM, CC:VM, Dietrichstrasse 3, tel. 0651/45712, fax 0651/978-2449).

For affordable beds near the train station, try **Hotel Monopol** (S-75 DM, Sb-90 DM, D-130 DM, Db-150 DM, buffet breakfast, Bahnhofsplatz 7, tel. 0651/714-090, fax 0651/714-0910). **Hotel Zum Christopher**, central and Old World, will be closed much of '98 for renovation (S-50 DM, Sb-75 DM, D-100 DM, Db-130 DM, CC:V; 4 blocks from the station, facing the TI and Roman gate, tel. 0651/74041, fax 0651/74732).

## Transportation Connections—Trier
**By train to:** Cochem (hrly, 45 min), **Köln** (9/day, 2.5 hrs),
**Koblenz** (hrly, 75 min).

## KÖLN (COLOGNE) AND THE UNROMANTIC RHINE
Romance isn't everything. Bonn and Köln are urban Jacuzzis
that keep the Rhine churning. The small town of Remagen had
a bridge that helped defeat Hitler in WWII, and unassuming
Aachen (near the Belgian border) was once the capital of
Europe.

## Getting Around the Unromantic Rhine
Fast and frequent super-trains connect Bonn, Köln, Trier,
Koblenz, and Frankfurt. All major sights are within a reason-
able walk from each city's train station.

## KÖLN
Germany's fourth largest city, big, no-nonsense Köln has a
compact and lively center. The Rhine was the northern boundary of the Roman Empire and, 1,700 years ago, Constantine,
the first Christian emperor, made "Colonia" the seat of a
bishop. Five hundred years later, under Charlemagne, it
became the seat of an archbishop. With 40,000 people living
within its walls, it was an important cultural and religious center throughout the Middle Ages. To many, the city is most
famous for its toilet water. "Eau de Cologne" was first made
here by an Italian chemist in 1709. Even after World War II
bombs destroyed 95 percent of it, Köln has remained, after a
remarkable recovery, a cultural and commercial center, as well
as a fun, colorful, and pleasant-smelling city.

### Orientation (tel. code: 0221)
**Tourist Information:** Köln's TI, opposite the church entry,
has a list of reasonable private guides (Monday–Saturday
8:00–22:30, Sunday 9:00–22:30, closes at 21:00 in winter, tel.
0221/19433).

    **Arrival in Köln:** Köln couldn't be easier to visit: its three
important sights cluster within 2 blocks of its train station and
TI. This super pedestrian zone is a constant carnival of people.
If you drive to Köln, follow signs to "Zentrum" and then to
the huge Dom/Rhein pay lot under the cathedral.

## Sights—Köln

▲▲**Cathedral**—The Gothic Dom, or cathedral, is far and away Germany's most exciting church (100 yards from the station, open 7:00–19:00). In 1998, the church celebrates its beginnings 750 years ago with a new organ and refurbished museum. Inside the church, under its 500-foot-tall spire, don't miss the amazingly realistic and 300-years-ahead-of-its-time "Gero Crucifix," sculpted in 976. The "Shrine of the Magi" is a lavish gold altarpiece containing the "bones of the three kings," which, by some stretch of medieval Christian logic, justified the secular power of the local king. These important relics, acquired in the 12th century, made Cologne a big enough stop on the pilgrimage trail to merit the construction of this magnificent cathedral. Take a careful look at the cathedral's fine stained glass and the cupboards of relics (mostly skulls) on each side of the nave. For 509 steps and 3 DM you can enjoy a fine city view from the cathedral's south tower. From the Glockenstube (only 400 steps) you can see the Dom's nine huge bells.

The square in front of the cathedral has been a busy civic meeting place since medieval times. Look for the giant replica tip of a spire, the north gate of the Roman city from A.D. 50, and postcards of the church after the 1945 bombing. As you face the church, the shopping pedestrian zone stretches to your right (at 3:00). The red brick building (at 2:00) is the Diocesan Museum. The Roman museum is ahead on the right (at about 1:00), and the art museum is behind that.

The Diocesan Museum has some of the cathedral's finest art (free, Friday–Wednesday 10:00–17:00, closed Thursday). It's an easy opportunity for a close-up view of exquisite medieval church art; an English sheet identifies each of the religious subjects.

▲▲**Römisch-Germanisches Museum**—Germany's best Roman museum offers not a word of English among its elegant and fascinating display of Roman artifacts: fine glassware, jewelry, and mosaics (7 DM, Tuesday–Friday 10:00–17:00, Thursday until 20:00, Saturday and Sunday 11:00–17:00). Cheapskates can view its prize piece, a fine mosaic floor, free from the front window.

▲▲**Wallraf-Richartz and Ludwig Museums**—Next door and more enjoyable, these two museums come in a slick and modern architectural package for one steep ticket price. The Richartz, on the first floor, features a world-class collection of old masters arranged chronologically, from medieval to northern Baroque and Impressionist. The Ludwig Museum (second and ground floors) is a stimulating trip through the art of our century (10 DM, Tuesday 10:00–20:00, Wednesday–Friday 10:00–18:00, Saturday–Sunday 11:00–18:00, closed Monday, buy the .50 DM "Museumsplan," classy but expensive cafeteria with a reasonable salad bar, tel. 0221/221-2382).

## Transportation Connections—Köln
**By train to: Cochem** (every 2 hrs, 1.75 hr), **Bacharach** or **St. Goar** (hrly, 1.5 hrs with one change), **Koblenz** (5/hr, 1 hr), **Bonn** (4/hr, 20 min), **Trier** (9/day, 2.5 hrs), **Aachen** (3/hr, 45 min), **Paris** (2/day, 6 hrs), **Amsterdam** (8/day, 2.5 hrs).

## Sights—Unromantic Rhine
▲**Bonn**—Bonn was chosen for its sleepy, cultured, and peaceful nature as a good place to plant Germany's first post-Hitler government. Now that Germany is one again, Berlin will resume its position as capital in 1999. Apart from the tremendous cost of switching the seat of government, more than 100,000 jobs are involved, and lots of Bonn families will have some difficult decisions to make.

Today Bonn is sleek, modern, and by big-city standards, remarkably pleasant and easygoing. Stop here not to see the sparse exhibit at **Beethoven's House** (8 DM, Monday–Saturday 10:00–17:00, Sunday 11:00–16:00, free English brochure, tel. 0228/981-7525) but to come up for a smoggy breath of the real world after the misty, romantic Rhine.

The pedestrian-only old town stretches out from the station and makes you wonder why the United States can't trade in its malls for real, people-friendly cities. The market square and Münsterplatz—filled with street musicians—are a joy. People-watching doesn't get much better. The TI is directly in front of the station (Monday–Friday 9:00–18:30, Saturday 9:00–17:00, Sunday 10:00–14:00, room-finding service for 5 DM, tel. 0228/773-466).

**Hotel Eschweiler** is plain but well-located, just off the market square on a pedestrian street next to Beethoven's place above a taco joint. Donka, the Bulgarian woman who runs the hotel, is a sweetheart (S-60 DM, Ss-70 DM, Sb-95 DM, Ds-120 DM, Db-140 DM, show this book for a 10 percent discount, great breakfasts, seven-minute walk from the station,

Bonngasse 7, tel. 0228/631-760 or 0228/631-769, fax 0228/694-904).

▲**Remagen**—Midway between Koblenz and Köln are the scant remains of the Bridge at Remagen, of World War II (and movie) fame. But the memorial and the bridge stubs are enough to stir the emotions of Americans who remember when it was the only bridge that remained, allowing the Allies to cross the Rhine and race to Berlin in 1945. The small museum tells the bridge's fascinating story in English. Built during World War I to help supply the German forces on the Western Front, it's ironic that this was the bridge Eisenhower said was worth its weight in gold for its service against Germany. Hitler executed four generals for their failure to blow it up. Ten days after the Americans arrived, it did collapse, killing 28 Americans (2.50 DM, daily March–October 10:00–17:00, on Rhine's west bank, south side of Remagen town, follow "Brücke von Remagen" signs). Remagen TI tel. 02642/22572.

▲**Aachen (Charlemagne's Capital)**—This city was the capital of Europe in A.D. 800, when Charles the Great (Charlemagne) called it Aix-la-Chapelle. The remains of his rule include an impressive Byzantine/Ravenna-inspired church with his sarcophagus and throne. The city also has a headliner newspaper museum and great fountains, including a clever arrange-'em-yourself version.

## Sightseeing Lowlights
**Heidelberg**—This famous old university town attracts hordes of Americans. Any surviving charm is stained almost beyond recognition by commercialism. It doesn't make it in Germany's top 20 days.

**Mainz, Wiesbaden, and Rüdesheim**—These towns are all too big or too famous. They're not worth your time. Mainz's Gutenberg Museum is also a disappointment.

# BERLIN

No tour of Germany is complete without a look at its historic and newly united capital, a construction zone called Berlin. Stand over ripped-up tracks and under a canopy of cranes and wonder where the city is going. Enjoy the thrill of walking over what was The Wall and through Brandenburg Gate. Crossing "into the East" is now like stepping on a dead dragon, no longer mysterious and foreboding—just ugly. That thrill is gone.

Berlin has shut the door on a tumultuous 50-year chapter in its 750-year history. It was devastated in World War II, then divided by the Allied powers, with the American, British, and French sectors being West Berlin, and the Russian sector, East Berlin. The division was set in stone when the East built the Berlin Wall in 1961. In 1989, The Wall fell, and in 1990, Germany was formally reunited.

Today the city is like a man who had a terrible accident, and half the body was given the best of care and the other was denied therapy. But Dr. Capitalism has arrived, and the East is on the mend.

The new right-wing city government is eager to charge forward with little nostalgia for anything that was "Eastern." Big corporations and the national government have moved in, and the dreary swath of land that was The Wall will soon again be the city center. City planners are boldly taking the reunification of the city and the return of the national government (in the year 1999) as a good opportunity to make Berlin a great capital once again.

But unification has a negative side. In some ways the soul of the city is gone. To many, the city is a sprawling, provincial, spoiled brat. The "Ossies" (less-than-flattering slang for East-erners) miss their security. The "Wessies" (Westerners) miss their easy ride. And The Wall survives in the minds of the peo-ple. Taxes and prices are sky high. Westerners no longer get their 8 percent bonus for living behind the "iron curtain." The metro—cheery as a New York subway—is filled with tired peo-ple. Hitler's dreams of a grand post-war Berlin seem to be resur-rected on the "Berlin 2005" posters. I fear a *Blade Runner* future.

## Planning Your Time

Because of its location and the cost of hotels, I'd enter and leave by either night train or plane. On a three-week trip through Germany, Austria, and Switzerland, I'd give Berlin two days and spend them this way:

**Day 1:** Arrive early on the overnight train. Visit the TI and check into a hotel. Do the Bus #100 orientation tour with a walk from Brandenburg Gate down Unter den Linden. (For a guided version of this orientation, take the Guide Friday tour or join a Berlin Walk). After lunch near Alexanderplatz, tour the Pergamon Museum, then spend the afternoon strolling Kurfürstendamm, visiting the Memorial Church and KaDeWe.

**Day 2:** Check out of hotel, leave bags there. Divide the morning between your choice of the paintings of the Gemälde-galerie (and nearby Kulturforum museums), the Egyptian Museum, Charlottenburg Palace, or the zoo. After lunch, sub-way to Hermannplatz and ride bus #129 through Kreuzberg to Haus am Checkpoint Charlie. Tour the museum, see remains of The Wall, tour the *Topography of Terror* exhibit. Depart on an overnight train.

## Orientation (tel. code: 030)

Berlin is huge, with 3.5 million people. But the tourist's Berlin can be broken into digestible chunks:

1. The area around Bahnhof Zoo and the grand Kurfürsten-damm Boulevard (transportation, tours, information, hotel, shopping, and nightlife hub).

2. Former downtown East Berlin (Brandenburg Gate, Unter den Linden Boulevard, Pergamon Museum, Wall-related sights, and nearby Potsdamer Platz).

3. Charlottenburg museums and palace.

Chunks 1 and 2 can be done on foot or with bus #100. Catch the U-Bahn to 3.

## Western Berlin

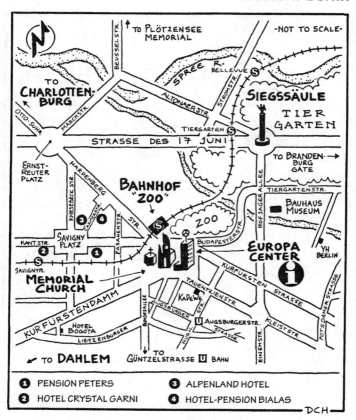

Legend:
1. PENSION PETERS
2. HOTEL CRYSTAL GARNI
3. ALPENLAND HOTEL
4. HOTEL-PENSION BIALAS

## Tourist Information

The two TI offices are run by a for-profit agency working for the city's big hotels. The main TI office is five minutes from the Bahnhof Zoo train station, in the Europa Center (with Mercedes symbol on top, enter outside to the left, on Budapesterstrasse, Monday–Saturday 8:00–22:00, Sunday 9:00–21:00, tel. 030/250-025). A smaller TI is at Brandenburg Gate, actually in the gate (daily 9:30–18:00). The TIs, which offer a room-finding service for 5 DM, also sell city maps (1 DM); the *Berlin Programm*, a German-language monthly listing upcoming events and museum hours, with a decent map (2.80 DM); and

## Eastern Berlin

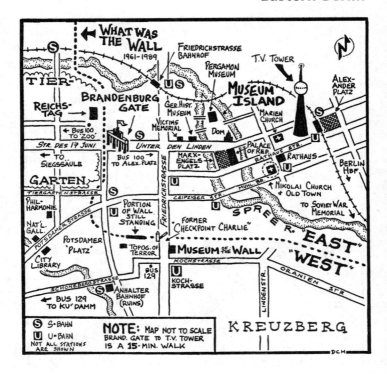

the German-English quarterly *Berlin* magazine, with good reading on Berlin, a partial calendar of events, and a centerfold map (3.50 DM). Most hotels have free city maps.

## Arrival in Berlin

**By Train:** Berlin's central station is called Bahnhof Zoo (Bahnhof Zoologischer Garten), because it's near Berlin's famous zoo. Berlin has three stations (described in Transportation Connections, at the end of chapter). Coming from western Europe, you'll probably land at Zoo (rhymes with "toe"). Stop by the handy EurAide office in the station for maps and answers (Monday–Saturday 8:00–12:00, 13:00–16:30).

To get to the TI from Bahnhof Zoo, follow signs to Hardenbergplatz—a busy square filled with city buses, taxis, the transit office, and derelicts. Across the square find the giraffe and the McDonald's. Tiptoe through the riffraff (studiously avoiding eye contact) to the big intersection on the right. Looking left down Hardenbergstrasse, you'll see the black bombed-out hulk of the Kaiser-Wilhelm Memorial Church and the Europa Center (with the Mercedes symbol spinning on its roof) that houses the main TI. Facing the church, most of the hotels I recommend are behind you to your right. Just ahead amid the traffic is the BVG transport information kiosk. (Buy the 7.50 DM day pass here and pick up a free subway map.) After checking into your hotel, return to Hardenbergplatz to catch bus #100 for the intro tour. If you arrive at Berlin's other train stations (Hauptbahnhof or Lichtenberg), get to Bahnhof Zoo by using the S-Bahn or U-Bahn (runs every few minutes).

**By Plane:** See Transportation Connections.

## Getting Around Berlin

Berlin, with sights spread far and wide, is miserable on foot. Right from the start, commit yourself to the fine public transit system. Taxis are expensive.

**By Subway and Bus:** The U-Bahn, S-Bahn, and all buses have been consolidated into one "BVG" system which uses the same tickets. (S-Bahn free with a Eurailpass).

The basic ticket, called a "Gesamtnetz Erwachsener," gives you two hours of travel on buses or subways (3.60 DM, *Erwachsener* means adult; to the BVG, that's anyone 14 or older). A day pass, called a "Tages Karte," covers zone A and B—the city proper—but not outlying destinations such as Potsdam (7.50 DM, good till 3:00 the morning after). For a single short ride (a distance of six bus stops or three subway stations, with one transfer), get the *Kurzstrecke Erwachsener* ticket (2.50 DM).

The "Berlin/Potsdam WelcomeCard" gives you three days of transportation and three days of minor sightseeing discounts for 29 DM (valid for an adult and up to three kids).

Buy your tickets or cards from machines at U- or S-Bahn stations or at any BVG office like the little BVG pavilion in front of Bahnhof Zoo. The WelcomeCard is also available at the TI. Validate any ticket or card (and avoid a 60-DM fine) by punching it in a clock machine. The double-decker buses are a joy (can buy ticket on bus), and the subway is a snap.

**By Bike:** Several places rent bikes in Berlin. Zweirad

Bahrdt im Zentrum is closest to my recommended hotels (15 DM/24 hours, 300 DM or credit-card imprint for deposit, Kantstrasse 88, near intersection with Windscheidstrasse, S-Bahn: Charlottenburg, tel. 030/323-8129).

## Helpful Hints

City museums are free on the first Sunday of each month. Some sights are closed on Monday: Pergamon Museum, art museums (Gemäldegalerie and New National Gallery), Charlottenburg sights (palace, museums), and the outlying Sanssouci Palace. Save Monday for Berlin Wall sights, other museums, the do-it-yourself orientation tour (see below), walking/bus tours, Kruezburg, churches, zoo, or shopping (Ku'damm, KaDeWe).

Many Berlin streets are numbered with odd and even numbers on the same side of the street, often with no connection to the other side (i.e., Ku'damm #212 can be across the street from #14). To save steps, check the white street signs on curb corners; many list the street numbers covered on that side of the block. Wasch Salon, a handy Laundromat, is at Leibnizstrasse 72 (near intersection with Kantstrasse, daily 6:00–22:00, 8–16 DM wash and dry).

## Do-It-Yourself Orientation Tour

Here's an easy ▲▲▲ introduction to the city. Half the tour is by bus, the other half is on foot. Berlin's bus #100 is a sightseer's dream, stopping at Bahnhof Zoo, Europa Center/Hotel Palace, Siegessaüle, Reichstag, Brandenburg Gate, Unter den Linden, Pergamon Museum, and Alexanderplatz. If you have the 30 DM and 90 minutes for a Guide Friday tour, take that instead. But this 3.60-DM, 30-minute tour is a winning intro to the city. Buses leave from Hardenbergplatz in front of the Zoo station (and nearly next door to the Europa Center TI, in front of the Hotel Palace). Jump on and off liberally. Buses come every ten minutes, and single tickets are good for two hours. Climb aboard, stamp your ticket (giving it a time), and grab a seat on top. You could ride the bus all the way, but I'd get out at the Brandenburg Gate and walk from there.

### Part 1: By Bus #100 from Bahnhof Zoo to Brandenburg Gate

This segment of the ride takes only about ten minutes.

• Around the corner, then straight ahead, before descending

into the tunnel: the bombed-out hulk of the Kaiser-Wilhelm Memorial Church, with its new sister church (described below) and the Europa Center.

• At the stop in front of the Hotel Palace: on the left, the Berlin Zoo entrance and its aquarium (described below).

• Driving down Kurfürstenstrasse, turning left into Tiergarten: The Victory Column, or Siegessaüle, (with the gilded angel, described below) towers above a vast city park.

• On the left a block after leaving the Siegessaüle: The 18th-century late-Rococo Bellevue Palace is the new German "White House," the residence of the federal president. If the flag's flying, he's home.

• Driving along the Spree River: This park area was a residential district before WWII. Soon it will be filled with the buildings of the new national government. Construction has already started. A Henry Moore sculpture floats in front of the slope-roofed "House of World Cultures" (left side). The modern tower (next on left) is a carillon with 68 bells (1987).

• Big black building on left: The Reichstag Building, while barely 100 years old, is as full of history as its bullet-riddled and patched-up complexion suggests. It was from this Parliament building that the German Republic was proclaimed in 1918. In 1933, Hitler burned this symbol of democracy to frame the Communists and grab power. And it was in here that the last 1,500 Nazis made their last stand, extending WWII in Europe by two days. For its 101st birthday, in 1995, the Bulgarian artist Christo wrapped it up. The Reichstag is being renovated in 1998 to serve as the Parliament building when Berlin resumes its status in 1999 as the capital of Germany.

• From here, things go fast and furiously. While you could continue by bus #100, it's better on foot. After driving along what was The Wall, the bus goes under the Brandenburg Gate and stops on Pariser Platz. Leap out there.

### Part 2: Walking Tour from Brandenburg Gate up Unter den Linden to Alexanderplatz

Allow a comfortable hour for this walk (including dawdling but not museum stops).

▲▲**Brandenburg Gate**—The historic Brandenburg Gate (1791, the last survivor of 14 gates in the old city wall), crowned by a majestic four-horse chariot with the Goddess of Peace at the reins, was the symbol of Berlin and then the symbol of divided Berlin. It sat, part of a sad circle dance called The Wall, for more than 25 years. Now postcards all over town show the ecstatic day—November 9, 1989—when the world enjoyed the sight of happy Berliners jamming the gate like flowers on a parade float. A carnival atmosphere continues (except on Sundays), as tourists stroll past hawkers with "authentic" pieces of The Wall, DDR flags, and military paraphernalia, to the traditional rhythm of an organ grinder. Step aside for a minute, and think about struggles for freedom—past and present.

**Pariser Platz**—From Pariser Platz, face the gate. Look left and right. The space used to be filled with important government buildings, bombed to smithereens, and later replaced by The Wall. The U.S. embassy is being built on the left, and a Holocaust Memorial will be completed by 2000. Beyond that is Potsdamer Platz (one U-Bahn stop or a long walk down Ebertstrasse), formerly the busiest square in Europe, then for decades a vacant lot, now being entirely rebuilt (see below).

Brandenburg Gate, the center of old Berlin, sits on a major city axis. This stretches 10 miles, with a grand boulevard leading past the Siegessaüle in one direction to the Charlottenburg Palace. Head the opposite direction, up Unter den Linden, into the heart of old imperial Berlin and what was once the palace of Prussian emperor Frederick the Great.

▲▲**Unter den Linden and Alexanderplatz**—This is the heart of East Berlin. In Berlin's good old days, Unter den Linden was one of Europe's grand boulevards. In the 15th century, this horseway led from the palace to the hunting lodge. In the 17th century, Hohenzollern princes and princesses moved in, building their palaces here to be near the Prussian emperor. Linden trees still give it a pleasant strolling ambience. This was the most elegant street of Prussian Berlin and the main drag of East Berlin.

Walking toward the giant TV tower, the first big building on your right is the Hotel Adlon. Once hosting such notables as Charlie Chaplin, Albert Einstein, and Greta Garbo (this was where she said "I want to be alone," during the filming of *Grand Hotel*), this grand hotel was rebuilt in 1996 after being destroyed in WWII.

On your right, several doors down, is the guarded Russian embassy—not quite as important now as it was a few years ago. It flies the Russian white, red, and blue. Continue past the

Aeroflot Airline offices. If you hear opera, it's coming from the Komische Oper (comic opera, program posted in window).

A few blocks ahead, the large equestrian statue in the street is of **Frederick II** ("the Great"; his statue might be removed in 1998 for restoration). He ruled from 1740 to 1786 and established Prussia as a military power. Most of the buildings around you were from his governmental center. His palace (torn down by the Communists since it symbolized the imperialist past) would have been just ahead.

**Humboldt University**, on the left, was one of Europe's greatest. Marx and Lenin (not the brothers or the sisters) studied here. Opposite the university is a square called Bebelplatz, bordered by the German State Opera, former state library, and the round Catholic St. Hedwig's church. It was on this square in 1933 that Hitler built a bonfire of 20,000 newly forbidden books. (Look for the empty shelves through the glass square in the middle.) The next square on your right holds the Opernpalais (see Eating, below).

On the university side of Unter den Linden, the Greek temple-like building is the **New Watch** (from the early 1800s). When The Wall fell, this memorial to the victims of fascism became a national memorial for the German victims of war and authoritarianism (from either end of the political spectrum). Step inside where the Käthe Kollwitz statue, *Mother with Her Dead Son*, is surrounded by thought-provoking silence. A plaque (just outside) tells the story in English. The **German History Museum** in the Zeughaus features Prussian military history and changing exhibits (free, Thursday–Tuesday 10:00–18:00, closed Wednesday, next door at Unter den Linden 2, tel. 030/215-020).

Cross the bridge to **Museum Island**, home of Germany's first museums and today famous for its Pergamon Museum (described below). The museum complex starts with the neoclassical facade on the left. The huge church is the 100-year-old **Berlin Cathedral**, or *Dom* (5-DM concerts offered daily at 15:00, confirm at TI). Inside, the great reformers stand around the dome like stern saints guarding their theology.

Across the street (with the copper-tinted windows) is the **Palace of the Republic**, the grand center and international showcase of East Berlin. Debate rages over whether to tear it down, though preservation is winning out (asbestos removal has begun). It sits on the spot of the original palace of the Prussian emperor. Some want to rebuild the palace.

As you cross another bridge, look left in the distance to see the gilded New Synagogue, rebuilt after WWII bombing (about 2 km away at Oranienburger Strasse 31; the message on its facade, *"Vergesst es nie,"* means "Never forget").

After crossing the bridge, you'll leave Museum Island. On your right, the pointy twin spires of the 13th-century Nikolai Church mark the center of medieval Berlin. Newly restored and gentrified, many enjoy strolling this *Nikolaiviertel* (district). But with limited time, I'd skip it. The red-brick building with the square tower is the city hall, built after the revolution of 1848 and arguably the first democratic building in the city. Next to this were the DDR presidential palace and Communist party headquarters. The much closer stone Marien Church dates back to 1270.

The 1,200-foot-tall **Fernsehturm TV Tower** offers a fine view from 600 feet at the deck and café (7 DM, daily 8:00–24:00). Built in 1969, the tower was meant to show the power of the state at a time when DDR leaders were having the crosses removed from church domes and spires. But when the sun shines on their tower, the greatest spire in East Berlin, a huge cross is reflected on the mirrored ball. ("The Pope's Revenge," as the cross is called, is best seen from a distance.)

Farther east, pass under the train tracks into **Alexanderplatz**. This (especially the Kaufhof) was the commercial pride and joy of East Berlin. Today it's still a landmark, with a major U-Bahn station surrounded by a few wurst stands. Most of the buildings around the square are slated for destruction.

For a ride through workaday eastern Berlin, with its stark Lego-hell apartments, hop back on bus #100 from here and ride to the end of the line (30-minute round-trip). Are the people different? They are politically free. Are they economically free? How's the future? (At the end of the line, get out. At the same stop, in a few minutes, another bus will take you back to Alexanderplatz, or even back to the start at Zoo.)

## Tours of Berlin

▲**City Walking Tours**—"Berlin Walks" offers an introductory walk every morning (15 DM, 10 DM if you're under 26 or have a WelcomeCard, 2.5 hrs, meet at 10:00 at taxi rank in front of Zoo station, April–December, confirm schedule at TI or with Nick or Serena at 030/301-9194). These fluent-in-English guides also offer tours on the Third Reich and Jewish

Life in Berlin. Since Nazi sights are so hard to find and really understand, the Third Reich walk is the best way to cover this slice of Berlin.

▲**City Bus Tours**—Several companies do quick, two-hour, 30-DM orientation bus tours as well as longer tours. They're fairly competitive, offer live narration in both German and English, and run daily, mostly departing from Kurfürsten-damm (Ku'damm). Some offer get-on-get-off services on an eight- to 12- stop route; look for the logo "City-Circle Sight-seeing" on the front of the bus or ask the guide. Severin & Kühn intro tours leave from Ku'damm 216 (4/day in summer, tel. 030/880-4190), and BVG buses from Ku'damm 225 (tel. 030/885-9880). The TI has all the brochures. I'm a Guide Friday fan. They are established throughout Britain and now have 90-minute, fast-talking tours of Berlin (30 DM, buses every 45 minutes departing from in front of the bombed-out memorial church on Tauenzienstrasse; you can get off at one stop and catch the next bus, tel. 030/4999-8030). These tours do the basic predictable circle from east to west, and on a sunny day when the double-decker buses go topless, they are a photographer's delight. Ask about Guide Friday's "nightseeing" tour covering the same basic route with a focus on nightspots (30 DM, summers, on request only).

## Sights—Western Berlin

▲**Kurfürstendamm**—In the 1850s, when Berlin became a wealthy and important capital, her new rich chose Kurfürsten-damm as their street. Bismarck made it Berlin's Champs-Elysées. In the 1920s, it became a chic and fashionable drag of cafés and boutiques. During the Third Reich, as home to the international community of diplomats and journalists, it enjoyed more freedom than the rest of Berlin. Throughout the Cold War, economic subsidies from the West made sure that capitalism thrived on Ku'damm, as western Berlin's main drag is popularly called. And today, while much of the old charm has been hamburgerized, Ku'damm is still the place to feel the pulse of the city and enjoy the elegant shops (around Fasanen-strasse), department stores, and people-watching. Ku'damm, starting at Kaiser Wilhelm Memorial Church, does its commercial can-can for more than 2 miles.

▲**Kaiser Wilhelm Memorial Church (Gedächtniskirche)**—Originally a memorial to the first emperor of Germany, who died in 1888, its bombed-out ruins have been left standing as a memorial to the destruction of Berlin in WWII. Under a mosaic ceiling, a small exhibit features interesting photos about the bombing (free, Monday–Saturday 10:00–16:00). Next to it, a new church (1961) offers a world of 11,000 little blue-glass windows. The square between this and the Europa Center (a shiny high-rise shopping center, built as a showcase of Western capitalism during the Cold War) is generally a lively busker scene.

▲**Käthe Kollwitz Museum**—This local artist (1867–1945), who experienced much of Berlin's most tumultuous century, conveys some powerful and mostly sad feelings about motherhood, war, and suffering through the black-and-white faces of her art (8 DM, Wednesday–Monday 11:00–18:00, closed Tuesday, a block off Ku'damm at Fasanenstrasse 24).

▲**Kaufhaus des Westens (KaDeWe)**—The "department store of the West" is the biggest department store in continental Europe. It takes a staff of more than 3,000 to help you find and purchase what you need from the vast selection of more than 200,000 items. You can get everything from a haircut and train ticket to souvenirs (fourth floor). The sixth floor is a world of taste treats. This biggest selection of deli and exotic food in Germany offers plenty of free samples and classy opportunities to sit down and eat. Ride the glass elevator to the seventh floor's glass-domed self-service cafeteria (Monday–Friday 9:30–20:00, Saturday 9:30–16:00, closed Sunday, tel. 030/21210, U-Bahn: Wittenbergplatz).

**Berlin Zoo**—More than 1,500 different kinds of animals call Berlin's famous zoo home—or so the zookeepers like to think (11 DM, 18 DM with the world-class aquarium, daily 9:00–18:30, feeding times posted at entry, morning is the best visiting time, enter near Europa Center in front of Hotel Palace, Budapesterstrasse 32, tel. 030/254-010).

**Erotic Art Museum**—From graphic 18th-century Oriental art to erotic films from the early 1900s, this museum is sure to offend most Americans. Security cameras insure a museum atmosphere (10 DM, daily 9:00–24:00, memorable gift shop, at corner of Kantstrasse and Joachimstalerstrasse, 1 block from Zoo train station). It's a stimulating stop before catching a night train out.

## Sights—Central Berlin
**Tiergarten/Siegessaüle**—Berlin's "Central Park" stretches about 2 miles from the Zoo train station to the Brandenburg

Gate. Its centerpiece, the Siegessaüle (Victory Column), was built to commemorate the Prussian defeat of France in 1870. The pointy-helmeted Germans rubbed it in, decorating the tower with French cannons and paying for it all with francs received as war reparations. The three lower rings commemorate Bismark's victories. Had Hitler won, his victory would have been honored here. Statues of Moltke and other German military greats goose-step around the angel at night. You can climb its 285 steps for a fine Berlin-wide view (2 DM, Monday 13:00–18:00, Tuesday–Sunday 9:00–18:00, bus #100). From the tower, the grand Strasse des 17 Juni leads to the Brandenburg Gate (via a thriving flea market each Saturday and Sunday).

**German Resistance Memorial Center (Gedenkstätte Deutscher Widerstand)**—This memorial and museum tell the story of the German resistance to Hitler. "The Benderblock" was a military headquarters where an ill-fated attempt to assassinate Hitler was plotted. Stauffenberg and his co-conspirators were shot in the courtyard. While explanations are in German only, the spirit that haunts the place is multilingual (free, Monday–Friday 9:00–18:00, weekends 9:00–13:00, just south of the Tiergarten at Stauffenbergstrasse 13, tel. 030/265-42-202).

**Berlin's Potsdamer Platz**—The Times Square of Berlin, arguably the busiest square in Europe, was cut in two by The Wall and left a deserted no-man's-land for 40 years. Sony, Daimler Benz, Starbucks, and other huge corporations are turning it once again into a center of Berlin. This huge complex will contain cinemas, restaurants, offices, apartments, retail shops, and a casino. The bright orange-red building, perched on black stilts, is called the Info Box. Take the stairs or the elevator for a rooftop view of the vast construction site (2 DM). Inside the "Box" are displays of all that's happening on the square (free, daily 9:00–19:00, Thursday till 21:00, lots of photos, models, multimedia shows, some descriptions in English).

**Kulturforum**—On Potsdamer Platz, this is the cultural center of 21st-century Berlin. It's the home of the **New National Gallery** featuring 20th-century art (Neue Nationalgalerie, 8 DM, free on the first Sunday of each month, Tuesday–Friday 9:00–17:00, weekends 10:00–17:00, closed Monday, Potsdamerstrasse 50, tel. 030/266-2662). Potsdamer Platz also hosts the new **Museum of Arts and Crafts**, the **National**

**Library** (free, huge, English periodicals), and the **Philharmonic Concert Hall** (S- and U-Bahn: Potsdamer Platz).
▲▲**Gemäldegalerie**—Germany's top collection of 13th-through 18th-century European paintings will reopen sometime in 1998 at its new location on Potsdamer Platz. To find out when, ask the TI or call 030/830-1465. The museum features 600 canvases by famous guys like Dürer, Titian, Botticelli, El Greco, Goya, Rubens, Vermeer, and Bruegel. Its collection of Rembrandts is one of the world's greatest. *The Man with the Golden Helmet*, recently determined not to have been painted by Rembrandt, still shines (4 DM, free on first Sunday of each month, Tuesday–Sunday 9:00–17:00, closed Monday, S- and U-Bahn: Potsdamer Platz).

## Sights—Eastern Berlin
▲▲**Pergamon Museum**—Of the museums on Museuminsel (Museum Island), just off Unter den Linden, only the Pergamon Museum is essential. Its fantastic Pergamon Altar, from a second-century B.C. Greek temple, features the Greeks under Zeus and Athena beating the giants in a dramatic pigpile of mythological mayhem. Check out the action spilling out on the stairs. The Babylonian Ishtar Gate (from sixth century B.C.) and many ancient Greek and Mesopotamian treasures are also impressive (8 DM, free on the first Sunday of each month, Tuesday–Sunday 9:00–17:00, closed Monday, café, tel. 030/2090-5555). Try the excellent audio tours of the museum's highlights (free except on first Sunday of month, when museum is free; then audio tour costs 7 DM). To get to the museum from Unter den Linden, walk along the canal. Passing the first bulky neoclassical building on your right, cross a bridge and follow the canal to the next bulky neoclassical building.
▲▲▲**The Museum of The Wall (Haus am Checkpoint Charlie) and a chunk of The Wall**—The 100-mile "Anti-Fascist Protective Rampart," as it was called by the DDR, was erected almost overnight in 1961 to stop the outward flow of people (3 million leaked out between 1949 and 1961). It was 13 feet high with a 16-foot tank ditch, 160 feet of no-man's-land, and 300 sentry towers. In its 28 years there were 1,693 cases when border guards fired, 3,221 arrests, 5,043 documented successful escapes (565 of these were DDR guards), and 80 deaths.
    **Checkpoint Charlie**, the famous American military

border crossing, is being buried under new construction. A block to the west, the fascinating **Haus am Checkpoint Charlie** museum tells the gripping history of The Wall and the many ingenious escape attempts. A visit includes plenty of video and film coverage of those heady days when people-power tore it down (7.50 DM, daily 9:00–22:00, U-Bahn to Kochstrasse, Friedrichstrasse 44, tel. 030/251-1031).

When it fell, The Wall was literally carried away by the euphoria. Little remains. From Checkpoint Charlie, Zimmerstrasse leads to a small surviving stretch. The park behind the wall marks the site of the command center of Hitler's Gestapo and SS (explained by English plaques throughout). It's been left undeveloped as a memorial to the tyranny once headquartered here. At the edge of this park is . . .

The *Topography of Terror*, built in an excavated air-raid shelter (which was used as an interrogation room) next to what was the Gestapo headquarters, tells the story of Nazism in Germany (free, daily 10:00–18:00, English translation 2 DM, tel. 030/2548-6703). Portraits of its most famous victims—who disappeared—line the walls.

**East Side Gallery**—The biggest remaining stretch of The Wall is now "the world's longest art gallery," stretching for a mile and covered with murals painted by artists from around the world, mostly in celebration of The Wall's demise. While not impressive, and in dire need of restoration, it does make for a thought-provoking walk. From Schlesisches Tor (end of Kreuzberg) walk across the river on the pedestrian bridge, turn left, and follow The Wall to Berlin Hauptbahnhof (a train station two stops from Alexanderplatz).

**Kreuzberg**—This poorer district along The Wall, with old restored and unrestored buildings and plenty of student and Turkish street life, offers the best look at melting-pot Berlin in a city where original Berliners are as rare as old buildings. Berlin is the fourth-largest Turkish city in the world, and this is its "downtown." But to call it a "little Istanbul" insults the big one. You'll see mothers wearing scarves, *döner kebab* stands, and spray paint–decorated shops. For a dose of Kreuzberg without getting your fingers dirty, you can joyride on bus #129. (Take U-8 to Hermannplatz; you'll ascend through the Karstadt department store's great cafeteria; #129 buses wait immediately outside its door, leaving every five minutes. After leaving Kreuzberg, they stop right at the Checkpoint Charlie

Museum and go all the way to KaDeWe and Ku'damm.) Wander the area between the Kottbusser Tor and Schlesisches Tor subway stops, ideally on Tuesday and Friday afternoons from 12:00–18:00 when the Turkish Market sprawls along the bank of the Maybachufer Canal (U-Bahn: Kottbusser Tor).

**Oranienburger Strasse**—On this bizarre street, hopelessness is hip, and rust and rot are a happening. Take the U-Bahn to Oranienburger Strasse, check out the New Synagogue (gilded dome), and stroll the Strasse to Oranienburger Tor U-Bahn stop. Dip into art gallery/cafés. Oren, a popular kosher/vegetarian café is next to the synagogue (see Eating, below).

**Natural History Museum (Museum für Naturkunde)**—Worth a visit just to see the largest dinosaur skeleton ever assembled. While you're there, meet "Bobby," the stuffed ape (5 DM, Tuesday–Sunday 9:30–17:00, closed Monday, U-6 to Zinnowitzer Strasse, at Invalidenstrasse 43).

## Sights—Around Charlottenburg Palace

**Charlottenburg Palace (Schloss)**—This only surviving Hohenzollern Palace is Berlin's top Baroque palace. If you've seen the great palaces of Europe, this one comes in at about tenth place, especially since its center is tourable only with a German guide. For a quick look, the Knöbelsdorff Wing (5 DM) is set up to let you wander on your own, a substantial hike through restored-since-the-war, gold-crusted white rooms filled with Frederick the Great's not-so-great collection of Baroque paintings (8 DM, Tuesday–Friday 9:00–17:00, weekends 10:00–17:00, closed Monday, U-1 to Sophie-Charlotte Platz and a ten-minute walk, or bus #145 direct from Bahnhof Zoo, tel. 030/320-911).

▲▲**Egyptian Museum**—Across the street from the palace is a little museum of Egyptian treasures. It offers one of the great thrills in art appreciation—gazing into the still-young and beautiful face of 3,000-year-old Queen Nefertiti, the wife of King Akhenaton (8 DM, Tuesday–Friday 9:00–17:00, weekends 10:00–17:00, Schlosstrasse 70).

▲**Bröhan Museum**—Wander through a dozen beautifully furnished Art Nouveau (Jugendstil) and art deco living rooms. If you're tired, the final rooms are not worth six flights of stairs (6 DM, Tuesday–Sunday 10:00–18:00, closed Monday, next to Egyptian Museum, across the street from Charlottenburg Palace).

## Sights—Near Berlin

**Sanssouci Palace, Potsdam**—With a lush park strewn with the extravagant whimsies of Frederick the Great, the sleepy town of Potsdam has long been Berlin's holiday retreat. Frederick's super-Rococo Sanssouci Palace is one of Germany's most dazzling. His equally extravagant New Palace (Neues Palais), built to disprove rumors that Prussia was running out of money after the costly Seven Years' War, is on the other side of the park. While Potsdam is easy to get to (30 minutes direct on S-Bahn from Bahnhof Zoo to Potsdam Stadt), Sanssouci Palace can be visited only by German-language tour—which can be booked up for hours. Even though Sanssouci means "without a care," get your appointment immediately upon arrival so you know how much time to kill (or if you need to come back and try again tomorrow). The TI's German/English bus tour includes Sanssouci (39 DM, Tuesday–Sunday at 11:00).

Sanssouci Palace (10 DM, Tuesday–Sunday 9:00–17:00, closed Monday, shorter hours off-season, tel. 0331/969-4190) and the New Palace (8 DM, Wednesday–Monday 9:00–17:00, closed Tuesday, tours not required) are a 30-minute walk apart. The palaces of Vienna, Munich, and even Würzburg offer equal sightseeing thrills with fewer headaches (Potsdam TI: tel. 0331/291-100). Potsdam's much-promoted Wannsee boat rides are torturously dull.

## Late-Night Berlin

*Zitty* and *Tip* (sold at kiosks) are the top guides to youth and alternative culture. The TI's *Berlin Programm* lists the nonstop parade of concerts, plays, exhibits, and cultural events. Tourists stroll the Ku'damm after dark. But the eastern part of town is where post-modern Berliners loiter away evenings now that the government has dropped their swizzle sticks. Oranienburger Strasse (described above) is an interesting new scene.

## Sleeping in Berlin
**(1.7 DM = about $1, tel. code: 030)**
Sleep Code: **S**=Single, **D**=Double/Twin, **T**=Triple, **Q**=Quad, **b**=bathroom, **t**=toilet only, **s**=shower only, **CC**=Credit Card (**V**isa, **M**asterCard, **A**mex).

Since reunification, costs in Berlin have skyrocketed: 40-DM hostel beds; 80-DM dumpy hotel doubles; 130-DM pleasant, small, pension doubles; 180-DM "normal" hotel doubles. Because of the cost of lodging and the distance necessary to travel to Berlin, I try to come and go by night train.

My listings are in decent, comfortable neighborhoods. Nearly all are a couple of flights up in big, run-down buildings. Inside they are clean, quiet, and big enough so that their well-worn character is actually charming. Rooms in back are on quiet courtyards. Unless otherwise noted, hall showers are free, breakfast is included, they speak English, and take no credit cards. Prices are usually soft in winter and for longer stays.

## Discount Business Hotels

For the most comforts at the least cost, arrive without a reservation (ideally in the morning) and let the TI book you a room in a fancy hotel on their push list. When there are no conventions or fairs (most of the summer), rather than go empty, business hotels rent rooms through the TI to lowly tourists for around half price. A modern, all-the-comforts, 300-DM business hotel double with a buffet breakfast within walking distance of the TI can be had for around 180 DM. The little pensions recommended below can't afford to play the discount game.

## Sleeping near Zoo Station at Savignyplatz
### (zip code: 10623)

These hotels and pensions are a five- to 15-minute walk from Bahnhof Zoo. S-Bahn stop: Savignyplatz. Hotels on Kantstrasse have street noise. Ask for a quieter room in back.

**Pension Peters**, run by a German-Swedish couple, is sunny and central. Decorated sleek Scandinavian, with every room renovated, it's a winner (S-70–80 DM, Ss-110 DM, D-90–110 DM, Ds-120–130 DM, extra bed-30 DM, kids under 12 free, group discounts, TVs in rooms, CC:VMA, 10 yards east of Savignyplatz, on second floor of Kantstrasse 146, tel. 030/3150-3944, fax 030/312-3519, SE). Downstairs in the same building, the **Pension Viola Nova** is similar, but prompts the question, "Why pay more?" (S-90 DM, Sb-160 DM, D-120 DM, Ds-150 DM, Db-160 DM, breakfast-10 DM, CC:VMA, tel. 030/313-1457, fax 030/312-3314).

**Hotel Crystal Garni** is professional with comfortable rooms and *vollkorn* breakfast room (S-70 DM, Sb-80 DM, D-90 DM, Ds-110 DM, Db-130–150 DM, CC:VMA, a block past Savignyplatz at Kantstrasse 144, tel. 030/312-9047, fax

030/312-6465, run by John and Dorothy Schwartzrock).
**Alpenland Hotel** is a classy hotel with a fine restaurant.
The big, bright but showerless doubles are the best value
(showers down the hall). Many rooms are on the fourth floor
and there's no elevator (S-75–90 DM, Ss-110 DM, Sb-
130–140 DM, D-120 DM, Db-170–200 DM, extra person-65
DM, CC:VM, just off Savignyplatz on a quiet street, Carmerstrasse 8, tel. 030/312-3970, fax 030/313-8444).

    **Hotel-Pension Bialas**, renovated for '98, has 40 big,
bright, airy rooms and offers discounts to school groups (S-65
DM, Sb-95 DM, D-95 DM, Db-135 DM, T-135 DM, Tb-185
DM, CC:VMA, reservations best by fax, Carmerstrasse 16, tel.
030/312-5025, fax 030/312-4396).

## Sleeping near Zoo Station, south of Ku'damm
### (zip code: 10707)

**Hotel-Pension Funk** is the former home of a 1920s silent-
movie star, offering 14 elegant, richly furnished old rooms for
a great price (S-65 DM, Ss-80 DM, Sb-100 DM, D-100 DM,
Ds-125 DM, Db-140–160 DM, extra person-45 DM,
CC:VMA, reserve early, Fasanenstrasse 69, a long block south
of Ku'damm, tel. 030/882-7193, fax 030/883-3329, fax is best).

    **Hotel Bogota** has big, bright, modern rooms in a spacious
old building half a block south off Ku'damm. The service is
brisk and hotelesque (S-78 DM, Ss-100 DM, Sb-130 DM, D-
125 DM, Ds-145 DM, Db-170–190 DM, extra person-45 DM,
elevator, CC:VMA, Schlüterstrasse 45, tel. 030/881-5001, fax
030/883-5887, e-mail: hotel.bogota@t-online.de).

    **Hotel Austriana** shares a building (and elevator) in a
charming, café-studded neighborhood 300 yards south of Ku'-
damm (S-75 DM, Ss-85 DM, Sb-110 DM, Ds-120 DM, Db-
160 DM, cheaper off-season, CC:VMA, Pariser Strasse 39, tel.
030/885-7000, fax 030/885-70-088) with two other pensions:
the simpler **Hotel Rügen** (Ds-115–125 DM, CC:VM, Pariser
Strasse 39, tel. 030/884-3940, fax 030/884-39-437) and **Pension Curtis**, also basic, but hip, with red comforters and light-
pine furniture (S-70 DM, Ds-110–130 DM, Pariser Strasse 39,
tel. 030/883-4931, fax 030/885-0438). Across the street is the
**Pension Parier-Eck**, faded and old-fashioned, with big homey
rooms (S-70 DM, Ss-80 DM, D-95 DM, Ds-115 DM, Ts-150
DM, extra bed-50 DM, Pariser Strasse 19, tel. 030/881-2145,
fax 030/883-6335). On the same street, the almost-too-modern

**Hotel Alexander** is an art-deco splurge with all the comforts (Ss-110–130 DM, Sb-160–210 DM, Db-180–210 DM, Tb-210 DM, breakfast-20 DM, prices soft if it's a slow time, CC:VMA, Pariser Strasse 37, tel. 030/881-6091, fax 030/881-6094).

## Sleeping near Augsburgerstrasse U-Bahn Stop

These pensions are about a 15-minute walk from the station, or two U-Bahn stops (with a transfer at Wittenbergplatz).

**Hotel-Pension Nürnberger Eck** has eight big, plush but worn rooms. Call first (S-80 DM, Sb-100 DM, D-130 DM, Db-150 DM, extra bed-50 DM, CC:VM, Nürnberger Strasse 24a, 10789 Berlin, tel. 030/235-1780, fax 030/2351-7899). Just upstairs, **Pension Fischer** is rundown, simple, and the best I've found in its price range (S-60 DM, D-80–90 DM, Ds-90–100 DM, extra person-35 DM, breakfast-8 DM, Nürnberger Strasse 24a, tel. 030/218-6808, fax 030/213-4225).

**Hotel Arco**, on a quiet street, newly renovated and well-run, caters to a mixed clientele of gays, straights, and families (S-75 DM, Sb-120–140 DM, D-125 DM, Ds-135 DM, Db-150–175 DM, extra person-40 DM, cheaper off-season and for longer stays, CC:VMA, some ground-floor rooms, Geisberger-strasse 30, tel. 030/235-1480, fax 030/211-3387). The garden is a cheery place for breakfast. Nearest U-Bahn stop: Witten-bergplatz, then a five-minute walk.

## Sleeping near Güntzelstrasse U-Bahn Stop

This U-Bahn stop is three stops from Zoo on the U-9 line. With your back to the metro exit, the first two listings are on your left, and the Finck is on your right.

**Hotel Pension München** is bright, lovingly run, and filled with modern art sculpted by the owner (S-60 DM, D-80 DM, Db-125 DM, extra bed-35 DM, breakfast-9 DM, elevator, cheaper off-season, third floor of Güntzelstrasse 62, 10717 Berlin, tel. 030/857-9120, fax 030/8579-1222). At the same address, **Pension Güntzel** rents eight decent rooms (Ss-80 DM, Sb-100 DM, Ds-110–130 DM, Db-130–150 DM, extra adult-30 DM or child-15 DM, tel. 030/857-9020, fax 030/853-1108). **Pension Finck** has 12 big, bright rooms in a more tra-ditional building (D-90 DM, Ds-110 DM, extra person-70 DM, elevator, Güntzelstrasse 54, tel. 030/861-2940, fax 030/861-8158, little English spoken).

## Hostel
**Studenten Hotel Berlin** is open to all, with no curfew (D-84 DM, 38-DM-per-bed quads with sheets and breakfast, near City Hall on JFK Platz, Meiningerstrasse 10, U-Bahn: Rathaus Schoneberg, tel. 030/784-6720, fax 030/788-1532).

# Eating in Berlin
Berlin has plenty of fun food places, both German and imported. Colorful pubs, called *Kneipe*, offer light meals and the fizzy local beer, Berliner Weiss. Ask for it *mit Schuss* for a shot of syrup in your suds. If the kraut is getting wurst, try one of the many Turkish, Italian, or Balkan restaurants. Eat cheap at Imbiss snack stands, bakeries (sandwiches), and falafel/kebab places. Bahnhof Zoo has several bright, modern fruit and sand-wich bars and a grocery (daily 6:00–24:00).

## Self-Service Cafeterias near Bahnhof Zoo
Check out the big department stores. **Wertheim**, a half block from the memorial church, has cheap basement food counters and a fine Le Buffet self-service cafeteria with a view up six banks of escalators (Monday–Friday 9:30–20:00, Saturday 9:00–16:00, closed Sunday, U-Bahn: Ku'damm). **KaDeWe's** top floor also holds a Le Buffet view cafeteria, and its sixth-floor deli food department is a picnicker's nirvana (hours simi-lar to Wertheim's). Its arterials are clogged with more than 1,000 kinds of sausage and 1,500 types of cheese. Put together a picnic and enjoy a sunny bench by the memorial church. The **Marche**, popping up in big cities all over Germany, is another decent self-service cafeteria, within a half block of the church (daily 8:00–24:00, CC:VMA, Ku'damm 14, enter on ground floor of mini-mall).

## Eating German-style near Recommended Hotels
**Pavilion Am Loretta** is a leafy, colorful Munich-style beer garden a block off the Ku'damm where Knesebeckstrasse hits Lietzenburg Strasse (nightly till late). **Schildkröte,** the "tur-tle," is worth the investment (daily 11:30–24:00, CC:A, 100 feet south of Ku'damm on Uhlandstrasse, tel. 030/881-6770). The **Lindner** deli next door is perfect (but not cheap) for lazy picnickers. Colorful eateries abound just off Savignyplatz (along Carmerstrasse, Grolmanstrasse, and Knesebeckstrasse). **Dirke Wirtin** has a good *Kneipe* atmosphere and famous

*Gulash Suppe* for 6 DM (opens daily at noon, closes late, Carmerstrasse 9).

### Eating along Unter den Linden near Pergamon Museum

The **Opernpalais**, preening with fancy pre-war elegance, hosts a number of pricey restaurants. Its Operncafé has the best desserts (across from the university and War Memorial at Unter den Linden 5). The shady beer/tea garden in front has a cheap self-service Imbiss (wurst, meatball sandwiches, etc.) and a creperie. **Oren** is a popular, stylish kosher/vegetarian restaurant (daily 10:00–24:00, north of Museum Island about 5 blocks away at Oranienburger Strasse 28, tel. 030/282-8228).

## Transportation Connections—Berlin

Berlin has three train stations. Bahnhof Zoo was the West Berlin train station and still serves Western Europe (Frankfurt, Munich, Hamburg, Paris, Amsterdam). The Hauptbahnhof (former East Berlin's main station) still faces east, serving Prague, Warsaw, Vienna, and Dresden. The Lichtenberg Bahnhof (eastern Berlin's top U- and S-Bahn hub) also handles a few eastbound trains. Expect exceptions. All stations are conveniently connected by subway. Train info: tel. 030/19419.

**By train to: Frankfurt** (14/day, 5 hrs) **Munich** (8/day, 8.5 hrs), **Köln** (hrly, 6.5 hrs), **Amsterdam** (8/day, 9 hrs), **Budapest** (3/day, 13 hrs), **Copenhagen** (4/day, 8 hrs), **London** (4/day, 15 hrs), **Paris** (6/day, 13 hrs), **Zurich** (12/day, 10 hrs), **Prague** (10/day, 4.5 hrs), **Warsaw** (4/day, 8 hrs), **Vienna** (2/day, 12 hrs—via Czech Republic, Eurailers pay an extra 66 DM for second class; otherwise, take the three-hour train to Hannover and sleep through Eurail country to Vienna).

Berlin is connected by overnight trains from Bonn, Köln, Frankfurt, Munich, and Vienna. A *Liege-platz*, or berth, is money well spent (26 DM in a six-bed cabin; or 45 DM on InterCity night train with breakfast). The beds cost the same whether you have a first- or second-class ticket or railpass. Trains are rarely full, but get your bed reserved a few days in advance from any travel agency or major train station in Europe.

## Berlin's Three Airports

**Tegel Airport** handles most flights from the U.S.A. and Western Europe (6 km from center, catch bus X9 to Bahnhof

Zoo, or bus #109 to Ku'damm and Bahnhof Zoo for 3.70 DM, tel. 030/41011). Flights from the east usually arrive at **Schöne-feld Airport** (20 km from center, short walk to S-Bahn, catch S-9 to Zoo station, tel. 030/60910). **Templehof Airport** is getting more domestic and European business (in Berlin, bus #119 to Ku'damm or U-Bahn 6 or 7, tel. 030/6951-2289). Allow at least 30 DM for a taxi ride to or from any airport. British Air (tel. 0180/334-0340), Delta (tel. 0180/333-7880), SAS (tel. 695-12-491), Lufthansa (tel. 0180/380-3803).

# AUSTRIA
## (ÖSTERREICH, THE KINGDOM OF THE EAST)

- 32,000 square miles (the size of South Carolina, or two Switzerlands)
- 7.6 million people (235 per square mile and holding, 85 percent Catholic)
- 12 Austrian schillings (AS) = about $1 (figure 8 cents each)

**Austria**

During the grand old Habsburg days, Austria was Europe's most powerful empire. Its royalty built a giant kingdom of more than 50 million people by making love, not war (having lots of children and marrying them into the other royal houses of Europe).

Today this small, landlocked country does more to cling to its elegant past than any other in Europe. The waltz is still the rage. Austrians are very sociable; it's important to greet people in the breakfast room and those you pass on the streets or meet in shops. The Austrian's version of "Hi" is a cheerful *"Grüss Gott"* ("May God greet you"). You'll get the correct pronunciation after the first volley—listen and copy.

While they speak German and talked about unity with Germany long before Hitler ever said "*Anschluss,*" the Austrians cherish their distinct cultural and historical traditions. They are not Germans. Austria is mellow and relaxed compared to Deutschland. *Gemütlichkeit* is the local word for this special Austrian cozy-and-easy approach to life. It's good living—whether engulfed in mountain beauty or bathed in lavish high culture. The people stroll as if every day were Sunday, topping things off with a cheerful visit to a coffee or pastry shop.

It must be nice to be past your prime—no longer troubled by being powerful, able to kick back and celebrate life in the clean, untroubled mountain air. While the Austrians make less money than their neighbors, they enjoy a short work week and a long life span.

The Austrian schilling (S or AS) is divided into 100 groschen. To convert prices from schillings into dollars, drop the last zero and subtract one-fifth (e.g., 450 AS = about $36). About 8 Austrian schillings equal 1 deutsche mark (DM). While merchants and waiters near the border are happy to accept DM, you'll save money if you use schillings. Prices in Austria are lower than in Germany and much lower than in Switzerland. Shops are open from 8:00 to 17:00 or 18:00.

Austrians eat on about the same schedule we do. Treats include *Wiener Schnitzel* (breaded veal cutlet), *Knödel* (dumplings), *Apfelstrudel*, and fancy desserts like the *Sachertorte*, Vienna's famous chocolate cake. Service is included in restaurant bills, but it's polite to leave a little extra (less than 5 percent).

In Austria, all drivers are required to buy a sticker for their car (70 AS for one week, 150 AS for two months, 550 AS for one year). Get it at a border gas station or your car rental agency.

In this section of the book, I'll cover Austria's top cities *except* for Reutte in Tirol. Look for Reutte in the Bavaria and Tirol chapter.

# VIENNA
# (WIEN)

Vienna is a head without a body. For 600 years the capital of the once-grand Habsburg Empire, she started and lost World War I and, with it, her far-flung holdings. Today you'll find an elegant capital of 1.6 million people (20 percent of Austria's population) ruling a small, relatively insignificant country. Culturally, historically, and from a sightseeing point of view, this city is the sum of its illustrious past. The city of Freud, Kafka, Brahms, a gaggle of Strausses, Maria Theresa's many children, and a dynasty of Holy Roman emperors is right up there with Paris, London, and Rome.

Vienna has always been the easternmost city of the West. In Roman times it was Vindobona, on the Danube facing the Germanic barbarians. In medieval times Vienna was Europe's bastion against the Ottoman Turks (a "horde" of 300,000 was repelled in 1683). While the ancient walls held out the Turks, World War II bombs destroyed 22 percent of the city's buildings. In modern times Vienna took a big bite out of the USSR's Warsaw Pact buffer zone. Read a coin—it says "Österreich." That's "Kingdom of the East."

The truly Viennese person is not Austrian but a second-generation Habsburg cocktail, with grandparents from the distant corners of the old empire—Polish, Serbian, Hungarian, Romanian, Czech, or Italian. Vienna is the melting-pot capital of an empire of 60 million—of which only 8 million are Austrian.

In 1900, Vienna's 2.2 million inhabitants made it the world's fifth-largest city (after New York, London, Paris, and Berlin). But the average Viennese mother has 1.3 children and the population is down to 1.6 million. (Dogs are the preferred "child.")

Of the Habsburgs who ruled Austria from 1273 to 1918, Maria Theresa (ruled 1740–1765) and Franz Josef (ruled 1848–1916) are the most famous. People are quick to remember Maria Theresa as the mother of 16 children (12 survived). This was actually no big deal back then (one of her daughters had 18 kids and a son fathered 16). Maria Theresa's reign followed the Austrian defeat of the Turks, when Europe recognized Austria as a great power. She was a strong and effective queen. (Her rival, the Prussian emperor, said, "When at last the Habsburgs get a great man, it's a woman.") She was a great social reformer. During her reign she avoided wars and expanded her empire by skillfully marrying her children into the right families. With daughter Marie Antoinette's marriage into the French Bourbon family (to Louis XVI), for instance, a country that had been an enemy became an ally. (Unfortunately for Marie, she arrived in time for the Revolution and lost her head.) In tune with her age and a great reformer, Maria Theresa's "Robin Hood" policies helped Austria slip through the "age of revolution" without turmoil. She taxed the church and the nobility and provided six years of obligatory education to all children and free health care to all in her realm. She also welcomed the boy genius Mozart into her court.

As far back as the 12th century, Vienna was a mecca for musicians—both secular (troubadours) and sacred. The Habsburg emperors of the 17th and 18th centuries were not only generous supporters of music but fine musicians and composers themselves. (Maria Theresa played a mean double bass.) Composers like Haydn, Mozart, Beethoven, Schubert, Brahms, and Mahler gravitated to this music-friendly environment. They taught each other, jammed together, and spent a lot of time in Habsburg palaces. Beethoven was a famous figure, walking—lost in musical thought—through Vienna's woods.

After the defeat of Napoleon and the Congress of Vienna (in 1815, which shaped 19th-century Europe), Vienna enjoyed its violin-filled belle époque, which shaped our romantic image of the city (fine wine, chocolates, cafés, and waltzes). The waltz was the rage, and "Waltz King" Johann Strauss and his brothers kept Vienna's 300 ballrooms spinning.

This musical tradition (that continues in our century) leaves some prestigious Viennese institutions for today's tourists to enjoy: the opera, the boys' choir, and the great Baroque halls and churches, all busy with classical and waltz concerts.

## Planning Your Time

As far as big cities go, Vienna has to be one of Europe's most pleasant and laid-back. Vienna is worth two days and two nights. Not only is it packed with great sights, but it's also a joy to spend time in. It seems like Vienna was designed to help people simply meander through a day. To be grand-tour efficient, you could sleep in and sleep out on the train (Berlin, Venice, Rome, the Swiss Alps, Paris, and the Rhine are each handy night trains away). But then you'd miss the Danube and Melk. I'd come in from Salzburg via Hallstatt, Melk, and the Danube and spend two days this way:

**Day 1:**

9:00    Circle the Ring by tram, following the tour explained below (or take this tour the night before with a stop at the Kursalon for Strauss).

10:00   Stroll Kärntner Strasse (take care of TI and ticket needs, possibly tour Kaisergruft tombs).

11:00   Tour the Opera (lunch at Rosenberger).

13:00   Tour Hofburg visiting Augustinian church, royal apartments, treasury, Neue Burg).

16:00   Walk Kohlmarkt, take Graben to the cathedral, then tour cathedral.

19:00   Choose classical music, Heuriger wine garden, Prater amusement park, or an Opera performance. Spend some time wandering the old center.

**Day 2:**

9:00    Schönbrunn Palace (possibly, if by car, on way out of town before five-hour drive to Hall near Innsbruck).

13:00   Kunsthistorisches Museum after lunch.

16:00   Strauss waltz coffee concert at Kursalon?

## Orientation (tel. code within Austria: 0222; from outside: 1)

Vienna, or *Wien* (VEEN) in German, is bordered on three sides by the Vienna Woods (*Wienerwald*) and the Danube (*Donau*). To the southeast is industrial sprawl. The Alps, which arc across Europe from Marseilles, end at Vienna's wooded hills. These provide a popular playground for walking and new-wine drinking. This greenery's momentum carries on into the city. You'll notice more than half of Vienna is park land, filled with ponds, gardens, trees, and statue memories of Austria's glory days.

Think of the city map as a target. The bull's-eye is the cathedral, the first circle is the Ring, and the second is the Gürtel. The old town snuggles around towering St. Stephan's Cathedral south of the Donau, bound tightly by the Ringstrasse. The Ring, marking what was the city wall, circles the first district (or *Bezirk*). The Gürtel, a broader ring road, contains the rest of downtown (Bezirkes 2–9).

Addresses start with the Bezirk, followed by street and building number. Any address higher than the ninth Bezirk is beyond the Gürtel, far from the center. The middle two digits of Vienna's postal codes show the district, or Bezirk. The address "7, Lindengasse 4" is in the seventh district, #4 on Linden Street. Its postal code would be 1070. Nearly all your sightseeing will be done in the core first district or along the Ringstrassse. As a tourist, concern yourself only with this small old center, and sprawling Vienna suddenly becomes manageable.

## Tourist Information

The "tourist offices" at the train stations and airport are hotel agencies in disguise. Vienna's real tourist office, near the Opera House at Kärntner Strasse 38, is excellent (daily 9:00–19:00, tel. 0222/211-140 or 0222/513-8892). Stop here first with a list of needs and questions, to confirm your sight-seeing plans, and to pick up the free and essential city map (best of its kind in Europe—use the town center inset), the museum brochure (listing hours, phone numbers), the monthly program of concerts, and the fact-filled *Young Vienna Scene* magazine. Consider investing in the handy 50-AS *Vienna from A to Z* booklet. Every important building has a numbered flag banner that keys into this guidebook. *A to Z* numbers are keyed into the TI's city map. When lost, find one of the "famous-building flags" and match its number to your map. If you're at a "famous building," check the map to see what other key numbers are nearby, then check the *A to Z* book to see if you want to drop in. Many of my recommended accommodations keep enough tourist maps and brochures on hand to make a TI trip unnecessary. The much-promoted 180-AS "Vienna Card" gives you a three-day transit pass (worth 130 AS) and tiny dis-counts at museums on the push list (which you probably won't visit). Skip it.

## Arrival in Vienna

**By Train at the West Station:** Most train travelers arrive at the Westbahnhof. Pick up a free city map at the "Reisebüro am Bahnhof" at the station. To get to the city center (and most likely, your hotel), catch the U-3 subway. Buy a 24-hour pass from the *Tabak* (tobacco) shop in the station or from a machine in the underground (50 AS, good on trams and buses, too). The subway has an entrance within the station. Follow the U-3 signs down the long escalator. If you still need a ticket or pass, stop at a VOR-Fahrkarten machine, push the yellow "24-Stunden" button, and the window display will read "50 AS." Insert 50 AS in coins (or a 100 AS bill and get change) and get your 24-hour ticket (individual tickets cost 17 AS). On the same level as the ticket machines, you'll see an "Information/Vorverkauf" office, where you can get transit advice, tickets and passes, and a tiny, free metro map. One more level down takes you to the U-3 tracks. Catch a train in the direction of U-3-Erdberg. Ride five stops to Stephansplatz, escalate in the exit direction "Stephansplatz," and you hit the cathedral. The TI is a five-minute stroll down the busy Kärntner Strasse pedestrian street.

The Westbahnhof station has a grocery store (daily 6:00–22:50), change offices, storage facilities, and rental bikes (see Getting Around, below).

**By Plane:** The airport (16 km from town) is connected by 70-AS shuttle buses (3/hr) to either the Westbahnhof (35 min) or the City Air Terminal (20 min) near the river in the old center. Taxis into town cost about 400 AS.

## Getting Around Vienna

**By Bus, Tram, and Subway:** To take simple and economical advantage of Vienna's fine transit system of buses, trams, and sleek, easy subways, buy the 24-hour (50-AS) or 72-hour (130-AS) subway/bus/tram pass at a station machine or at Tabak shops near any station. Take a moment to study the eye-friendly city center map on metro station walls to internalize how the metro and tram system can help you. I use it mostly to zip along the Ring (tram #1 or #2) and subway to more outlying sights or hotels. The 15-AS transit map is overkill. The necessary routes are listed on the free tourist city map. Without a pass, either buy individual tickets (17 AS, good for one journey with necessary changes) from metro ticket windows or buy blocks of five tickets for 85 AS (17 AS apiece). If you buy from the bus driver, you'll pay 20 AS per ticket. Eight-strip, eight-day, 265-AS transit passes, called "8 Tage Umwelt Streifennet-zkarte," can be shared (for instance, four people for two days each, a 33 percent savings over the cheap 24-hour pass).

Stamp your pass as you enter the system or tram (which puts a time on it). Rookies often miss stops because they fail to open the door. Push buttons, pull latches, do whatever it takes to get on or off. Study your street map before you exit the subway; by choosing the right exit, you'll save yourself lots of walking.

**By Taxi:** Vienna's comfortable, honest, and easy-to-flag-down taxis start at 26 AS and mount quickly; you'll pay about 60 AS for a five-minute ride (tel. 0222/40106).

**By Bike:** Good as the city's transit system is, you may want to rent a bike at any train station (daily 4:00–midnight, 90 AS/day with railpass or train ticket, 150 AS without; rent early in morning before supply runs out). Pedal Power offers rental bikes (350 AS/day for "trekking" bike, 395 AS includes delivery and pick-up from your hotel) and four-hour city tours (daily at 10:00, 280 AS includes bike and guide, Austellungsstrasse 3, U-1 to Praterstern, tel. 0222/729-7234, run by American Rick Watts and others).

**By Buggy:** Rich romantics get around by traditional horse and buggy. You'll see the *Fiakers* clip-clopping tourists on 20-minute (500 AS) or 40-minute (800–1,000 AS) tours.

## Helpful Hints

**Bank Alert:** There is a mix of decent and rip-off banks in the city and at the airport. Save 5 percent by checking the rates at three before changing. Avoid the rip-off Rieger "Bank." Bank hours are roughly Monday through Friday from 8:00 to 15:00 and until 17:30 on Thursday. After hours, you can change money at train stations, the airport, the main post office on Postgasse in the city center (open 24 hours daily, also has handy metered phones), or the Verkehrsbüro at Stephansplatz 10 (daily 9:00–18:30). Commissions of 80 AS are sadly normal. A happy exception is the American Express office, which charges no commissions to change Amex checks (Monday–Friday 9:00–17:30, Saturday 9:00–12:00, Kärntner Strasse 21-23, tel. 0222/51540).

**English Bookstores:** The British Bookshop is at the corner of Weihburggasse and Seilerstätte (Monday–Friday

9:00–18:30, Saturday 10:00–17:00), and Shakespeare & Co. is at Sterngasse 2, north of the Höher Markt square (Monday–Friday 9:00–19:00, Saturday 9:00–17:00, tel 535-50-5354; as a bonus for coming here at noon, the clock in Höher Markt does a musical act with moving figures).

## Do-It-Yourself Bus Orientation Tour

▲▲Ringstrasse Tour—In the 1860s, Emperor Franz Josef had the city's ingrown medieval wall torn down and replaced with a grand boulevard 190 feet wide, arcing nearly 3 miles around the city's core. The road predates all the buildings that line it. So what you'll see is neo-Gothic, neoclassical, and neo-Renaissance. One of Europe's great streets, it's lined with many of the city's top sights. Trams #1 and #2 circle the whole route and so should you.

In fact, start your Vienna visit with this do-it-yourself, 20-AS, 30-minute circular tour. "Tours" leave every five minutes. Tram #1 goes clockwise; tram #2, counterclockwise. Since most of the sights are on the outside of the Ring, tram #2 is best (sit on the right in the front of the front car). Ideally, catch it at the Opera House at Opernring and Kärntner Strasse (but anywhere will do). With a 24-hour ticket, you can jump on and off as you go. This is great, since trams come every few minutes. (Otherwise, buy your 20-AS ticket, good for only one ride, as you board.) All described sights on this tour are on the right unless I say "on left." Let's go:

• Just past the Opera (on left): The city's main pedestrian drag, Kärntner Strasse, leads to the zigzag roof of St. Stephan's Cathedral. This tour makes a 360-degree circle, staying about this far from that spire.

• At the first bend: Look towards the tall fountain. Schwartzenberg Platz—with its equestrian statue of Prince Charles Schwartzenberg, who battled Napoleon—leads to the Russian monument (behind the fountain). This monument was built in 1945 as a forced thanks to the Soviets for liberating Austria from the Nazis. Formerly a sore point, now it's just ignored.

• Going down Schubertring: The white and yellow concert hall behind the trees is the Kursalon, opened in 1867 by the Strauss brothers, who directed many waltzes here. (See below for concert times.) The huge Stadtpark (city park) honors 20 great Viennese musicians and composers with statues.

• Immediately after next stop: In the park, the gilded statue of Waltz King Johann Strauss holds his violin as he did when he conducted his orchestra.

• While at next stop at end of park: On the left, a green and white statue of Dr. Karl Lueger honors the popular man who was mayor of Vienna until 1910.

• At next bend in road: The quaint building with military helmets decorating the windows was the Austrian ministry of war, back when that was a serious operation. Field Marshal Radetzky, a military big-shot in the 19th century under Franz Josef, still sits on his high horse.

• At next corner: The white-domed building is the Urania, Franz Josef's 1910 observatory. Lean forward and look behind it for a peek at the huge red cars of the giant 100-year-old Ferris wheel in Vienna's Prater Park.

• Now you're rolling along the Danube Canal. This "Baby Danube" is one of the many small arms of the river that once made up the Danube at this point. The rest have been gathered together in a mightier modern-day Danube, farther to the right. This was the site of the original Roman town, Vindobona. In 3 long blocks, on the left (opposite the BP station), you'll see the ivy-covered walls and round Romanesque arches of St. Ruprechts, the oldest church in Vienna (built in the 11th century on a bit of Roman ruins). By about 1200, Vienna had grown to fill the area within this ring road.

• Leaving the canal, turning up Schottenring, at first stop: On the left, the pink and white neo-Renaissance temple of money, the Börse, is Vienna's stock exchange.

• Next stop, at corner: The huge frilly neo-Gothic church is a "votive church," built in 1853 as a thanks to God when an assassination attempt on Emperor Franz Josef failed. Ahead on the right is the Vienna University building, which faces (on the left, behind the gilded angel) a chunk of the old city wall.

• At next stop: The neo-Gothic city hall, flying the flag of Europe, towers over Rathaus Platz, a festive site of outdoor movies and concerts. Immediately across the street (on left) is the Hofburg Theater.

• At next stop: The neo-Greek temple of democracy houses the Austrian Parliament. The lady with the golden helmet is Athena, goddess of wisdom. Across the street (on left) is the royal park called the Volksgarten.

• At next stop: Ahead on the right is the Natural History

# Vienna

HOTELS:
- ❶ NOSSEK
- ❷ ACLON
- ❸ PERTSKY
- ❹ NEUER MARKT
- ❺ SUZANNE
- ❻ WIENER STAATS
- ❼ DR. GEISSLER
- ❽ SCHWEIZER SOLDERER

HOFBURG DETAILS:
- Ⓐ NEUE BURG
- Ⓑ IN DER BURG SQUARE
- Ⓒ ALBERTINA

Ⓤ U-BAHN STATION

Museum, the first of Vienna's huge twin museums. Next door is the Kunsthistorisches Museum, containing the city's greatest collection of paintings. A statue of Empress Maria Theresa sits between the museums, facing the grand gate to the Hofburg, the emperor's palace (on your left). Of the five arches, only the emperor used the center. The gate, a modern addition, is located where Vienna's medieval city wall once stood.
• Fifty yards after the next stop, through a gate in the black iron fence: On the left is the statue of Mozart in the Burggarten, which until 1880 was the private garden of the emperor. A hundred yards later (on your left), Goethe sits in a

big thought-provoking chair playing Trivia with Schiller (on
your right). Behind the statue of Schiller is the Academy of Fine
Arts. Vienna had its share of intellectual and creative geniuses.
• Hey, there's the Opera again. Jump out and see the rest of
the city. (In front of the Opera there's a person who'd love to
take you on a bus tour of what you just did . . . for 220 AS.)

## Sights—Vienna's Old Center
(These sights are in walking order.)

▲▲▲**Opera**—The Staatsoper, facing the Ring, just up from
Stephansdom and next to the TI, is a central point for any visitor. While the critical reception of the building 130 years ago
led the architect to commit suicide, and it's been rebuilt since
the World War II bombings, it's a dazzling place (60 AS, by
guided 35-minute tour only, offered daily in English, July and
August at 11:00, 13:00, 14:00, 15:00, and often at 10:00 and
16:00; other months, afternoons only). Tours are often canceled for rehearsals and shows, so check the posted schedule or
call 0222/51444.

The Vienna State Opera, with the Vienna Philharmonic
Orchestra in the pit, is one of the world's top opera houses.
There are performances almost nightly, except in July and
August (when the singers are on vacation, but music still trills
in Vienna—see Summer Music Scene, below). Expensive seats
and shows are normally sold out. Unless Pavarotti is in town,
it's easy to get one of 500 *Stehplatz* (standing-room spots,
which are 20–30 AS; the downstairs spots are best). Join the
Stehplatz lineup at the Abendkasse side door, where the number of available places is posted. The ticket window opens an
hour before each performance. Buy your place at the padded
leaning rail. Since the spots aren't numbered, tie your belt or
scarf to the rail and you can slip out for a snack and return to
enjoy the performance. If less than 500 people are in line,
there's no need to line up early.

Between the Opera and the TI is Philharmoniker Strasse;
take a left to the Sacher Café, home of every chocoholic's fan-
tasy, the Sachertorte (100 AS for cake and coffee). Continue
past the café to the . . .

**Monument against War and Fascism**—Behind the Opera
House, on Albertinaplatz, a modern white split statue is Vien-
na's monument remembering the victims of the 1938–1945
Nazi rule of Austria. In 1938, Germany annexed Austria,

saying Austrians were wanna-be-Germans anyway. Austrians are *not* Germans—never were, never will be. They're quick to tell you that while Austria was founded in 976, Germany wasn't born until 1870. For seven years (1938–1945) there was no Austria. In 1955, after ten years of joint occupation by the victorious Allies, Austria regained her independence.

Across the street, the **Albertina Museum**, with its great collection of sketches and graphic art, sits atop the Augustiner Beerhall (colorful lunch place; see Eating, below). This building is the beginning of the huge Hofburg Palace complex.

To get to the pedestrian street, Kärntner Strasse, either retrace your steps or take Maysedergasse, off Albertinaplatz, passing the recommended Rosenberger Markt (see Eating, below).

▲**Kärntner Strasse**—This grand but hamburgerized mall (traffic-free since 1974) is the people-watching delight of this in-love-with-life city. It points south in the direction of the southern Austrian state of Kärnten (for which it's named). Starting from the Opera, you'll find the TI, city Casino (at #41, the former Esterhazy Palace), many fine stores, pastry shops, the American Express office (#21–23), and the cathedral.

▲▲**St. Stephan's Cathedral**—Stephansdom is the Gothic needle around which Vienna spins. It's survived all of Vienna's many wars and symbolizes the city's freedom. Locals call it "Steve" (*Steffl*). Hundreds of years of history are carved in its walls and buried in its crypt (40 AS, open at odd times, tel. 0222/515-52-526). Tours are usually in German, but English tours are offered in July and August. The information board near the entry has tour schedules and the time of the impressive 50-minute daily Mass. You can ascend both towers, the north (via crowded elevator) and the south (by spiral staircase). The north shows you a big bell (the 21-ton Pummerin, cast from the cannon captured from the Turks in 1683) but a mediocre view (40 AS, daily 9:00–18:00, enter inside). The 450-foot high south tower, also called St. Stephan's Tower, offers a great view—343 tightly wound steps away, up the spiral staircase at the watchman's lookout, 246 feet above the postcard stand (25 AS, daily 9:00–17:00, enter outside and burn about one Sachertorte of calories). From the top, use your *Vienna from A to Z* to locate the famous sights. The church is open daily from 6:00 to 22:00.

Outside, the last bit of the 11th-century Romanesque church can be seen in the west end (above the entry): the portal and the round windows of the towers. The church survived the bombs of WWII but, in the last days of the war, fires from the street-fighting between Russian and Nazi troops leapt to the rooftop; the original timbered Gothic rooftop burnt, and the cathedral's huge bell crashed to the ground. With a financial outpouring of civic pride, the roof of this symbol of Austria was rebuilt in its original splendor by 1952. The ceramic tiles are purely decorative (and each has the name of a local who contributed money to the rebuilding). Photos of the war damage can be seen inside.

The interior is grand in general, but it's hard to get thrilled about any particular bit. An exception is the Gothic sandstone pulpit in the middle of the nave (on left or north). A spiral stairway winds up to the lectern surrounded and supported by the four Latin Church Fathers: St. Ambrose, St. Gerome, St. Gregory, and St. Augustine. The work of Anton Pilgram, this has all the elements of Flamboyant Gothic in miniature. But this was 1515. The Italian Renaissance was going strong in Italy and, while Gothic persisted in the north, the Renaissance spirit had already arrived. Pilgram included a rare self-portrait bust in his work (the guy with sculptor's tools, looking out a window under the stairs). Gothic art was to the glory of God. Artists were anonymous. In the more humanist Renaissance, man was allowed to shine—and artists became famous.

The peaceful **Cathedral Museum** (Dom und Diözesan Museum) gives a close-up look at piles of religious paintings, statues, and a treasury (40 AS, Tuesday–Saturday 10:00–16:00, behind the church and past the buggy stand, Stephansplatz 6). Near the church entrance, descend into the Stephansplatz subway stop for a peek into the 13th-century Virgilkapelle.

▲▲**Stephansplatz, Graben, and Kohlmarkt**—The atmosphere of the church square, Stephanplatz, is colorful and lively. At the nearby Graben Street (which was once a Graben or "ditch"), topnotch street entertainment dances around an exotic plague monument. In medieval times, people did not understand the causes of plagues and figured they were a punishment from God. It was common for survivors to thank God with a monument like this one from the 1600s. Just beyond the monument is a fine set of Jugendstil public toilets (5.50 AS). St. Peter's Church faces the toilets. Step into this festival of Baroque (from 1708) and check out the jeweled skeletons—

anonymous martyrs donated by the pope. Kohlmarkt (at the end of Graben), Vienna's most elegant shopping street, leads left to the palace. Wander down here, checking out the edible window displays at Demel (Kohlmarkt 14). Then drool through the interior (coffee and cake for 100 AS). Shops like this one and the one across the street boast "K. u. K." This means a shop considered good enough for the *Köenig und Kaiser* (king and emperor—same guy). Kohlmarkt leads to Michaelerplatz. The stables of the Spanish Riding School face this square. Notice the Roman excavation in the center. Enter the Hofburg Palace by walking through the gate and into the first square (In der Burg).

## Sights—Vienna's Hofburg Palace

▲▲**Hofburg**—The complex, confusing, imposing Imperial Palace, with 640 years of architecture, demands your attention (and with so many turnstiles, a lot of your money). This first Habsburg residence (13th century) grew in an ad-lib manner until 1913, when the new wing (Neue Burg) was opened. The winter residence of the Habsburg rulers until 1918, it's still the home of the Spanish Riding School, the Vienna Boys' Choir, the Austrian President's office, and several important museums.

While you could lose yourself in its myriad halls and courtyards, I'd focus on three things: the apartments, treasury, and new palace. Orient yourself to the complex from the In der Burg square. The statue is of Emperor Franz II (grandson of Maria Theresa and grandfather of Franz Josef). Behind him is a tower with three kinds of clocks (the yellow disc shows the stage of the moon tonight). On the right, a door leads to the imperial apartments and Hofburg model. Franz II is facing the oldest part of the palace. The gate (which used to have a drawbridge) leads to the 13th-century Swiss Court (named for the Swiss mercenary guards who used to be stationed here) with the Schatzkammer (treasury) and the palace chapel (Hofburgkappelle), where the boys' choir sings the Mass. Continuing out opposite the way you entered In der Burg, you'll find the Hero's Square and the Neue Burg. The *A to Z* book sorts out this time-blackened, jewel-stained mess. Or, if overwhelmed, tour the Imperial Apartments first; here you can buy a big, glossy, detailed Hofburg guidebook in English with great photos and special emphasis on apartments (95 AS).

Leave In der Burg for the Imperial Apartments, where you'll find a marvelous model of the whole darn place under a glass pyramid. Study that.

▲▲**Imperial Apartments (Kaiserappartements)**—These lavish, Versailles-type "wish-I-were-God" royal rooms are a small, downtown version of the grander Schönbrunn Palace. If rushed, see one palace or the other. These suffice. The Apartments are next to the Silver and Porcelain Collection (Silberkammer). You can tour either for 80 AS or get a Kombi-Ticket for 95 AS and see them both (daily 9:00–17:00, from courtyard through St. Michael's Gate, just off Michaelerplatz, tel. 0222/533-7570). An optional guided tour, in German only, costs 20 AS extra.

▲▲**Treasury**—The Weltliche and Geistliche Schatzkammer (secular and religious treasure room) is expensive, but if you want historic and lavish jewels, these are by far the best on the Continent. Reflect on the glitter of 21 rooms filled with scepters, swords, crowns, orbs, weighty robes, a 96-inch-tall and 500-year-old unicorn horn (or maybe the horn of a narwhal), double-headed eagles, gowns, dangles, and gem-studded bangles. Remember that these were the Holy Roman Emperor's—the divine monarch's. The highlight is Room 11, with the Reichskrone—the tenth-century crown of the Holy Roman Emperor—and two cases of Karls des Grossen (Charlemagne's) riches (80 AS, Wednesday–Monday 10:00–18:00, closed Tuesday, follow Schatzkammer signs through the red/gold/black arch leading from the main courtyard into the Schweizerhof, tel. 0222/533-7931). Included with your admission is an Art-guide; strap this infrared computer around your neck and point it at display cases to get information (deposit: passport or 500 AS).

▲**Neue Burg (New Palace)**—This is the last and most impressive addition to the palace. Dating from this century, it was built for Franz Ferdinand but never used. Its grand facade arches around Heldenplatz, or Hero's Square. The featured heroes are Prince Eugene of Savoy (who saved the city from the Turks) and Archduke Charles Schwartzenberg (first to beat Napoleon in a battle, breaking Nappy's image of invincibility and heralding the end of the Napoleonic age). The palace houses three museums: an armory, historical musical instruments, and classical statuary from ancient Ephesus. The musical instruments are particularly entertaining, and free radio headsets (when they work) play appropriate music in each room. Wait at the orange dots for the

German description to finish, and you might hear the instruments you're seeing. Stay tuned in, as graceful period music accompanies your wander through the neighboring halls of medieval weaponry—a killer collection of crossbows, swords, and armor. An added bonus is the chance to wander all alone among those royal Habsburg halls, stairways, and painted ceilings (30 AS for all three collections, Wednesday–Monday 10:00–18:00, closed Tuesday, almost no tourists).

## More Sights—Vienna

▲▲▲Kunsthistorisches Museum—This exciting museum near the Hofburg Palace showcases the great Habsburg collection of work by Dürer, Rubens, Titian, Raphael, and especially Brueghel. There's also a fine display of Egyptian, classical, and applied arts, including a divine golden saltshaker by Cellini. The museum sells a pamphlet on the top 21 paintings (20 AS) and offers English tours (usually at 11:00 and 15:00 Tuesday–Sunday April–October). The paintings are hung on one floor, and clear charts guide you (95 AS, higher depending on special exhibitions, Tuesday–Sunday 10:00–18:00, Thursday until 21:00, closed Monday, tel. 0222/525-240).

Natural History Museum—In the twin building facing the art museum, you'll find moon rocks, dinosaur stuff, and the *Venus of Willendorf*—at 30,000 years old, the world's oldest sex symbol, found near Vienna in the Danube Valley (Wednesday–Monday 9:00–18:00, closed Tuesday; off-season 9:00–15:00).

▲Academy of Fine Arts—This small but exciting collection includes works by Bosch, Botticelli, and Rubens; a Venice series by Guardi; and a self-portrait by 15-year-old Van Dyck (30 AS, Tuesday, Thursday, and Friday 10:00–14:00, Wednesday 10:00–13:00 and 15:00–18:00, Saturday and Sunday 9:00–13:00, three minutes from the Opera at Schillerplatz 3, tel. 0222/588-16-225).

▲Kaisergruft, the Remains of the Habsburgs—Visiting the imperial remains is not as easy as you might imagine. These original organ donors left their bodies—147 in all—in the Kaisergruft (Capuchin Crypt, 40 AS, daily 9:30–16:00, a block behind the Opera on Neuer Markt, 5-AS map with a Habsburg family tree and a chart locating each coffin), their hearts in St. George Chapel in the Augustinian Church (church open daily, but to see the goods you'll have to talk to a priest; near the Hofburg, Augustinerstrasse 3), and their entrails in the crypt below St. Stephan's Cathedral. Don't tripe. Rather than chasing down all these body parts, remember that the magnificence of this city is the real remains of the Habsburgs. Pan up. Watch the clouds glide by the ornate gables of Vienna.

Nearby, step into the Augustinian Church, where the Habsburg weddings took place. Don't miss the exquisite Canova tomb (neoclassical, 1805) of Maria Theresa's favorite daughter, Maria Christina, with its incredibly sad white-marble procession. The church has the burial vault for the hearts of the Habsburgs (by appointment only).

▲**Belvedere Palace**—The elegant palace of Prince Eugene of Savoy (the still-much-appreciated conqueror of the Turks), and later home of Franz Ferdinand, houses the Austrian Gallery of 19th- and 20th-century art. Skip the lower palace and focus on the garden and the top floor of the upper palace (Oberes Belvedere) for a winning view of the city and a fine collection of Jugendstil art, Klimt, and Kokoschka (60 AS, Tuesday–Sunday 10:00–17:00, closed Monday, entrance at Prince Eugen Strasse 27, tel. 0222/795-570). Your ticket includes the Austrian Baroque and Gothic art in the Lower Palace.

▲▲▲**Schönbrunn Palace**—Schloss Schönbrunn is second only to Versailles among Europe's palaces. Located 7 kilometers from the center, it was the Habsburgs' summer residence. It is big—1,441 rooms—but don't worry, only 40 rooms are shown to the public. (The families of 260 civil servants actually rent simple apartments in the rest of the palace.)

While the exterior is Baroque, the interior was finished under Maria Theresa in the Rococo style. The chandeliers are either of hand-carved wood with gold-leaf gilding or of Bohemian crystal. Thick walls hid the servants as they ran around stoking the ceramic stoves from the back, and so on. Most of the public rooms are decorated in neo-Baroque as they were under Franz Josef (1890). While WWII bombs rained on the city and the palace grounds, the palace itself took only one direct hit; that bomb, which crashed through three floors, including the sumptuous central ballroom, was a dud.

There are two different tours you can take. Both come with free headphones that describe the sights in English as you walk through the rooms on your own. The Imperial Tour covers 22 rooms (90 AS) and the Grand Tour covers those 22 rooms plus 18 others (120 AS). Both include the special Empress Elizabeth exhibit. Optional guided tours in English are scheduled roughly every two hours (25 AS extra); you can call in advance for tour times or you can just show up and kill waiting time in the gardens or coach museum (palace open 8:30–17:00, until 16:30 off-season; from the Westbahnhof, either take bus #58 or take subway U-6 to Längenfeldstrasse, then transfer to U-4 and get off at Schönbrunn stop—take exit "Schönbrunn Palace" at train level, tel. 0222/8111-3239). The palace is the most crowded right at opening time and on weekends; it's least crowded from 12:00 to 14:00 and after 16:00.

Wagenburg, the adjacent coach museum, is impressive, with more than 50 royal carriages and sleighs, including a death-black hearse carriage and an extravagantly gilded job, pulled by a dozen horses, that seems pumpkin-bound (30 AS, daily 9:00–18:00; off-season 10:00–16:00 and closes on Monday). The sculpted gardens (with a palm house) lead up to the Gloriette, a purely decorative monument celebrating an obscure Austrian military victory and offering a fine city view (and an expensive cup of coffee). The park is free and open until dusk.

▲City Park—Vienna's Stadtpark is a waltzing world of gardens, memorials to local musicians, ponds, peacocks, music in bandstands, and local people escaping the city. Notice the Jugendstil entry at the Stadtpark subway station. The Kursalon orchestra plays Strauss waltzes daily in summer: 16:00–18:00, 20:00–21:00, and 21:30–22:30 (tel. 0222/713-2181). You can buy a front-row seat or join the local seniors and ants on the grass for free.

▲Prater—Vienna's sprawling amusement park tempts any visitor with its huge 220-foot-high, famous, and lazy Ferris wheel (Riesenrad), roller coaster, bumper cars, Lilliputian railroad, and endless eateries. This is a fun, goofy place to share the evening with thousands of Viennese (daily 9:00–24:00 in summer, subway: Praterstern). For a local-style family dinner, eat at Schweizerhaus (great beer) or Wieselburger Bierinsel.

Sunbathing—Like most Europeans, the Austrians worship the sun. Their lavish swimming centers are as much for tanning as for swimming. For the best man-made island beach scene, head for the "Danube Sea," Vienna's 20 miles of beach along Danube Island (subway: Donauinsel).

▲Naschmarkt—Vienna's ye olde produce market bustles daily, near the Opera along Wienzeile Street. It's likeably seedy and surrounded by sausage stands, Turkish döner kebab stalls, cafés, and theaters. Each Saturday it's infested by a huge flea market where, in olden days, locals would come to hire a monkey to pick little critters out of their hair (Monday–Friday 6:00–18:30, Saturday 6:00–17:00). For a picnic park, walk 1 block down Schleifmuhlgasse.

**City Tours**—Get the *Walks in Vienna* brochure at the TI. Of Vienna's many guided walks, only a few are in English (126 AS, not including admissions, 90 min, tel. 0222/51450, ext. 257). The 75-minute "Getting Acquainted" German/English bus tour is essentially what I covered above in the Ring Tour, with a detour to the Upper Belvedere Palace (220 AS, daily from the Opera at 10:30, 11:45, 15:00, and, in summer, 16:30; no reservations necessary; tel. 0222/712-4683). While pricey, it's intensely informative and a good introduction if you're lazy. Cut out at the palace (which is near the end) if you'd like to see its collection of Klimt and Art Nouveau. The TI has a booklet listing all city tours. Eva Prochaska can book you an excellent private guide who charges 1,180 AS for a half-day (1, Weihburggasse 13-15, tel. 0222/513-5294).

**KunstHausWien**—This "make yourself at home" modern-art museum, opened in 1990, is a real hit with lovers of modern art. It features the work of local painter/environmentalist Hundertwasser (90 AS, daily 10:00–19:00; 3, Weissgerberstrasse 13, nearest metro: U-3 Landstrasse, tel. 0222/712-0491). Nearby, the one-with-nature Hundertwasserhaus (at Löwengasse and Kegelgasse) is a complex of 50 lived-in apartments. This was built in the 1980s as a breath of architectural fresh air in a city of blocky, suicidally predictable apartment complexes. It's not open to visitors but worth visiting for its fun-loving exterior, the Hundertwasser festival of shops across the street, and for the pleasure of annoying its residents.

▲**Jugendstil**—Vienna gave birth to its own curvaceous brand of Art Nouveau around the turn of the century. Jugendstil art and architecture are popular around Europe these days, and many come to Vienna solely in search of it. The TI has a brochure laying out Vienna's 20th-century architecture. The best of Vienna's scattered Jugendstil sights include the Belvedere Palace collection, the clock on Höher Markt (which does a musical act at noon), that WC on the Graben, and the Karlsplatz subway stop, where you'll find the gilded-cabbage-domed gallery with the movement's slogan: "To each century its art and to art its liberty." Klimt, Wagner, and friends (who called themselves the Vienna Succession) first exhibited their "liberty style" art here in 1897.

**Spanish Riding School**—Performances are usually sold out in advance (tickets 250–900 AS, standing room 200 AS), but training sessions in a chandeliered Baroque hall are open to the public (100 AS at the door, Tuesday–Saturday 10:00–12:00 roughly February–June, September, and mid-October–December; long line; Innerer Burghof in the Hofburg).

**Honorable Mention**—There's much, much more. The city museum brochure lists everything. If you're into butterflies, Esperanto, undertakers, tobacco, clowns, fire-fighting, or the homes of dead composers, you'll find them all in Vienna. Several good museums that try very hard but are submerged in the greatness of Vienna include: **Historical Museum of the City of Vienna** (Tuesday–Sunday 9:00–16:30, Karlsplatz), **Folkloric Museum of Austria** (8, Laudongasse 15, tel. 0222/438-905), and **Museum of Military History**, one of Europe's best if you like swords and shields (Heeregeschichtliches Museum, Saturday–Thursday 10:00–16:00, closed Friday; 3, Arsenal, Objekt 18). The best-value shopping street, with more than 2,000 shops, is Mariahilfer Strasse. For a walk in the Vienna Woods, catch the U-4 subway to Heiligenstadt then bus #38A to Kahlenberg, where there are great city views and a café terrace overlooking the city. From there it's a peaceful 45-minute downhill hike to the Heurigen of Nussdorf or Grinzing to enjoy some wine.

## Vienna's Cafés and Wine Gardens

▲**Viennese Coffeehouse**—In Vienna the living room is the coffeehouse down the street. This tradition is just another example of the Viennese expertise in good living. Each of Vienna's many long-established (and sometimes even legendary) coffeehouses has its individual character (and characters). They offer newspapers, pastries, sofas, elegance, a smoky ambience, and a "take all the time you want" charm for the price of a cup of coffee. You may want to order *malange* (with a little milk) rather than *schwarzer* (black).

Some of my favorites are: **Café Hawelka**, with a rumpled, "brooding Trotsky" atmosphere, paintings on the walls by struggling artists who couldn't pay, a saloon-wood flavor, chalkboard menu, smoked velvet couches, an international selection of newspapers, and a phone that rings for regulars

(8:00–2:00, Sunday from 16:00, closed Tuesday, Dorotheergasse 6, just off the Graben); the **Café Central,** with Jugendstil
decor and great *Apfelstrudel* (8:00–20:00, closed Sunday, Her-
rengasse 14); the Jugendstil **Café Sperl**, dating from 1880
(7:00–23:00, closed Sunday in summer, Gumpendorfer 11, just
off Naschmarkt); and the basic, untouristy **Café Ritter** (daily
8:00–20:00, Mariahilfer Strasse 73, at the Neubaugasse subway
stop near several of my recommended hotels).

▲**Wine Gardens**—The *Heurige* is a uniquely Viennese institution celebrating the *Heuriger,* or new wine. It all started when
the Habsburgs let Vienna's vintners sell their own wine tax-
free for 300 days a year. Several hundred families opened
*Heurigen* wine-garden restaurants clustered around the edge of
Vienna, and a tradition was born. Today they do their best to
maintain their old-village atmosphere, serving the homemade
new wine (the last vintage, until November 11th) with light
meals and strolling musicians.

Of the many Heurigen suburbs, **Grinzing** (tram #38 or
#38A) is the most famous and lively—but it comes with tour
buses. **Nussdorf** is less touristy but still characteristic and popular with locals (two fine places are right at the end of tram D).
For more crowds and music with your meal, visit **Beethoven's
home** in Heiligenstadt (on Pfarrplatz, tram #38A or #37 and a
ten-minute walk, tel. 0222/371-287). While Beethoven lived
here in 1817 (to be near a spa he hoped would cure his worsen-
ing deafness), he composed his Sixth Symphony ("Pastoral").
These suburbs are all within a 15-minute stroll of each other.

At any Heurige you'll fill your plate at a self-serve cold-cut
buffet (75–125 AS for dinner). Waitresses will then take your
wine order (30 AS per quarter-liter). Many locals claim it takes
several years of practice to distinguish between Heuriger and
vinegar. For a near-Heurigen experience right downtown, drop
by Gigerl Stadtheuriger (see Eating, below).

## Summer Music Scene

Vienna is Europe's music capital. It's music *con brio* from October through June, with things reaching a symphonic climax
during the Vienna Festival each May and June. Sadly, in July
and August, the Boys' Choir, the Opera, and many more music
companies are—like you—on vacation. But Vienna hums year-
round with live classical music. In the summer, you have these
basic choices:

**Touristy Mozart and Strauss concerts**—Quality but touristy powdered-wig orchestra performances are given almost nightly in grand traditional settings (400–600 AS). Music is becoming a tourist trap in Vienna. Pesky wigged and powdered Mozarts peddle tickets in the streets. At the touristy Wiener Mozart Konzerte, the orchestra, clad in historic costumes and looking better than it sounds, performs Mozart's greatest hits, including his famous opera arias. The Strauss concerts feature formal waltzers and the Salon Orchestra of the "Wiener Volksoper" inside the Kursalon, where the Waltz King himself directed wildly popular concerts 100 years ago.

▲▲**"Programm"**—Serious concerts, including the Opera, are listed in the "Programm," a free monthly brochure available at the TI. Events cost between 150 and 700 AS. Tickets booked in advance or through a box office come with a stiff 25 percent booking fee (one's next to the TI behind the Opera). If you call a concert hall directly, they can advise you on the availability of (cheaper) tickets at the door. Vienna takes care of its starving artists (and tourists) by offering cheap standing-room tickets to top-notch music and opera.

▲**Free music**—For a festive and free slice of the local music scene, ask about free concerts at the Rathaus (city hall) and on the big screen in front of the Opera. You can also freeload on the Kursalon outdoor Strauss concerts by sitting in the fringes.

▲**Strauss in the Kursalon**—This is your easiest, most affordable option, with daily concerts (April–mid-October) and all your three-quarter favorites in a romantic outdoor setting (weather permitting). Check schedule by calling 0222/713-2181. Pay at the door. Seats are always available (40 AS for orchestra only from 16:00–18:00, or 195 AS for orchestra, dancers, and champagne: 20:00–21:00 or 21:30–22:30 ).

▲**"Summer of Music" Festival**—This assures that even from June through September you'll find lots of top-notch concerts, choirs, and symphonies (special "Klang Bogen" brochure at TI; tickets at the Wien Ticket pavilion on Kärntner Strasse next to the Opera House, or go direct to the location of the particular event; tel. 0222/4000-8410 for information).

▲▲**Vienna Boys' Choir**—The boys sing (heard but not seen, from a high balcony) at Mass in the Imperial Chapel of the Hofburg (entrance at Schweizerhof) at 9:15 on Sundays, except from July through mid-September. Seats must be reserved at least two months in advance (60–280 AS), but standing room is free and open to the first 60 or 70 who line up. Concerts (on stage in the Konzerthaus, or Concert Hall) are also given Fridays at 15:30 in May, June, September, and October (390–430 AS, fax 011-431-587-1268 from U.S.A. or write Reisebüro Mondial, Faulmanngasse 4, 1040 Wien). They're nice kids but, for my taste, not worth all the commotion.

## Nightlife
If old music or new wine isn't your thing, Vienna has plenty of alternatives. For an up-to-date rundown on fun after dark, get the TI's free *Young Vienna Scene* booklet. An area known as the Bermuda Dreieck (Triangle), north of the cathedral between Rotenturmstrasse and Judengasse, is the hot local nightspot, with lots of classy pubs or *Beisles* (such as Krah Krah, Salzamt, and Kitch and Bitter) and popular music spots such as the disco P1 (Rotgasse 9, tel. 0222/535-9995) and Jazzland (Franz Josefs-Kai 29, tel. 0222/533-2575). Most lively on a balmy summer evening is the scene at Danube Island.

## Sleeping in Vienna
**(12 AS = about $1, tel. code within Austria: 0222; from outside: 1)**
Sleep Code: **S**=Single, **D**=Double/Twin, **T**=Triple, **Q**=Quad, **b**=bathroom, **t**=toilet only, **s**=shower only, **CC**=Credit Card (**V**isa, **M**asterCard, **A**mex). English is spoken at each place.

Call accommodations a few days in advance. If you're calling from outside Austria, replace the "0222" area code with "1." Most places will hold a room without a deposit if you promise to arrive before 17:00. My recommendations stretch along the likeable Mariahilfer Strasse from the Westbahnhof (West Station) to the town center. Unless otherwise noted, prices include a sparse continental breakfast.

Street addresses start with the district. Postal code is 1XX0, with XX being the district.

### Sleeping Outside the Ring, along Mariahilfer Strasse
Lively Mariahilfer Strasse connects the West Station with the center. The U-3 subway line, starting at the Westbahnhof, goes down Mariahilfer Strasse to the cathedral. While most places are on stern and quiet no-nonsense side roads, the nearby and very Viennese Mariahilfer Strasse is a comfortable and vibrant area filled with local shops and cafés.

**Privatzimmer F. Kaled** is bright, airy, homey, quiet, and has TVs (with CNN) in each of the four rooms. Hardworking Tina is a mini tourist information service. Being Hungarian, she has good contacts for people visiting Budapest (S-400 AS, Sb-450 AS, D-550 AS, Db-650 AS, T-800 AS, 150 AS for extra bed, skip the 75-AS breakfast in bed, prices through 1998, secure reservation with CC, but room bills must be paid in cash, tell Tina or Fred when you'll arrive; 7, Lindengasse 42, 1070 Wien, near intersection with Neubaugasse, tel. & fax 0222/523-9013). Across the street, Zur Lindenwirtin is a hole-in-the-wall serving big salads and reasonable meals. The Zimmer is a 15-minute walk from the station or a quick two-stop metro ride on U-3 to Neubaugasse (exit to Neubaugasse at train level).

**Pension Lindenhof** is worn but clean, filled with plants, and run with a unique combination of Bulgarian and Armenian warmth (S-360 AS, Sb-460 AS, D-600 AS, Db-820 AS, cheaper in winter, hall showers-20 AS, most rooms are spacious; 7, Lindengasse 4, 1070 Wien, metro: U-3 Neubaugasse—take "Stiftgasse" exit, tel. 0222/523-0498, fax 0222/523-7362).

**Pension Hargita**, with 19 generally small, bright, and tidy rooms (mostly twins), is handy—right at the U-3 Zieglergasse stop—and next to a sex shop (S-400 AS, Ss-450 AS, D-550 AS, Ds-650 AS, Db-800 AS, Ts-800 AS, Tb-1,000 AS, Qb-1,100 AS, breakfast-40 AS extra, cheaper for longer stays off-season, corner of Mariahilfer Strasse and Andreasgasse at 7, Andreasgasse 1, 1070 Wien, tel. 0222/526-1928, fax 0222/526-0492).

**Budai Ildiko**, in a Jugendstil building with a vintage elevator, has high-ceilinged rooms and classy furnishings (small S-350 AS, D-560 AS, T-820 AS, Q-1,050 AS, laundry-20 AS; 7, Lindengasse 39/5, 1070 Wien, tel. 0222/523-1058, tel. & fax 0222/526-2595, run by a charming Hungarian woman).

**Hotel Kummer** is a 100-room turn-of-the-century hotel with all the comforts (Sb-990–1,490 AS, Db-1,250–2,400 AS, the upper price range applies in May, September, and October, show book to get lower price outside those months, elevator, some no-smoking rooms, CC:VMA, right at the U-3 Neubaugasse stop, 6, Mariahilfer Strasse 71A, 1060 Wien, tel. 0222/58895, fax 0222/587-8133, e-mail: kummer@austria-hotels.co.at).

**Privatzimmer Hilde Wolf**, 3 blocks off Naschmarkt near U-2 Karlsplatz, is a homey place one floor above an ugly entry, with four huge rooms like old libraries. Hilde loves her

## Vienna: Hotels Outside The Ring

❶ FUNFHAUS
❷ F. KALED
❸ LINDENHOF
❹ HARGITA
❺ KUMMER
❻ QUISIANA
❼ HILDE WOLF
❽ HOSTELS
❾ BELIEVE IT OR...
❿ WILD
⓫ ANDREAS

Ⓤ U-BAHN

work, will do your laundry if you stay two nights, and even offers to baby-sit if traveling parents need a break. Her helpful husband, Otto, speaks English. From West Station, take tram #6 or #18 five stops to Eichenstrasse, then tram #62 six stops to Paulanergasse (two stops from Opera). For a real home in Vienna, unpack here (S-450 AS, D-650 AS, T-955 AS, Q-1,225 AS, with a big, friendly, family-style breakfast, prices through 1998; 4, Schleifmühlgasse 7, 1040 Vienna, tel. 0222/586-5103, reserve by telephone and CC; if you can't make it, call to cancel).

**Pension Quisisana** is tired and ramshackle, but is a fine value for bohemians in search of the old days and a clean dive (S-330 AS, Ss-380 AS, D-520 AS, Ds-600–640 AS, Db-700–740 AS, 640 AS for a big corner room, third person-260

AS, prices through 1998 with this book, Db rooms are a better value than the D rooms with head-to-toe twin beds; a block south of Mariahilfer Strasse at 6, Windmuhlgasse 6, 1060 Wien, tel. 0222/587-7155, fax 0222/587-715-633).

West of the Westbahnhof, **Pension Funfhaus** is big, clean, stark, and quiet, with 97 beds split between the main building and an annex. Although the neighborhood is run-down, this place is a great value, especially the spacious and bright doubles with bathrooms (S-390 AS, Sb-470 AS, D-560 AS, Db-640 AS, T-840 AS, Tb-910 AS, two-bedroom apartments for four-1,120 AS, free and easy street parking, closed mid-November–February; 15, Sperrgasse 12, 1150 Wien, tel. 0222/892-3545 or 0222/892-0286, Frau Susi Tersch SE, her mama doesn't). From the station, either ride tram #52 or #58 two stops or walk 7 blocks away from downtown on Mariahilfer Strasse, to Sperrgasse.

### Sleeping North of Mariahilfer Strasse
These listings are 4 to 8 blocks north of Mariahilfer Strasse.

**Jugendherbergen Myrthengasse/Neustiftgasse** is actually two hostels near each other. Both are cheery and well-run, will hold rooms until 16:00, have a lock-out period from 9:00–16:00 and a 1:00 curfew, and offer 60-AS meals. The **IYHF** hostel charges 165 AS per person plus 40 AS for non-members (includes sheets and breakfast, three- to six-bed rooms; 7, Myrthengasse 7, 1070 Wien, tel. 0222/523-6316, fax 0222/523-5849). Across the street is **Believe It Or Not,** a friendly and basic place with two big coed rooms for up to ten travelers under age 30. It's locked up from 10:30 to 12:30, has kitchen facilities, and has no curfew (160 AS per bed, 110 AS November–Easter; 7, Myrthengasse 10, no sign, ring apt. #14, tel. 0222/526-4658, run by Gosha).

**Pension Wild** has 14 fine rooms (though a few have a stale smell) and a good, "keep-it-simple-and-affordable" attitude. There are handy extras, like an elevator, full kitchen facilities on each floor, and cheap passes to the health club downstairs (S-450 AS, Ss-550 AS, D-590 AS, Ds-690 AS, Db-790 AS, T-860 AS, Ts-960 AS, reserve with CC:VMA but pay cash, near U-2 Rathaus; 8, Langegasse 10, 1080 Vienna, tel. 0222/406-5174, fax 0222/402-2168).

**Pension Andreas** is past-its-prime classy and quiet, but a bit smoky (St-580–690 AS, Ds-780–850 AS, Db-890–930 AS, big Db-990 AS, elevator, CC:VMA, near U-2 Rathaus at 8, Schlösselgasse 11, 1080 Wien, tel. 0222/405-3488, fax 0222/405-348-850).

## Sleeping Within the Ring, in the Old City Center

These places offer less room per schilling but are comfortable, right in the town center, elevatored, with easy subway connections from West Station. The first four are nearly in the shadow of St. Stephan's Cathedral, on or near the Graben, where the elegance of Old Vienna strums happily over the cobbles. The next two listings are near the Opera (subway: Karlsplatz) just off the famous Kärntner Strasse, near the tourist office and five minutes from the cathedral.

At **Pension Nossek**, an elevator takes you above any street noise into Frau Bernad's and Frau Gundolf's world, where the children seem to be placed among the lace and flowers by an interior designer. Street musicians, a pedestrian mall filled with cafés, and the plague monument are outside your door. This is the best value of these first three (Ss-650 AS, Sb-800–900 AS, small Db-1,050 AS, big Db-1,100 AS, apartment-1,500 AS; 1, Graben 17, tel. 0222/5337-0410, fax 0222/535-3646). This pension borders on the square with the Jugendstil WCs.

**Pension Aclon** is quiet, elegant, sternly run, a block off the Graben, and above a classic Vienna café. The owner, Frau Michlmayer, is curt (S-500 AS, Sb-730 AS, D-860 AS, Db-1,200 AS, T-1,230 AS, Tb-1,620, Q-1,600, Qb-2,000; 1, Dorotheergasse 6-8, tel. 0222/512-79-400, fax 0222/513-8751).

**Pension Pertschy** is more hotelesque than the others. Its big rooms are huge (ask to see a couple), and those on the courtyard are quietest (Sb-800 AS, Db-1,180–1,440 AS depending on size, apartments with kitchenette for the same price—just ask, cheaper off-season, extra person-300 AS, CC:VM; 1, Habsburgergasse 5, tel. 0222/53449, fax 0222/534-4949).

**Pension Neuer Markt**, also just off Graben, has cheap-looking doors but the rooms are comfy and pleasant and the location is great (Ss-900 AS, St-800 AS, Sb-1,100 AS, Ds-1,050 AS, Dt-980 AS, Db-1,380 AS, prices soft if business is slow, TVs and phones, CC:VMA; 1, Seilergasse 9, 1010 Wien, tel. 0222/512-2316, fax 0222/513-9105). Ask for a view of Naschmarkt.

**Pension Suzanne**, as Baroque and doily as you'll find in this price range, is wonderfully located a few yards from the

Opera. Suzanne is quiet, with pink elegance bouncing on every bed (Sb-850–880 AS, Db-1,050–1,300 AS, third person-500 AS, TV and phones, reserve with CC but cash preferred; 1, Walfischgasse 4, 1010 Wien, tel. 0222/513-2507, fax 0222/513-2500). From the Westbahnhof, take U-3 to Volkstheater, then transfer to U-2 and get off at Karlsplatz (Opera exit).

**Hotel zur Wiener Staatsoper** is quiet, rich, and hotelesque. Its rooms come with high ceilings, chandeliers, and fancy carpets on parquet floors—a great value for this locale and ideal for people whose hotel taste is a cut above mine (Sb-1,100 AS, Db-1,600 AS, Tb-1,850 AS, CC:VMA; 1, Krugerstrasse 11, 1010 Wien, tel. 0222/513-1274, fax 0222/513-127-415). Take subway to Karlsplatz, or walk five minutes from U-3: Stephansplatz.

**Schweizer Pension Solderer**, in the family for three generations, is warmly run by two friendly sisters, Monica and Anita. Enjoy the homey feel, comfortable rooms, parquet floors, and lots of tourist info (S-430 AS, Ss-650 AS, Sb-700 AS, D-700 AS, Ds-860 AS, Db-980 AS, quirky elevator costs 1 AS, laundry-150 AS, non-smoking, Heinrichsgasse 2, 1010 Wien; from West station, take U-3 to Volkstheater, then U-2 to Schottenring; tel. 0222/533-8156, fax 0222/535-6469).

**Pension Dr. Geissler** has attractive rooms, indifferent staff, and the same cheap doors and same owner as Pension Neuer Markt (S-450–580 AS, Sb-650–850 AS, D-600–780 AS, Ds-620–980 AS, Db-800–1,180 AS, prices vary with season, CC:VMA, north of central post office; 1, Postgasse 14, 1010 Wien; from West station, take U-3 to Stephansplatz, then U-1 to Schwedenplatz; tel. 0222/533-2803, fax 0222/533-2635).

### Sleeping Outside the Center
**Turmherberge "Don Bosco"** is far away, but I stayed there in 1973, and it's still the cheapest place in Vienna (with some of the same staff). Catholic-run, it's closed from 12:00 to 17:00 and in winter (95-AS dorm beds and sheets with IYHF card, no breakfast; 3, Lechnerstrasse 12, tel. 0222/713-1494). From South Station, take tram #18 to the last stop. From West Station, take U-3 to Kardinal Nagl Platz.

## Eating in Vienna
The Viennese appreciate the fine points of life, and right up there with the waltz is eating. The city has many atmospheric

restaurants. As you ponder the menus, remember that Vienna's diverse empire may be gone, but its flavor lingers. You'll find Slavic and Eastern European specialties here, along with wonderful desserts and local wine.

On nearly every corner you can find a colorful *Beisl* (Viennese tavern) filled with poetry teachers and their students, couples loving without touching, housewives on their way home from cello lessons, and waiters who thoroughly enjoy serving hearty food and good drink at an affordable price. Ask at your hotel for a good *Beisl*.

All my recommended eateries are within a five-minute walk of the cathedral.

These **wine cellars** are fun and touristic but typical, in the old center of town, with painless prices and lots of smoke. **Zu den Drei Hacken** is famous for its local specialties (Monday–Friday 9:00–24:00, Saturday 10:00–24:00, closed Sunday, indoor/outdoor seating, CC:VA, Singerstrasse 28). The less touristy **Pürstner** restaurant is pleasantly drenched in Old World atmosphere but doesn't encourage lingering (daily 11:00–24:00, indoor/outdoor seating, 150-AS meals, a block away at Riemergasse 10, tel. 0222/512-6357). **Melker Stiftskeller**, the least touristy, is a *Stadtheuriger* in a deep and rustic cellar with hearty, inexpensive meals and new wine (Monday–Saturday 17:00–24:00, closed Sunday, halfway between Am Hof and the Schottentor subway stop at Schottengasse 3, tel. 0222/533-5530).

For a near-Heuriger experience (a la Grinzing, see above) without leaving the center, eat at **Gigerl Stadtheuriger**. Just point to what looks good. Food is sold by the weight (cheese and cold meats cost about 35 AS/100 grams, salads are about 15 AS/100 grams). They also have menu entrees, along with spinach strudel, quiche, *Apfelstrudel*, and, of course, the new and local wines. Meals run 100–150 AS (daily 11:00–24:00, indoor/outdoor seating, near the cathedral, a block off Kärntner Strasse, a few cobbles off Rauhensteingasse on Blumenstock, tel. 0222/513-4431).

**Brezel-Gwölb**, a wonderfully atmospheric wine cellar with outdoor dining on a quiet square, serves delicious, moderately priced light meals, fine *Krautsuppe*, and local dishes. It's ideal for a romantic late-night glass of wine (daily 11:30–1:00, Ledererhof 9, take Drahtgasse off Am Hof). Around the corner, **Zum Scherer Sitz u. Stehbeisl** is just as untouristy, with indoor or outdoor seating, a soothing woody atmosphere, intriguing decor, and local specialties (Monday–Saturday 11:00–1:00, Sunday 17:00–24:00, Judenplatz 7, near Am Hof).

**Augustinerkeller** is fun, inexpensive, and touristy (daily 10:00–24:00, next to the Opera under the Albertina Museum on Augustinerstrasse). **Figlmüller** is a popular *Beisl* famous for its giant schnitzels (one can easily feed two) near St. Stephan's Cathedral (daily 11:00–22:30, just down the Stephansplatz 6 alley at Wollzeile 5, watch for thieves and rip-off waiters).

For a fast, light, and central lunch, **Rosenberger Markt Restaurant**, a popular highway chain, has an elegant super-branch a block toward the cathedral from the Opera. This place, while not cheap, is brilliant: friendly and efficient, with special theme rooms to dine in, offering a fresh and healthy cornucopia of food and drink and a cheery break from the heavy, smoky, traditional eateries (daily 11:00–23:00, lots of fruits and vegetables, just off Kärntner Strasse at Mayseder-gasse 2, head downstairs). You can stack a small salad or veggie plate into the tower of gobble for 30 AS.

**Buffet Trzesniewski** is justly famous for its elegant and cheap finger sandwiches (9 AS) and small beers (9 AS). Three sandwiches and a *kleines Bier* (Pfiff) make a fun, light lunch (Monday–Friday 8:30–19:30, Saturday 9:00–17:00, just off the Graben, nearly across from the brooding Café Hawelka, on Dorotheergasse).

**Naschmarkt**, five minutes beyond the Opera, is Vienna's best Old World market, with plenty of fresh produce, cheap eateries, cafés, and döner kebab and sausage stands (Monday–Friday 6:00–18:30, Saturday until 17:00, closed Sunday). For about the cheapest hot meal in town, lunch at the nearby Technical University's **Mensa** (cafeteria) in the huge, modern, light-green building just past Karlsplatz (Monday–Friday 11:00–14:30, Wiedner Hauptstrasse 8-10, second floor). Anyone is welcome to eat here with a world of students. The snack bar is less crowded, but the bigger mensa on the same floor has a more interesting selection. The popular **Italian Eis** at Schwedenplatz has great gelato; survey the evening scene from their sidewalk benches.

Wherever you're eating, some vocabulary will help. Three interesting drinks to try are *Grüner Veltliner* (dry white wine, any time), *Traubenmost* (a heavenly grape juice on the verge of wine, autumn only, sometimes just called *Most*), and *Sturm* (barely fermented *Most*, autumn only). The local red wine (called *Portuguese*) is pretty good. Since the Austrian wine is often very sweet, remember the word *Trocken* (German for "dry"). You can order your wine by the *Viertel* (quarter-liter) or *Achtel* (eighth-liter). Beer comes in a *Krugel* (.5 liter) or *Seidel* (.3 liter).

## Transportation Connections—Vienna

Vienna has two main train stations: the Westbahnhof, serving Munich, Salzburg, Switzerland, and Budapest; and the Südbahnhof, serving Italy, Budapest, and Prague. The third station, Franz Josefs, serves Krems and the Danube Valley. Subway line U-3 connects the Westbahnhof with the center, tram D takes you from the Südbahnhof and from the Franz Josefs to downtown, and tram #18 connects West and South Stations. Train info: tel. 0222/1717.

By train to: **Melk** (hrly, 75 min), **Krems** (10/day, 1 hr), **Salzburg** (hrly, 3 hrs), **Innsbruck** (3/day, 5.5 hrs), **Budapest** (3/day, 4 hrs), **Prague** (4/day, 5.5 hrs), **Munich** (10/day, 4.5 hrs), **Berlin** (2/day 14 hrs), **Zurich** (4/day, 9 hrs), **Rome** (3/day, 14 hrs), **Venice** (6/day, 9 hrs), **Frankfurt** (7/day, 7.5 hrs), **Amsterdam** (2/day, 14 hrs).

To Eastern Europe: Vienna is the natural springboard for a quick trip to Prague and Budapest. Vienna is four hours by train from Budapest (360 AS, 580 AS round-trip, free with Eurail) and 5.5 hours from Prague (488 AS one-way, 976 AS round-trip, 652 AS with Eurail). Visas are not required. Train tickets are purchased easily at most travel agencies (such as Intropa, next to the TI on Kärntner Strasse).

# DANUBE VALLEY

The Danube is at its romantic best just west of Vienna. Mix a cruise with a bike ride through the Danube's Wachau Valley, lined with ruined castles, beautiful abbeys, small towns, and vineyard upon vineyard. After touring the glorious abbey of Melk, douse your warm, fairy-tale glow with a bucket of Hitler at the Mauthausen concentration camp.

## Planning Your Time

For a day trip from Vienna, catch the early train to Melk, tour the abbey, eat lunch and split the afternoon trip along the river from Melk to Krems by boat and rented bike. From Krems, catch the train back to Vienna. Remember, the boat goes much faster downstream (east). While this region is a logical day trip from Vienna, with good train connections to both Krems and Melk, spending a night in Melk is a winning idea. Melk is on the main Munich/Salzburg/Vienna train line. Mauthausen, farther away, should be seen en route to or from Vienna. On a three-week trip through Germany, Austria, and Switzerland, I'd see only one concentration camp. Mauthausen is more powerful than the more convenient Dachau.

## Cruising the Danube

By car, bike, or boat, the 38-kilometer stretch of the Danube between Krems and Melk is as pretty as they come. You'll cruise along Danube's wine road, seeing wine gardens all along the river. Those hanging out a wreath of straw or greenery are inviting you in to taste. St. Michael has a small wine garden and an old tower you can climb for a view. In local slang, someone who's feeling his wine is "blue." Blue Danube?

**By Boat:** Boats run between Krems and Melk (5/day in each direction, April–October, 170 AS for a day ticket), departing from Melk at 9:05, 11:00, 13:50, 14:10, and 16:00 (1.5-hour ride downstream). Boats depart from Krems at 10:20, 10:55, 12:45, 15:45, and 15:55 (because of the 6-knot flow of the Donau, the same ride upstream takes three hours). The 16:00 departure from Melk and the 15:45 departure from Krems require an easy transfer in Spitz; the rest are direct. To confirm these times, call the DDSG boat-company office (tel. 0222/58880 in Vienna), the Melk TI (tel. 02752/2307), or Krems TI (tel. 02732/82676). On weekends, some boats start or end in Vienna if you'd like a longer cruise (April–October, tel. 0222/58880 in Vienna).

**By Bike:** There's a bike path all the way. Rent a bike at any train station (90 AS with a railpass or ticket, otherwise 150 AS). If you pay 40 AS extra, you can drop off your bike at a different train station. It's about a three-hour pedal from Krems to Melk. Pedal along the north bank (just off the main road; the "bike-in-a-red-border" signs mean "no biking"), following the TI's Cycle Track brochure. If you prefer, you can go half and half by cruising to Spitz and then hopping on a bike (or vice versa).

**By Bus:** The bus between Melk and Krems is a good budget or rainy day alternative to the boat (70 AS, catch bus at train station, buy ticket on bus, for best views sit on the driver's side from Melk to Krems, the non-driver's side from Krems to Melk).

## Sights—The Danube Valley

**Krems**—This is a gem of a town. From the boat dock, walk a few blocks to the TI (pick up a town map). Then stroll the traffic-free, shopper's-wonderland old town. If nothing else, it's a pleasant 20-minute walk from the dock to the train station (hourly trains, a one-hour ride into Vienna's Franz Josefs Bahnhof). The local TI can find you a bed in a private home (D-400 AS, Db-550 AS) if you decide to side-trip into Vienna from this small-town alternative (TI open Monday–Friday 9:00–19:00, weekends 10:00–12:00 and 13:00–18:00, less off-season, tel. 02732/82676). Melanie Stasny Gastezimmer is a super place to stay (D-560 AS, next to dock at Steiner Land-strasse 22, tel. 02732/82843).

**Durnstein**—This touristic flypaper lures hordes of visitors with its traffic-free quaintness and its one claim to fame (and

## Danube Valley

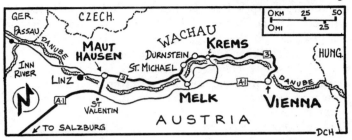

fortune): Richard the Lion-Hearted was imprisoned here in 1193. You can probably sleep in his bedroom.

**Willendorf**—Known among art buffs as the town where the oldest piece of European art was found. A few blocks off the river (follow the signs to "Venus") you can see the monument where the well-endowed, 30,000-year-old fertility symbol, the *Venus of Willendorf*, was discovered. (She's now in Vienna's Natural History Museum.)

▲**Melk**—Sleepy and elegant under its huge abbey that seems to police the Danube, the town of Melk offers a pleasant stop. The TI, near the traffic-free main square, has info on nearby castles and bike rides along the river (Monday–Saturday 9:00–19:00, Sunday 10:00–14:00, less off-season, good picnic garden with WC behind TI, tel. 02752/2307).

▲▲**Melk Abbey (Benediktinerstift)**—The newly restored abbey beaming proudly over the Danube Valley is one of Europe's great sights. The Abbey Church, with its 200-foot-tall dome and symmetrical towers, dominates the complex of abbey buildings. Freshly painted and gilded throughout, it's a Baroque dream, a lily alone. Established as a fortified Benedictine Abbey in the 11th century, it was destroyed by fire. What you see today is from the 18th century. Napoleon headquartered here in 1805 and 1809. Its lavish library, palace rooms, church, and the great Danube view from the balcony are highlights of the one-hour tour. Modern frescoes in the courtyard make the point that the abbey is a living institution.

After a grand restoration project (1978–1995), the abbey was completed in time to celebrate the "1,000 years of Ostarrichi" in 1996, the anniversary of the first reference to a country named Österreich (Austria).

German tours are available constantly. English tours are offered May through September, daily at 14:55 (55 AS, 70 AS with a tour, daily 9:00–18:00, last entry 17:00, tel. 02752/231-2232). Call to see if you can establish a tour. They'll schedule an English tour with a nucleus of eight people, then let others join in. It's worth the trouble. The abbey garden, café, and charming village below make waiting for a tour pleasant.

## Sleeping in Melk
**(12 AS = about $1, tel. code: 02752, zip code: 3390)**
Sleep Code: **S**=Single, **D**=Double/Twin, **T**=Triple, **Q**=Quad, **b**=bathroom, **t**=toilet only, **s**=shower only, **CC**=Credit Card (**V**isa, **M**asterCard, **A**mex). Breakfast is included, and at least some English is spoken.

Melk makes a fine overnight stop. **Hotel Fürst** is a fluffy, creaky old place with 15 rooms, run by the Madar family, right on the traffic-free main square with a fountain out your door and the abbey hovering overhead (Db-680 AS, Rathausplatz 3-5, tel. 02752/2343, fax 02752/23434). **Gasthof Goldener Stern**, traditional with a barn-flavored elegance, is also quiet and cozy on a pedestrian street in the center (D-520 AS, cheaper three- to five-bed rooms, Sterngasse 17, tel. 02752/2214). **Maria Atzmuller** runs a fine and friendly B&B a mile from the abbey (D-400 AS, Kreuzackerstrasse 32, tel. 02752/2163). **Pension Wachau**, near the autobahn exit, will pick you up at the station (Sb-475 AS, Db-730 AS, Wachberg 157, tel. 02752/52531, fax 02572/525-3113, some English spoken). The modern **hostel** is a few minutes' walk from the station (166-AS beds in quads with sheets and breakfast, easygoing about membership, tel. 02752/2681).

## Transportation Connections—Melk
Melk is on the autobahn and the Salzburg–Vienna train line.

**By train to: Vienna** (hrly, 1 hr; get off at Spittelau for direct connection to U-Bahn #4 and #6; only trams run from Franz Josef Bahnhof), **Salzburg** (hrly, 2 hrs), **Mauthausen** (nearly hrly, 75 min, transfer at St. Valentin).

# MAUTHAUSEN CONCENTRATION CAMP
More powerful and less tourist-oriented than Dachau, this slave-labor and death camp functioned from 1938 to 1945 for the exploitation and extermination of Hitler's opponents. More

than half of its 206,000 quarry-working prisoners were killed here. Set in a strangely beautiful setting next to the Danube, in a now-still and overgrown quarry, Mauthausen is open daily from 8:00 to 18:00 (25 AS, last entry an hour before closing, closes mid-December–January and at 16:00 off-season, tel. 07238/2269, TI tel. 07238/3860). Leave your passport to borrow a free tape-recorded 20-minute tour.

The camp barracks house a worthwhile museum at the far end of the camp on the right (some English labels, but the 35-AS English guidebook gives a complete translation). See the graphic 45-minute movie shown at the top of each hour. Ask for an English showing; if necessary, gather a group of English-speaking visitors. If it's running, just slip in.

The most emotionally moving rooms (described in English) and the gas chamber are downstairs. The spirits of the victims of these horrors can still be felt. Outside the camp each victim's country has erected a gripping memorial. Many yellowed photos sport fresh flowers. Walk to the barbed-wire memorial overlooking the quarry and the "stairway of death."

By visiting a concentration camp and putting ourselves through this emotional wringer, we heed and respect the fervent wish of the victims of this fascism—that we "never forget." Many people forget by choosing not to know.

## Sleeping in Enns, near Mauthausen

**Hotel Am Limes**, just off the autobahn in Enns, has comfortable rooms and an Italian/Austrian restaurant. Reinhard speaks English and picks up at the station (Sb-500 AS, Db-750 AS, Stadlgasse 2b, tel. 07223/6401, fax 07223/640164). Enns is about 6 km southwest of Mauthausen and 100 km west of Vienna.

## Transportation Connections—Mauthausen

Most trains stop at St. Valentin, midway between Salzburg and Vienna, where sporadic trains make the 15-minute ride to the Mauthausen station (get map from station attendant, camp is #9, baggage check-30 AS). To get to the camp, which is 3 miles from the Mauthausen station, you can hike (one hour), bike (90-AS rental at station with railpass or ticket, 150 AS without), or take a mini-bus taxi (100 AS, join other tourists, tel. 07238/2439). Train info: 07238/2207.

**St. Valentin by train to: Salzburg** (hrly, 2 hrs), **Vienna** (hrly, 2 hrs).

## Route Tips for Drivers

**Hallstatt to Vienna, via Mauthausen, Melk, and Wachau Valley (210 miles):** Leave Hallstatt early. Follow scenic Route 145 through Gmunden to the autobahn and head east. After Linz, take exit #155, Enns, and follow Mauthausen signs (8 km from the freeway). Go through Mauthausen town, and follow signs to Ehemaliges KZ-lager. From Mauthausen, the speedy route is the autobahn to Melk, but the curvy, scenic Route 3 along the river is worth the nausea. Cross the bridge and follow the signs, not into town (Zentrum Melk), but to Stift Melk, the Benediktinerstift (Benedictine Abbey).

The most scenic stretch of the Donau is the Wachau Valley, lying between Melk and Krems. From Melk (get a Vienna map at the TI), cross the river again (signs to Donaubrucke) and stay on Route 3. After Krems, it hits the autobahn (A22), and you'll barrel right into Vienna's traffic.

Navigating in Vienna, if you understand the Ring and Gürtel, isn't bad. Study the map and see how the two ring roads loop out from the Donau. As you approach the city from Krems, you'll cross the North Bridge and land right on the Gürtel, or outer ring. You can continue along the Danube canal to the inner ring, called the Ringstrasse (clockwise traffic only). Circle around either thoroughfare until you reach the "spoke" street you need.

**Vienna west to Hall in Tirol (280 miles):** To leave Vienna, follow the signs past the Westbahnhof to Schloss Schönbrunn, which is directly on the way to the West A-1 autobahn to Linz. The king had plenty of parking. Leave by 15:00, beating rush hour, and follow autobahn signs to West A-1, passing Linz and Salzburg, nipping through Germany, and turning right onto Route 93 in the direction of Kufstein, Innsbruck, and Austria at the Dreieck Inntal (autobahn intersection). Crossing back into Austria, you'll follow the scenic Inn River valley, stopping 5 miles east of Innsbruck at Hall in Tirol. There's an autobahn tourist information station just before Hall (daily 10:00–22:00 in season, working for the town's hotels but still helpful). This five-hour ride is nonstop autobahn. Gasthof Badl is just off the autobahn in Hall.

# SALZBURG, SALZKAMMERGUT, AND WEST AUSTRIA

Enjoy the sights and sounds of Salzburg, Mozart's hometown, then commune with nature in the Salzkammergut, Austria's *Sound of Music* country. Amid hills alive with the S.O.M., you'll find the tiny town of Hallstatt, as pretty as a postcard (and about the same size). Farther west, the Golden Roof of Innsbruck glitters—but you'll strike it rich in neighboring Hall, which has twice the charm and none of the tourist crowds.

## SALZBURG

With a well-preserved old town, gardens, churches, and lush surroundings, set under Europe's biggest intact medieval castle, its river adding an almost seaside ambience, Salzburg is forever smiling to the tunes of Mozart and *The Sound of Music*.

This town knows how to be popular. Eight million tourists crawl its cobbles each year. That's a lot of Mozart balls. But all that popularity has led to a glut of businesses hoping to catch the tourist dollar, and an almost desperate greediness. The town's creative energy is invested in ways to soak the tourist rather than share its rich cultural heritage. Salzburg makes for a pleasant visit, but for most, a day is plenty. With a few exceptions, it's hard to get English information, and music costs about 350 AS per event.

### Planning Your Time

While Vienna measures much higher on the Richter scale of sightseeing thrills, Salzburg is simply a joy. A touristy and expensive joy, but a joy nevertheless. If you're going into the nearby Salzkammergut lake country anyway, you don't need to take the *Sound of Music* tour. But this tour kills a nest of sight-seeing birds with one ticket (city overview, S.O.M. sights, a luge ride, and a fine drive through the lakes). If you're not planning a detour through the lakes, allow half a day for this tour. That means a minimum of two nights for Salzburg. Of course, the nights are important for concerts and swilling beer in atmospheric local gardens. The actual town sights are mediocre. It's the town itself—a Baroque treat—that you should enjoy. If you like things slow, bike down the river or hike across the Mönchsberg.

## Orientation (tel. code: 0662)

Salzburg, a city of 150,000 (Austria's fourth-largest) is divided into old and new. The old town, sitting between the Salzach River and the 1,600-foot-high hill called Mönchsberg, is a bundle of Baroque holding all the charm and most of the tourists.

**Tourist Information:** Salzburg's three tourist offices (at the train station; on Mozartplatz in the old center—daily 8:00–20:00; and on the freeway entrance to the city, tel. 0662/88987) are helpful. Ask for a city map, the "hotel plan" map, a list of sights with current hours, and a schedule of events. Book a concert upon arrival. The TIs also book rooms (30-AS fee, or 60 AS for three people or more).

**Arrival in Salzburg:** The Salzburg station makes getting set up easy. The TI is at track 2A. Downstairs is the place to leave bags, rent bikes, buy tickets, and get train information (at "Reisebüro am Bahnhof"). This lower street level faces the bus station (where buses 1, 5, 6, and 51 go to the old center; get off at the first stop after you cross the river). To walk downtown (15 minutes), leave the station ticket hall near window #8 through the door marked "Zentrum" and walk absolutely straight down Rainerstrasse, which leads you under the tracks past Mirabellplatz, changes its name to Dreitaltigkeitsgasse, and takes you to the *Staatsbrucke* (bridge) which deposits you in the old town. For a more dramatic approach, leave the same way but follow the tracks to the river, turn left, and walk the riverside path toward the castle.

**American Express:** The Amex office holds mail for their check- or credit card–users, and doesn't charge a commission for cashing Amex checks (Monday–Friday 9:00–17:30, Saturday 9:00–12:00, Mozartplatz 5, A-5010 Salzburg, tel. 0662/8080).

## Getting Around Salzburg

**By Bus:** Single-ride tickets are sold on the bus for 19 AS. Daily passes, called Tageskarte, cost 38 AS (good for one calendar day only). The "Salzburg Card" is not worth it for most (24-hour bus pass and 24 hours free entrance to all the city sights for 180 AS). Bus information: tel. 0662/872-145.

**By Bike:** Salzburg is bike-friendly. From 7:00 until midnight, the train station rents good road bikes for 50 AS and mountain bikes for 150 AS; without a railpass or train ticket, you'll pay 50 AS more (no deposit required, pay at counter #3, pick it up at "left luggage"). Georg, who runs Velo-Active, rents bikes on Residenzplatz under the glockenspiel in the old town. He offers carriers of this book a one-day rental for 100 AS (daily 9:00–18:00, passport number for security, extra charge for mountain bikes, tel. 0663/435-595).

**By Funicular and Elevator:** The old town is connected to Mönchsberg (and great views) via road, funicular, and elevator. The funicular whisks you up to the imposing Hohensalzburg fortress (32 AS round-trip, 67 AS includes fortress admission). The elevator on the east side of the old town propels you to Café Winkler, the recommended Naturfreundehaus (see Sleeping, below), and lots of wooded paths (27 AS round-trip).

## Sights—Salzburg's Old Town

▲▲**Old Town Walking Tour**—The two-language, one-hour guided walks of the old town are informative and worthwhile if you don't mind listening to a half-hour of German (80 AS, start at TI on Mozartplatz at 12:15, Monday–Saturday, May–October, tel. 0662/847-568), but you can easily do it on your own. Here's a basic old-town orientation walk (start on Mozartplatz in the old town):

**Mozartplatz** features a statue of Mozart erected in 1842. Mozart spent most of his first 20 years (1756–1777) in Salzburg. The tourist information office and American Express Company face this square. Salzburg was the greatest Baroque city north of the Alps. Walk to the next square with the huge fountain.

**Residenz Platz:** Salzburg's energetic Prince-Archbishop Wolf Dietrich (who ruled from 1587–1612) was raised in Rome, counted the Medicis as his buddies, and had grand Renaissance ambitions for Salzburg. After a convenient fire destroyed much of the old town, he set about building "the

Rome of the North." This square with his new cathedral and palace was the centerpiece of his new, Italian-designed Baroque city. A series of interconnecting squares lead from here through the old town.

For centuries, Salzburg's leaders were both important church leaders and princes of the Holy Roman Empire, hence their title mixing sacred and secular authority. Wolf Dietrich abused his power and spent his last five years imprisoned in the Salzburg castle.

The fountain is as Italian as can be, with a Triton matching Bernini's famous *Triton Fountain* in Rome. As the north became aware of the exciting things going on in Italy, things Italian were respected. Local architects even Italianized their names in order to raise their rates.

Dietrich's palace, the **Residenz**, is connected to the cathedral by a skyway. A series of fancy rooms are open to visitors but only with a German-language tour (not worth the boredom or the 50-AS price, English fact sheet available, tel. 0662/8042-2690). The Residenz also has an art gallery.

Opposite the Residenz is the new Residenz, which has long been a government administration building (and post office with a handy bank of pay phones). Atop the new Residenz is the famous **Glockenspiel**, or bell tower. Its carillon of 35 17th-century bells (cast in Antwerp) chimes throughout the day and plays a tune (that changes each month) at 7:00, 11:00, and 18:00. There was a time when Salzburg could afford to take tourists to the top of the tower to actually see the big adjustable barrel turn . . . pulling the right bells in the right rhythm—a fascinating show.

Look back past Mozart's statue to the 4,220-foot-tall Gaisberg (the forested hill with the television tower). A road leads to the top for a commanding view. It's a favorite destination for local bikers. Opposite the church is a picnic-friendly grocery store with an orange awning (Monday–Friday 8:30–18:00, Saturday 8:00–16:00). Walking under the Prince-Archbishop's skyway, step into Domplatz, the cathedral square.

**Salzburg Cathedral**, built in the 17th century, claims to be the first Baroque building north of the Alps (free, daily 6:00–20:00). The dates on the iron gates refer to milestones in the church's history: In 774 the previous church (long since destroyed) was founded by St. Virgil, to be replaced in 1628 by the church you see today. In 1959, the reconstruction was

## Salzburg

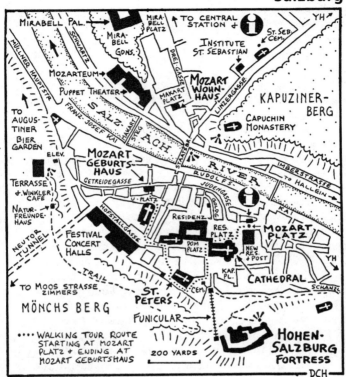

completed after a bomb blew through the dome in WWII.

Check out the organ draped over the entrance; it was played only when the archbishop walked in and out of the cathedral. Gape up. The interior is marvelous. Concert and Mass schedules are posted at the entrance; Sunday Mass (10:00) is famous for its music.

Under the skyway, a stairway leads down to the excavation site under the church with a few second-century Christian Roman mosaics and the foundation stones of the previous Romanesque and Gothic churches (20 AS, Wednesday–Sunday 9:00–17:00). The Cathedral (or *Dom*) Museum has a rich collection of church art (entry at portico).

The cathedral square is surrounded by "ecclesiastical palaces." The statue of Mary (1771) is looking away from the church, but if you stand in the rear of the square immediately under the middle arch, you'll see how she's positioned to be crowned by the two angels on the church facade.

From the arch, walk back across the square to the front of the cathedral and turn right (going past the underground public toilets) to the next square where you'll see locals playing chess on the giant board. Past the chessboard, a small road leads up to the castle (and castle lift). On the right, a gate reading "St. Peter's" leads past a traditional old bakery (near the waterfall) and into a cemetery.

**St. Peter's Cemetery** is a collection of lovingly tended mini-gardens (butted up against the Mönchberg's rock wall). The graves are cared for by relatives; anyone residing in the cemetery for over 30 years without living kin gets booted out. Early Christian catacombs are carved into the rock wall above the graveyard (12 AS, 10:00–17:00). This was where the Trapp family hid out in the S.O.M. movie. Walk through the cemetery and out the opposite end. Drop into St. Peter's Church, a Romanesque basilica done up beautifully Baroque. Continue through another square and past another church to Universität-splatz, with its busy open-air produce market. This is Salzburg at its liveliest and most real (mornings, daily except Sunday). Take one of several covered arcades from here to Getreidegasse.

**Getreidegasse** was old Salzburg's lively and colorful main drag. Famous for its old wrought-iron signs, it still looks much as it did in Mozart's day. *Schmuck* means jewelry. Wolfgang was born on this street. Find his very gold house.

▲**Mozart's Birthplace (Geburtshaus)**—Mozart was born here in 1756. It was in this building that he composed most of his boy-genius works. This most popular Mozart sight in town, filled with scores of scores, portraits, and old keyboard instruments and violins, is almost a pilgrimage. If you're a fan, you'll have to check it out. It's right in the old town on colorful Getreidegasse #9 (65 AS, or 100 AS for combined ticket to Mozart's Wohnhaus—see below, daily 9:00–19:00, shorter hours off-season).

▲**Hohensalzburg Fortress**—Built on a rock 400 feet above the Salzach River, this castle, one of Europe's mightiest, dominates Salzburg's skyline and offers great views of the city and surrounding hills. The castle interior is so-so unless you catch a tour (35 AS admission plus 30 AS for a tour; confirm that it will be in English as well as German). Check out the

sound-and-vision show. The museum has the noisiest floor-
boards in Europe, but even so, the princess had a chastity belt.
You can see it next to other gruesome torture devices that need
no explanation. Upstairs, the mediocre military museum on
WWI honors the nice-looking young men who fought in the
war Austria started. You can walk up to the fortress, but the
funicular is effortless (32 AS round-trip, every ten minutes, 69
AS includes fortress admission). The castle is open daily from
8:00 to 19:00, until 18:00 in the off-season (tel. 0662/842-430).
▲**The Hills are Alive Walk**—For a most enjoyable approach
to the castle, consider riding the elevator to the Café Winkler
and walking 20 minutes through the woods high above the city
to Festung Hohensalzburg (stay on the high paved paths, or
you'll have a needless climb back up to the castle).

## Sights—Across the River
▲**Mozart's Wohnhaus (a.k.a. Mozarts Ton- und Filmmu-
seum)**—Even better than the birthplace is this newly renovated museum, previously Mozart's second home (his family
moved here when he was 17). A headphone, free with admission, lets you hear English throughout. Along with the usual
scores and old pianos, the highlight is an intriguing film which
leaves you wanting to know more about Mozart and his
remarkable family (65 AS, or 100 AS for combined ticket to
birthplace, guidebook-58 AS, daily 10:00–18:00, just over the
river at Marktplatz 8, tel. 0662/8834-5440).
▲**Mirabell Gardens and Palace (Schloss)**—The bubbly gardens are always open and free. You may recognize the statues
featured in the S.O.M. To properly enjoy the lavish Mirabell
Palace, get a ticket to a *Schlosskonzerte*. Baroque music flying
around a Baroque hall is a happy bird in the right cage. Tickets
are around 360 AS and are rarely sold out (tel. 0662/848-586).

## More Sights—Salzburg
▲▲**Riverside Bike Ride**—The Salzach River has smooth, flat,
and scenic bike paths along each side. On a sunny day, I can
think of no more shout-worthy escape from the city. Hallein is
a pleasant destination (with a salt-mine tour, about 12 kilometers away, north or new-town side of river is most scenic).
Even a quickie ride from one end of town to the other gives
you the best possible views of Salzburg. In the evening, it's a
hand-in-hand, floodlit-spires world.

▲▲*Sound of Music* **Tour**—I took this tour skeptically (as part of my research chores) and liked it. It includes a quick but good general city tour, stops for a luge ride (in season, fair weather, 30 AS extra), hits all the S.O.M. spots (including the stately home, gazebo, and wedding church), and shows you a lovely stretch of the Salzkammergut. The Salzburg Panorama Tours Company charges 350 AS for the four-hour, English-only tour (from Mirabellplatz daily at 9:30 and 14:00, tel. 0662/874-029, e-mail: Panorama@alpin.or.at; ask for a reservation and a free hotel pickup if you like; travelers with this book who buy their ticket at the Mirabellplatz ticket booth get a 10 percent discount on this and any other tour they do). This is worthwhile for S.O.M. fans without a car, or those who won't otherwise be going into the Salzkammergut. Warning: Many think rolling through the Austrian countryside with 30 Americans singing "Doe, a deer" is pretty schmaltzy. And local Austrians don't understand all the commotion.

There are several similar and very competitive tour companies which offer every conceivable tour of and from Salzburg (Mozart sights, Berchtesgaden, salt mines, Salzkammergut lakes and mountains). Some hotels have their brochures and get a healthy commission. The only minibus tours going are Bob's Tours (two different tours: S.O.M. or Berchtesgaden and Bavarian Alps, Kaigasse 19, tel. 0662/849-511).

▲**Hellbrunn Castle**—The attractions here are a garden full of clever trick fountains and the sadistic joy the tour guide gets from soaking tourists. The archbishop's mediocre 17th-century palace is open by tour only (30 AS, hrly, 20 minutes). His Baroque garden, one of the oldest in Europe, is pretty enough, and now features the "I am 16, going on 17" gazebo (70 AS for the 40-minute tour and admission, daily 9:00–17:00, until 22:00 in July and August, until 16:30 in April and October, closed November–March, tel. 0662/820-372). The castle is 3 miles south of Salzburg (bus #55 from the station or downtown, twice hourly, 20-minute ride). It's most fun on a sunny day or with kids, but it's a lot of trouble for a few water tricks.

## Music Scene

▲▲**Salzburg Festival**—Each summer from late July to the end of August, Salzburg hosts its famous Salzburger Festspiele, founded in 1920 to employ Vienna's musicians in the summer. This fun and festive time is crowded, but there are plenty of beds (except for a few August weekends). Except for the big shows, tickets are normally available the day of the concert (ticket office on Mozartplatz). You can contact the Austrian National Tourist Office in the U.S.A. for specifics on this year's festival schedule and tickets (Box 1142 Times Square, New York, NY 10108-1142, tel. 212/944-6880, fax 212/730-4568, Web site: www.anto.com, e-mail: antonyc@ix.netcom.com), but I've never planned in advance and have enjoyed great concerts with every visit.

▲▲**Musical events outside of Festival time**—Salzburg is busy throughout the year with 2,000 classical performances in its palaces and churches annually. (While you may find folk evenings twice a week in the summer, Innsbruck is better for these.) Pick up the events calendar at the TI (free, comes out monthly). Whenever you visit, you'll have a number of concerts to choose from. There are nearly nightly concerts at the Mirabell Palace and up in the fortress (both with open seating and 360-AS tickets, concerts at 20:30, doors open at 20:00). The Schlosskonzerte at the Mirabell Palace offers a fine Baroque setting for your Mozart (tel. 0662/848-586). The fortress concerts, called *Festungskonzerte*, are held in the "prince's chamber" (usually chamber music—a string quartet, tel. 0662/825-858 to reserve, you can pick up tickets at the door). This medieval-feeling room atop the castle has windows overlooking the city. The extra 32-AS round-trip lift gives you a chance to enjoy a stroll through the castle courtyard and enjoy the grand city view.

The almost daily "5:00 Concert" next to St. Peter's is cheaper, since it features young artists (120 AS, daily except Wednesday, 45 minutes, tel. 0662/844-57-619). While the series is named after the brother of Joseph Haydn, it features music from various masters.

The Marionette Theater performs operas with fine marionettes and recorded music (250–400 AS, nearly nightly May–September, tel. 0662/872-406).

## Sights—Near Salzburg

▲**Bad Dürnberg Salzbergwerke**—Like its salty neighbors, this salt-mine tour and cable-car ride above the town of Hallein (12 kilometers from Salzburg) respects only the German speakers. You'll get information sheets or headphones but none of the jokes. Still, it's a fun experience wearing white overalls, sliding down the sleek wooden chutes, and crossing underground from Austria into Germany (daily 9:00–17:00, easy bus and train connections from Salzburg, tel. 06245/ 82121 or 06245/852-8515).

▲**Berchtesgaden**—This Alpine resort just across the German border (20 km from Salzburg) flaunts its attractions and you may find yourself in a traffic jam of desperate tourists trying to turn their money into fun. From the station and TI (tel. 08652/9670), buses go to the salt mines (a 30-minute walk otherwise) and the idyllic Königsee (21.50 DM, two-hour scenic cruises, 2/hr, stopovers anywhere, tel. 08652/963-618).

At the salt mines, you put on the traditional miners' outfits, get on funny little trains, and zip deep into the mountain. For one hour you'll cruise subterranean lakes; slide speedily down two long, slick, wooden banisters; and learn how they mined salt so long ago. Call for crowd-avoidance advice. You can buy a ticket early and browse through the town until your appointed tour time (19.50 DM, daily 9:00–17:00; winter Monday–Saturday, 12:30–15:30, tel. 08652/60020).

Hitler's famous (but overrated) "Eagle's Nest" towered high above Obersalzberg near Berchtesgaden. The site is open to visitors, but little remains of the Alpine retreat Hitler visited only five times. The bus ride up the private road and the lift to the top (a 2,000-foot altitude gain) cost 26 DM from the station, 20 DM from the parking lot. If the weather's cloudy, as it often is, you'll Nazi a thing.

Berchtesgaden is a train ride from Munich (hrly, 2.5 hrs, with one change). From Salzburg, ride the scenic and more-direct-than-train bus (2/hr, 60 min). Berchtesgaden caters to long-term German guests. During peak season, it's not worth the headaches for the speedy tourist.

## Sleeping in Salzburg
**(12 AS = about $1, tel. code: 0662, zip code: 5020)**
Sleep Code: **S**=Single, **D**=Double/Twin, **T**=Triple, **Q**=Quad, **b**=bathroom, **t**=toilet only, **s**=shower only, **CC**=Credit Card (**V**isa, **M**asterCard, **A**mex).

Finding a room in Salzburg, even during the music festival, is usually easy. Unless otherwise noted, all my listings come with breakfast and at least some English is spoken. The more expensive places charge more during the music festival (late July and August).

## Sleeping in or above the Old Town

**Gasthaus Zur Goldenen Ente**, run by the Family Steinwender, is a great splurge if you'd like to sleep in a 600-year-old building above a fine restaurant as central as you can be on a pedestrian street in old Salzburg. Somehow the 15 modern and comfortable doubles fit into this building's medieval-style stone arches and narrow stairs (Sb-680 AS and Db-980 AS with this book, higher prices in high season, extra person-450 AS, parking deals, CC:VMA, Goldgasse 10, tel. 0662/845-622, fax 0662/845-6229). The breakfast is buffet-big and their restaurant is a treat (see Eating, below).

**Hotel Restaurant Weisses Krentz** is a classy, comfy, family-run place on a cobbled back street near the castle (Sb-600 AS, Db-1,000 AS, Tb-1,400, reserve ahead, Bierjodlgasse 6, tel. 0662/845-641, fax 0662/845-6419).

**Gasthof Hinterbrühl** is a smoky, ramshackle old place with a handy location, minimal plumbing, and not a tourist in sight (S-420 AS, D-520 AS, T-600 AS, plus optional 50-AS breakfast, above a bar that can be noisy, workable parking, CC:V, on a village-like square just under the castle at Schanzlgasse 12, tel. 0662/846-798).

**Naturfreundehaus**, also called Gasthaus Bürgerwehr, is a local version of a mountaineer's hut. It's a great budget alternative in a forest guarded by singing birds and snuggled in the remains of a 15th-century castle wall overlooking Salzburg, with magnificent old-town and mountain views (D-280 AS, 120 AS per person in four- to six-bed dorms, breakfast-30 AS, dinner-68–108 AS, curfew-1:00, open May–September, Mönchsberg 19, two minutes from the top of the 27-AS round-trip Mönchsberg elevator, tel. 0662/841-729). High above the old town, it's the stone house to the left of the glass Café Winkler.

## Sleeping on Linzergasse and near Kapuzinerberg

All of these listings are a 15-minute walk from the train station in the "new" section of town, across the river from the old town. The first three are on lower Linzergasse, directly across the bridge from Mozartville. Its bustling crowds of shoppers overwhelm the few shy cars that venture onto it. The last two listings are farther from the city center (a ten-minute walk).

**Institute St. Sebastian** is close to the old town and newly renovated, offering the town's best doubles and dorm beds for the money (Sb-300 AS, Db-600 AS, Tb-870 AS, elevator, Linzergasse 41, enter through arch at #37, tel. 0662/871-386, fax 0662/8713-8685). They usually have rooms available, as well as 200-AS spots in ten-bed dorms (30 AS less if you have sheets, no lock-out time, lockers, free showers). Anyone is welcome to use the self-service kitchen on each floor. Fridge space is free; just ask for a key. This friendly, clean, historic building has lots of spacious public areas and a roof garden. The doubles come with modern baths and head-to-toe twin beds. Some Mozarts are buried in the courtyard.

**Hotel Pension Goldene Krone** is big, quiet, and creaky-traditional but modern, with comforts rare in this price range (Sb-500–570 AS, D-700–800 AS, Db-800–970 AS, Tb-1,100–1,300 AS, elevator, Linzergasse 48, tel. 0662/872-300).

Troglodytes love **Hotel zum Jungen Fuchs**. It's very plain but clean and wonderfully located in a funky, dumpy old building (S-280 AS, D-400 AS, T-500 AS, no breakfast, across from Institute St. Sebastian at Linzergasse 54, tel. 0662/875-496).

**Pension Bergland** is a classy oasis of calm, with rustic rooms and musical evenings (S-460 AS, Sb-530 AS, two dim D-620 AS, Db-820–880 AS depending on size, Tb-1,010 AS, music room open 17:00–21:30, bike rental, English library, Laundromat nearby, Rupertgasse 15, southeast of the station, tel. 0662/872-318, fax 0662/872-3188, e-mail: pknhn@sol.at, run by Peter Kuhn).

**Gasthaus Ganslhof**, 3 blocks away from the Bergland, is clean, comfortable, and back in the real world with Motel 6 ambience and a parking lot (Sb-480 AS, Db-800 AS, 150 AS more per person in the summer, elevator, TV and phone, CC:VMA, Vogelweiderstrasse 6, tel. 0662/873-853, fax 0662/873-85-323).

### Bed and Breakfasts

These are generally roomy, modern, comfortable, and come with a good breakfast. Off-season, competition softens prices. They are a bus ride from town, but with a day pass and the frequent service, this shouldn't keep you away. Unsavory Zimmer skimmers lurk at the station. If you have a reservation, ignore them. If you need a place . . . they need a customer.

**Brigitte Lenglachner** fills her big, traditional home with a warm welcome and lots of tourist information (S-270 AS, D-480 AS, bunk bed D-390 AS, Db-550 AS, T-690 AS, apartment available, two nights preferred, one night costs 10 percent more, breakfast served in room, tel. & fax 0662/438-044). It's in a chirpy neighborhood a ten-minute walk northwest of the station: From the station, cross the pedestrian Pioneer Bridge, turn right, pass the park, and take the third left to Scheibenweg 8.

**Trude Poppenberger**, near Brigitte's place, also offers lots of tourist info. It's three pleasant rooms share the same long balcony and a mountain view (S-280 AS, D-460 AS, T-690 AS; if you stay two nights she'll do your laundry for 80 AS; Wachtelgasse 9, tel. & fax 0662/430-094). It's a 20-minute walk northwest of the station (she will pick you up for free) and a short bus ride (on #49 or #95) into the old town.

**Zimmers on Moosstrasse:** The street called Moosstrasse, southwest of Mönchsberg, is lined with Zimmer. Those farther out are farmhouses. From the station, catch bus #1 and change to bus #60 immediately after crossing the river. From the old town, ride bus #60 (get off at "Marienbad," the stop after the American High School). If you're driving from the center, go through the tunnel, straight on Neutorstrasse, and take the fourth left onto Moosstrasse. **Maria Gassner** rents ten sparkling clean, comfortable rooms in her modern house (St-250 AS, Sb-400 AS, D-440 AS, Db-500 AS, big Db-600 AS, 10 percent more for one-night stays, family deals, CC:VM, 60-AS coin-op laundry, Moosstrasse 126-B, tel. 0662/824-990, fax 0662/822-075).

**Frau Ballwein** offers cozy, charming rooms in an old farmhouse (S-200 AS, Ss-240 AS, D-400 AS, Db-480 AS, farm-fresh breakfasts, Moosstrasse 69A, tel. 0662/824-029).

The **Ziller Family Farm** rents three huge rooms with kitchenettes in a kid-friendly, horse-filled environment (Db-600 AS, minimum two nights, Moosstrasse 76, tel. 0662/824-940, Gabi speaks English).

**Gästehaus Blobergerhof** is rural and comfortable (Sb-350 AS, Db-550 AS, 10 percent more for one-night stays, CC:VM; breakfast buffet, bike rental, will pick up at station, Hammerauerstrasse 4, Querstrasse zur Moosstrasse, tel. 0662/830-227, fax 0662/827-061).

**Helga Bankhammer** rents recently-renovated, pleasant rooms in a farmhouse with farm animals nearby (D-440–500 AS, most with private bath, Moosstrasse 77, tel. 0662/830-067).

## Sleeping near the Train Station

**Pension Adlerhof**, a plain and decent old place, is 2 blocks in front of the train station but a 15-minute walk from the sightseeing action. It has a quirky staff and well-maintained rooms (S-380–400 AS, Sb-490–540 AS, D-590–640 AS, Db-690–790 AS, Elisabethstrasse 25, tel. 0662/875-236, fax 0662/875-2366).

### Hostel

Salzburg has more than its share of hostels (and tourists). The TI has a complete listing (with directions from the station), and there are nearly always beds available. The most fun, handy, and American is **Gottfried's International Youth Hotel**, a.k.a. "the Yo-Ho" (D-360 AS, Q-160 AS per bed, or six- to eight-bed dorm-140 AS, sheets not required but rentable-20 AS, 5 blocks from the station towards the center at Paracelsusstrasse 9, tel. 0662/879-649). This easygoing place speaks English first, has cheap meals, lockers, a laundry, tour discounts, and no curfew; plays *The Sound of Music* free daily at 13:30; runs a lively bar; and welcomes anyone of any age. Expect a non-stop noisy, smoky, party atmosphere.

## Eating in Salzburg

Salzburg boasts many inexpensive, fun, and atmospheric places to eat. I'm a sucker for big cellars with their smoky Old World atmosphere, heavy medieval arches, time-darkened paintings, antlers, and hearty meals to match. These places are famous with visitors but also enjoyed by the locals.

**Gasthaus "Zum Wilder Mann"** is the place if the weather's bad and you're in the mood for Hofbräu atmosphere and a hearty, cheap meal at a shared table in one small, well-antlered room (Monday–Saturday 11:00–21:00, closed Sunday, two minutes from Mozart's place—enter from Getreidegasse 20 or Griesgasse 17, tel. 0662/841-787). For a quick 100-AS lunch, get the *Bauernschmaus*, a mountain of dumpling, kraut, and peasant's meats.

**Krimplestätter** employs 500 years of experience serving authentic old-Austrian food in its authentic old-Austrian interior or its cheery garden (10:00–24:00, closed Monday all year, closed Sunday September–April, Müllner Hauptstrasse 31, ten minutes north of the old town near the river). For fine food with a wild finale, eat here and drink at the nearby Augustiner Bräustübl.

**Augustiner Bräustübl**, a monk-run brewery, is so rustic and crude that I hesitate to show my true colors by recommending it, but I must. On busy nights it's like a Munich beer hall with no music but the volume turned up. When it's cool, you'll enjoy a historic setting with beer-sloshed and smoke-stained halls. On balmy evenings you'll eat under trees in a pleasant outdoor beer garden. Local students mix with tourists eating hearty slabs of schnitzel with their fingers or cold meals from the self-serve picnic counter. It'll bring out the barbarian in you (Augustinergasse 4, head up Müllner Hauptstrasse northwest along the river, and ask for "Müllnerbräu," its local nickname). Don't be fooled by second-rate gardens serving the same beer nearby—this huge, 1,000-seat place is in the Augustiner brewery (daily 15:00–23:30). Order carefully, prices can sting. Pick up a half-liter (28–32 AS) or full-liter mug (56–64 AS) of the great beer, pay the lady, and give Mr. Keg your empty mug. For dessert, after a visit to the strudel kiosk, enjoy the incomparable floodlit view of old Salzburg from the nearby pedestrian bridge and then stroll home along the river. Delicious memories.

**Stiftskeller St. Peter** has been in business for more than 1,000 years. It's classier (with strolling musicians), more central, and a good splurge for traditional Austrian cuisine in medieval sauce (daily 11:00–24:00, outdoor and indoor seating, meals 100–200 AS, CC:VMA, next to St. Peter's church at the foot of Mönchsberg, tel. 0662/841-268).

**Gasthaus Zur Goldenen Ente** (see Sleeping, above) serves great food. The chef, Robert, specializes in roast duck (*Ente*) and seafood, along with "Salzberger Nockerl," the mountainous sweet soufflé served all over town. It's big enough for four (Monday–Friday 11:00–21:00, closed Saturday and Sunday, Goldgasse 10, tel. 0662/845-622).

**Stieglkeller** is a huge, atmospheric institution which has several rustic rooms and outdoor garden seating with a great rooftop view of the old town (daily 10:00–22:00, 50 yards uphill from the lift to the castle, Festungsgasse 10, tel. 0662/842-681). They offer the latest S.O.M. spin-off, a *Sound of Music* Dinner Show, featuring songs from the movie and local dances (520 AS includes dinner, 360 AS for show only, daily May–September, tel. 0662/832-029). Since the Stieglkeller has lots of rooms, you can skip the show and still enjoy the restaurant.

**Picnics:** The University Square, just behind Mozart's house, hosts a bustling morning **produce market** daily except Sunday.

**Lunch:** Classy Salzburg delis serve good, cheap, sit-down lunches on weekdays. Have them make you a sandwich or something hot, toss in a carrot, a piece of fruit, yogurt, and a box of milk, and sit at a small table with the local lunch crowd.

**Café Glockenspiel**, on Mozartplatz 2, does a good, if pricey, lunch (80–160 AS). The following cheaper places are all just across the river from the old town: **Frauenberger** is friendly, picnic-ready, and inexpensive, with indoor or outdoor seating (Monday 8:00–14:00, Tuesday–Friday 8:00–14:00 and 15:00–18:00, Saturday 8:00–12:30, closed Sunday, across from Linzergasse 16); their take-out window is open until midnight. **Café Haydn Stube**, run by the local music school, is cheap and popular with students (Monday–Friday 9:00–18:00, later in summer, Mirabellplatz 1, at the entry to the Aicherpassage). **Mensa Aicherpassage** serves even cheaper meals in the basement (Monday–Friday 11:30–14:30, go under arch, enter metal door to "Mozarteum," and go down one floor).

## Transportation Connections—Salzburg

**By train to: Innsbruck** (every 2 hrs, 2 hrs), **Vienna** (2/hr, 3.5 hrs), **Hallstatt** (hrly, 50 min to Attnang Puchheim, 20-minute wait, 1.5 hrs to Hallstatt), **Reutte** (every 2 hrs, 4 hrs, transfer in Innsbruck), **Munich** (hrly, 2 hrs).

## SALZKAMMERGUT LAKE DISTRICT AND HALLSTATT

Commune with nature in Austria's Lake District. "The hills are alive," and you're surrounded by the loveliness that has turned on everyone from Emperor Franz Josef to Julie Andrews. This is *The Sound of Music* country. Idyllic, majestic, but not rugged, it's a gentle land of lakes, forested mountains, and storybook villages, rich in hiking opportunities and inexpensive lodging. Settle down in the postcard-pretty, fjord-cuddling town of Hallstatt.

## Planning Your Time

While there are plenty of lakes, Hallstatt is really the only one that matters. One night and two hours to browse is all you'll need to fall in love. To relax or take a hike in the surroundings, give it two nights and a day. It's a good stop between Salzburg and Vienna. A visit here (with a bike ride along the Danube) balances out your Austrian itinerary.

## Orientation (tel. code: 06134)

Lovable Hallstatt is a tiny town bullied onto a ledge between a selfish mountain and a swan-ruled lake, with a waterfall ripping furiously through its middle. It can be toured on foot in about ten minutes. The town is one of Europe's oldest, going back centuries before Christ. The charm of Hallstatt is the village and its lakeside setting. Go there to relax, nibble, wander, and paddle. (In August, tourist crowds trample much of Hallstatt's charm.) The lake is famous for its good fishing and pure water (8 km by 2 km, 125 meters deep at 508 meters altitude).

**Tourist Information:** The TI can always find you a room. Its hotel "guest card" gives you free parking and sight-seeing discounts (Monday–Friday 9:00–18:00, weekends 10:00–14:00, less off-season, tel. 06134/8208).

**Arrival in Hallstatt:** Hallstatt's train station is a wide spot on the tracks across the lake. *Stefanie* (a boat) meets you at the station and glides across the lake into town (20 AS, with each train until 18:35—don't arrive after that). The boat ride is gorgeous.

## Sights—Hallstatt

**Prehistory Museum**—The humble Prehistory Museum adjacent to the TI is interesting because little Hallstatt was the important salt-mining hub of a culture which spread from France to the Balkans during what archaeologists call the Hallstatt Period (800–400 B.C.). Back then Celtic tribes dug for precious salt and Hallstatt was, as its name means, the "salt mine." Your 40-AS Prehistory Museum ticket also gets you into the cute Heimat Museum of folk culture (daily 10:00–18:00 in summer). Historians like the English booklet that covers both museums (25 AS). The Janu sport shop across from the TI recently dug into a prehistoric site, and now its basement is another small museum.

▲▲**Hallstatt Church and Cemetery**—Hallstatt has two churches. The Protestant church is at lake level. The more interesting Catholic church, with a giant St. Christopher (protector of us travelers) on its outside wall, overlooks the town from above. From near the boat dock, hike up the covered wooden stairway to the church. The lovely church has 500-year-old altars and frescoes dedicated to the saints of mining and salt. Space is so limited in Hallstatt that bones have only 12 peaceful buried years in the church cemetery before making way for the freshly dead. The result is a fascinating chapel of bones in the cemetery (Beinhaus, 10 AS, daily 10:00–18:00). Each skull is lovingly named, dated, and decorated, with the men getting ivy, and the women, roses. They stopped this practice in the 1960s, about the same time the Catholic Church began permitting cremation.

▲▲**Salt Mine Tour**—If you have yet to do a salt mine, Hallstatt's is as good as any. You'll ride a frighteningly steep funicular high above the town (97 AS round-trip, 85 AS with guest card), take a ten-minute hike, put on old miners' clothes, take an underground train, slide down the banisters, and listen to an English tape-recorded tour while your guide speaks German (135 AS, 120 AS with guest card, daily 9:30–16:30, closes early off-season, no children under age 4, tel. 06134/8251). The well-publicized ancient Celtic graveyard excavation sites nearby are really dead. The scenic 50-minute hike back into town is (with strong knees) a joy.

▲**Boating, Hiking, and Spelunking**—Those into relaxation can rent a sleepy motorboat to enjoy town views from the water (75 AS/30 minutes, 120 AS/one hour, one or two people, two speeds: slow and stop, from Das Boot in the center or from the bus terminal just south of town). Mountain lovers, hikers, and spelunkers keep busy for days using Hallstatt as their home base. Get information from the TI on the various caves with their ice formations, the thunderous rivers, mountain lifts, nearby walks, and harder hikes. The best short and easy walk is the two-hour round-trip up the Echerhal Valley to a waterfall and back. With a car, consider hiking around nearby Altaussee (flat, three-hour hike) or along Grundlsee to Tolpitzsee. Regular buses connect Hallstatt with Gosausee for a pleasant walk around that lake. The TI can recommend a great two-day hike with an overnight in a nearby mountain hut.

## Sleeping in Hallstatt
**(12 AS = about $1, tel. code: 06134, zip code: 4830)**
Hallstatt's TI can almost always find you a room. July and August can be tight, and early August is worst. A bed in a private home costs about 200 AS with breakfast. It's hard to get a

## Salzkammergut and Hallstatt

one-night advance reservation. But if you drop in and they have a spot, they're happy to have you. Prices include breakfast, lots of stairs, and a silent night. *"Zimmer mit Aussicht?"* means "Room with view?"—worth asking for.

**Gasthof Simony** is my stocking-feet-tidy, 500-year-old favorite, right on the square with a lake view, balconies, creaky wood floors, slip-slidey rag rugs, antique furniture, a lakefront garden, and a huge breakfast. Call friendly Susan Scheutz for a reservation. For safety, reconfirm a day or two before you arrive (Sb-500 AS, Db-850 AS, price can vary according to the plumbing, view, season, and length of stay, 250 AS for third person, cheaper for families, Markt 105, tel. 06134/8231, SE). Downstairs Frau Zopf runs a traditional Austrian restaurant; try her delicious homemade desserts.

**Pension Seethaler** is a homey old lodge with 45 beds and a breakfast room mossy with antlers, perched above the lake on the parking-lot side of town (215 AS per person in S, D, T, or Q, 280 AS/person in rooms with private bath, cheaper if you stay more than one night, no extra for views, Dr. Morton Weg 22, tel. 06134/8421, fax 06134/84214; Frau Seethaler).

**Pension Sarstein** has 25 beds, mostly in rooms with flower-bedecked lake-view balconies, in a charming building a few minutes' walk along the lake from the center, run by friendly Frau Fisher. You can swim from her lakeside garden (D-420 AS, Ds-550 AS, Db-600 AS with this book; one-night stays cost 20 AS per person extra; Gosaumühlstrasse 83, tel. 06134/8217). Her sister, friendly **Frau Zimmermann**, runs a small Zimmer (as her name implies) in a 500-year-old ramshackle house with low beams, time-polished wood, and fine lake views just down the street (200-AS-per-person bed and breakfast in a double or triple, can be musty, Gosaumühlstrasse 69, tel. 06134/8309). These elderly ladies speak almost no English, but you'll find yourself caught up in their charm and laughing together like old friends.

**Helga Lenz** has a big, sprawling, woodsy house on top of the town with great lake and town views and a neat garden perch. It's ideal for those who sleep well in tree houses (180 AS per person in two-, three-, or four-bed rooms, 20 AS more for one-night stays, high above the paddleboat dock at Hallberg 17, tel. 06134/8508, SE).

**Gasthof Zauner** is a business machine offering modern pine-flavored rooms with all the comforts on the main square, and a restaurant specializing in grilled meat and fish (Db-1,190 AS, CC:VM, Marktplatz 51, tel. 06134/8246, fax 06134/82468).

**Gasthaus Mühle Naturfreunde-Herberge** has the best cheap beds in town and is clearly the place to eat well on a budget—great pizzas (145 AS per bed with sheets in two- to 20-bed coed dorms, 110 AS if you BYO hostel sheet, 40-AS breakfast, closed in November, the restaurant is closed on Wednesday, Kirchenweg 36, just below the tunnel car park, tel. & fax 06134/8318, run by Ferdinand Törö). "Nature's friends' houses" are found throughout the Alps. Like mountaineers' huts, they're a good, basic, fun bargain.

The nearby village of Obertraun is a peaceful alternative to Hallstatt in August. Check out the ice caves on a hot day. You'll find plenty of Zimmer and a luxurious hostel (135-AS beds with breakfast, tel. 06131/1360).

## Transportation Connections—Hallstatt

**By train to: Salzburg** (hrly, 90 min. to Attnang Puchheim, 10-to 30-min wait, 50 min to Salzburg), **Vienna** (hrly, 90 min. to Attnang Puchheim, 10- to 30-min wait, 2.5 hrs to Vienna). Daytrippers to Hallstatt can either check their bags or use the lockers at Attnang Puchheim station.

## INNSBRUCK

Innsbruck is world-famous as a resort for skiers and a haven for hikers. When compared to Salzburg and Vienna, it's stale strudel. Still, a quick look is easy and interesting.

Innsbruck was the Habsburgs' capital of the Tirol. Its medieval center, now a glitzy tourist-filled pedestrian zone, still gives you the feel of a provincial medieval capital. The much-ogled Golden Roof (Goldenes Dachl) is the centerpiece. Built by Emperor Maximilian in 1496, this balcony (with 2,657 gilded copper tiles) offered an impressive spot to view his medieval spectacles. From this square, you'll see the Golden Roof, the Baroque-style Helblinghaus, and the city tower (climb it for a great view, 20 AS). Nearby are the palace (Hofburg), church (Hofkirche), and Folklife Museum.

**Tourist Information:** Innsbruck has two TIs; one is downtown (daily 8:00–19:00, 3 blocks in front of the Golden Roof) and the other is at the train station (open until 21:15, tel. 0512/5356). The 200-AS one-day Innsbruck Card pays for itself only if you take the Mountain Lift (also covers Igls Lift, as well as the buses, trams, museums, zoo, and castle).

## Sights—Innsbruck

▲▲**Folklife Museum (Tiroler Volkskunst Museum)**—This offers the best look anywhere at traditional Tirolean lifestyles. Fascinating exhibits range from wedding dresses and gaily painted cribs and nativity scenes, to maternity clothes and babies' trousers. The upper floors show Tirolean homes through the ages (40 AS, Monday–Saturday 9:00–17:30 in summer, Sunday 9:00–12:00, hard to appreciate without the English guidebook).

**Maria-Theresa Strasse**—From the medieval center stretches the fine Baroque Maria-Theresa Strasse. St. Anne's Column marks the center of the old marketplace. At the far end, the Triumphal Arch is a gate Maria Theresa built to celebrate the marriage of her son, Leopold II.

▲**Ski Jump View**—The great ski jump of the 1964 and 1976 Olympics is an inviting side trip, overlooking the city just off the Brenner Pass road on the south side of town (follow signs to Bergisel). For the best view, hike to the Olympic rings under the dish that held the Olympic flame, where Dorothy Hamill and a host of others who brought home the gold are honored. Near the car park is a memorial to Andreas Hofer, the hero of the Tirolean battles against Napoleon.

**Mountain Lifts and Hiking**—A popular mountain-sports center and home of the 1964 and 1976 Winter Olympics, Innsbruck is surrounded by 150 mountain lifts, 1,250 miles of trails, and 250 hikers' huts. If it's sunny, consider riding the lift right out of the city to the mountaintops above (200 AS). If you stay at least one night in Innsbruck, ask your hotel or hostel for an Innsbruck Club card, which lets you take advantage of various discounts, bike tours, and free guided hikes. Hikers meet in front of Congress Innsbruck daily at 8:30; each day it's a different hike in the surrounding mountains and valleys (bring only lunch and water; boots, rucksack, and transport are provided).

**Alpenzoo**—This zoo is one of Innsbruck's most popular attractions (understandable when the competition is the Golden Roof). You can ride the funicular up to the zoo (free if you buy your zoo ticket before boarding) and get a look at all the animals that hide out in the Alps: wildcats, owls, elk, vultures, and more (70 AS, daily 9:00–18:00, special deal at the TI).

▲**Slap-Dancing**—For your Tirolean folk fun, Innsbruck hotels offer an entertaining evening of slap-dancing and yodeling nearly every summer night (200 AS includes a drink with the two-hour show, 20:45, tickets at the TI).

▲▲**Alpine Side Trip by Car to Hinterhornalm**—In Gnadenwald, a village sandwiched between Hall and its Alps, pay a 60-AS toll, pick up a brochure, then corkscrew your way up the mountain. Marveling at the crazy amount of energy put into such a remote road project, you'll finally end up at the rustic Hinterhornalm Berg restaurant (crude rooms, often closed, tel. 05223/52170). Hinterhornalm is a hang gliding

## Innsbruck and Hall

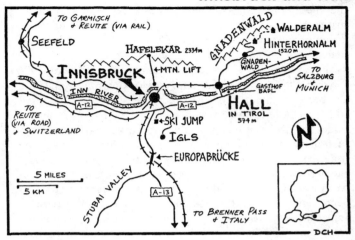

springboard. On good days, it's a butterfly nest. From there it's a level 20-minute walk to Walderalm, a cluster of three dairy farms with 70 cows that share their meadow with the clouds. The cows—cameras dangling from their thick necks—ramble along ridge-top lanes surrounded by cut-glass peaks. The ladies of the farms serve soup, sandwiches, and drinks (very fresh milk in the afternoon) on rough plank tables. Below you spreads the Inn River Valley and, in the distance, Innsbruck.

## Transportation Connections—Innsbruck

**To: Hall** (2 buses/hr, 30 min; hrly trains, 15 min), **Salzburg** (hrly trains, 2 hrs), **Vienna** (hrly trains, 5 hrs), **Reutte** (trains every 2 hrs, 2.5 hrs with one change; or by bus: 4/day, 2.5 hrs), **Bregenz** (6 trains/day, 3 hrs), **Zurich** (6 trains/day, 3.5 hrs), **Munich** (hrly trains, 2.5 hrs), **Paris** (1 train/day, 11 hrs), **Milan** (5 trains/day, 5.5 hrs), **Venice** (5 trains/day, 5.5 hrs). Train info: tel. 0512/1717.

## HALL IN TIROL

Hall was a rich salt-mining center when Innsbruck was just a humble bridge (*Brücke*) town on the Inn River. Hall actually has a larger old town than does its sprawling neighbor, Innsbruck. Hall hosts a colorful morning scene before the daily tour buses arrive, closes down tight for its daily siesta, and sleeps on Sunday. There's a farmer's market on Saturday mornings. The town tries hard and promises much, but in practice there usually are not enough tourists to make any of the scheduled tours happen. Tirolean folk evenings happen nearly nightly in Innsbruck and weekly in Absam, near Hall. (Drivers can use Hall as a convenient overnight stop on the drive from Vienna to Switzerland.)

## Orientation (tel code: 05223)

**Tourist Information:** Hall's TI is just off the main square (Monday–Friday 8:15–12:15 and 14:00–18:00, Saturday 9:00–12:00, closed Sunday, tel. 05223/56269).

**Bike Rental:** Bikes can be rented at the Camping Grounds (tel. 454-6475). The riverside bike path (11 km from Hall to Volders) is a real treat.

## Sights—Hall

**Hasegg Castle**—This was the town mint. As you walk over the old pedestrian bridge from Gasthof Badl into town, this is the first old building you'll see (you can pick up a town map and a list of sights here).

**Parish Church**—Facing the town square, this much-appended Gothic church is decorated Baroque, with fine altars, a twisted apse, and a north wall lined with bony relics.

**Salt Museum (Bergbaumuseum)**—Back when salt was money, Hall was loaded. Try catching a tour at this museum, where the town has reconstructed one of its original salt mines, complete with pits, shafts, drills, tools, and a slippery but tiny wooden slide (30 AS, by guided tour only, 30-minute tours depart on the hour from 14:00–17:00 if there are at least three people, English spoken, Monday–Saturday from April–October, closed Sunday, tel. 05223/56269).

**Walking Tours**—The TI organizes town walks in English (80 AS including admissions, 9:30 and 14:00, two hours, minimum four people. It's best to call first to confirm, tel. 05223/56269).

**Swimming**—To give your trip a special splash, check out Hall's magnificent Freischwimmbad, a huge outdoor pool with four diving boards, a giant lap pool, and a kiddies' pool, all surrounded by a lush garden, sauna, mini-golf, and lounging locals (38 AS).

## Sleeping and Eating in Hall
**(12 AS = about $1, tel. code: 05223)**

Lovable towns that specialize in lowering the pulse of local vacationers line the Inn Valley. Hall, while the best town, has the shortest list of accommodations. Up the hill on either side of the river are towns strewn with fine farmhouse hotels and pensions. Most Zimmer charge about 200 AS per person but don't accept one-night stays.

**Gasthof Badl** is a big, comfortable, friendly place run by sunny Frau Steiner and her daughter, Sonja. It's easy to find, immediately off the Hall in Tirol freeway exit with an orange-lit "Bed" sign. I like it for the convenience, the quiet, the big breakfast, the warm welcome, and the fact that they'll hold a room for a phone call (Sb-450 AS, Db-730 AS, Tb-1,050 AS, Qb-1,360 AS, elevator, CC:VM, Innsbruck 4, A-6060 Hall in Tirol, tel. 05223/56784, fax 05223/567-843, SE). Hall's kitchens close early, but Gasthof Badl's restaurant serves excellent dinners until 22:00 (from 120 AS, closed Tuesday). In the Gasthof Badl lobby, you'll find all the essential TI brochures and maps of Hall and Innsbruck in English.

For a cheaper room in a private home, **Frieda Tollinger** rents out three rooms and accepts one-nighters (220 AS per person with breakfast; across the river from Badl, and downstream about half a mile, follow Untere Lend, which becomes Schopperweg, to Schopperweg 8, tel. 05223/41366, NSE).

**Alpenhotel Speckbacherhof** is a grand rustic hotel set between a peaceful forest and a meadow with all the comforts, a pool, mini-golf, and so on (Db-840–880 AS, half-board 170 AS per person more, ask for 10 percent discount with this book, CC:VMA, A-6060 Gnadenwald/Tirol, tel. 05223/52511, fax 05223/525-1155, family Mayr). Drive ten minutes uphill from Hall to the village of Gnadenwald. It's across the street from the Hinterhornalm toll road.

### Sleeping near Hall in Reith

**Schloss Matzen** is a 12th-century castle about 40 km northeast of Hall/Innsbruck and 2 km off the autobahn, a good option for drivers. The friendly American hosts share their wealth of info on the area and its history (one Sb-$140, Db-$175–250, open February and mid-May–October, CC:VM, A-6230 Reith im Alpbachtal, U.S.A. tel. 888/837-0618 or 707/937-0618, e-mail: mfox@mcn.org).

## Transportation Connections—Hall

The nearest major train station is at Innsbruck. Hall and Innsbruck are connected by trains (hourly) and by bus #4 (4/hr, 30 min, 26 AS). Drivers staying in freeway-handy Hall can easily side-trip into Innsbruck using bus #4 (departs from just over the bridge or the Kurhaus at the top of town to the Innsbruck train station, a seven-minute walk from the old town center).

## Route Tips for Drivers

**Into Salzburg from Munich:** After crossing the border, stay on the autobahn, taking the Süd Salzburg exit in the direction of Anif. First you'll pass the Schloss Hellbrunn (and zoo), then the TI and a great park-and-ride service. Get sightseeing information and a day-long bus pass from the TI (daily 9:00–20:00), park your car (free), and catch the shuttle bus (19 AS, every five minutes) into town. Mozart never drove in the old town, and neither should you. If you don't believe in P&R, the easiest, cheapest, most central parking lot is the 1,500-car Altstadt lot in the tunnel under the Mönchsberg (160 AS per day, note your slot number and which of the twin lots you're in). Your hotel may have parking discount passes.

**From Salzburg to Hallstatt (50 miles):** Get on the Munich–Wien autobahn (blue signs), head for Vienna, exit at Thalgau, and follow signs to Hof, Fuschl, and St. Gilgen. The road to Hallstatt leads first past Fuschlsee (mediocre Sommerrodelbahn summer luge ride, 30 AS, open when dry, April–mid-October 10:00–17:00, at Fuschl an See), to St. Gilgen (pleasant but touristy), to Bad Ischl (the center of the Salzkammergut with a spa, salt-mine tour, casino, the emperor's villa if you need a Habsburg history fix, and a good tourist office, tel. 06132/23520), and along Hallstattersee to Hallstatt.

Hallstatt is basically traffic-free. Park in the middle of the tunnel at the P-1 sign and waterfall. If this is full, try the lakeside lot (P-2, a pleasant five-minute lakeside walk from the town center) just after the tunnel. If you're traveling off-season and staying downtown, you can drive in and park by the boat dock (your hotel "guest card" gives you permission).

**From Hall into Innsbruck and on to Switzerland:** For old Innsbruck, take the autobahn from Hall to the Innsbruck Ost exit, and follow the signs to Zentrum, then Kongresshaus, and park as close as you can to the old center on the river (Hofgarden).

Just south of Innsbruck is the Olympic ski jump (from the autobahn take the Innsbruck Süd exit and follow signs to "Bergisel"). Park at the end of the road near the Andreas Hofer Memorial and climb to the empty, grassy stands for a picnic.

Leaving Innsbruck for Switzerland (from ski jump, go down into town along huge cemetery, thoughtfully placed just beyond the jump landing, and follow blue A12, Garmisch, Arlberg signs), head west on the autobahn (direction: Bregenz). The 8-mile-long Arlberg tunnel saves you 30 minutes but costs 160 AS and lots of scenery. For a joyride and to save a few bucks, skip the tunnel, exit at St. Anton, and go via Stuben.

After the speedy Arlberg tunnel, you're 30 minutes from Switzerland. Bludenz, with its characteristic medieval quarter, makes a good rest stop. Pass Feldkirch (and another long tunnel) and exit the autobahn at Rankweil/Feldkirch Nord, following signs for Altstätten and Meiningen (CH). Crossing the baby Rhine River, you leave Austria.

To side trip to Liechtenstein, follow FL signs at Feldkirch (see Appenzell chapter).

**Side trip over Brenner Pass into Italy:** A short swing into Italy is fast and easy from Innsbruck or Hall (45-minute drive, easy border crossing, Austrian schillings accepted in the border region), but before you do it, check with your car rental company about coverage in Italy (theft insurance is required). To get to Italy, take the great Europa Bridge over Brenner Pass. It's expensive (about $15), but in 30 minutes you'll be at the border. (Note: Traffic can be heavy on summer weekends.) In Italy drive to the colorful market town of Vipiteno/Sterzing. The **Reifenstein Castle** is just south of town on the east side of the valley, down a small road next to the autobahn. The lady who lives at the castle gives tours (9:30, 10:30, 14:00, and 15:00, closed Friday) in German, Italian, and a little English. It's a unique and wonderfully preserved medieval castle (4,000L or 30 AS, tel. from Austria 00-39-472/765-879).

# SWITZERLAND
## (SCHWEIZ, SUISSE, SVIZZERA)

- 16,000 square miles (half the size of Ireland, or 13 Rhode Islands)
- About 6 million people (400 people per square mile, declining slightly)
- 1 Swiss franc (SF) = about 65 cents, 1.5 SF = about $1

Switzerland is one of Europe's richest, best-organized, and most expensive countries. Like Boy Scouts, the Swiss count cleanliness, neatness, punctuality, tolerance, independence, thrift, and hard work as virtues, and they love pocketknives. They appreciate the awesome nature that surrounds them and are proud of their little country's many achievements. Their high income, a great social security system, and the Alps give the Swiss plenty to be thankful for.

Switzerland is Europe's most mountainous country. Forty percent of the country consists of uninhabitable rocks, lakes, and rugged Alps. Its geography has given it distinct cultural regions and customs. Two-thirds of the people speak German, 20 percent French, 10 percent Italian, and a small group in the southeast speak Romansch, a direct descendant of ancient Latin. Within these four language groups, there are many dialects. The sing songy Swiss German, the spoken dialect, is quite a bit different from High German, which is Switzerland's written German. Most Swiss are multilingual, and English is widely spoken, but an interest in these regional distinctions will win the hearts of locals you meet. As you travel from one valley to the next, notice changes in architecture and customs.

Historically, Switzerland is one of the oldest democracies (yet women didn't get the vote until 1971). Born when three states, or "cantons," united in 1291, the Confederation Helvetica, as it was called in Roman times (the "CH" decal on cars doesn't stand for chocolate), grew to the 23 cantons of today. The government is decentralized, and cantonal loyalty is very strong.

Fiercely independent, Switzerland loves its neutrality and stayed out of both world wars. But it's far from lax defensively.

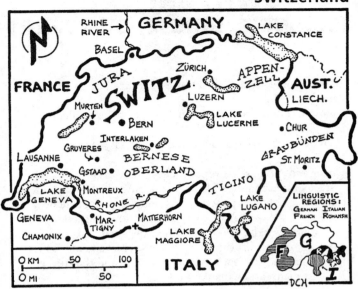

Every fit man serves in the army and stays in the reserve. Each house has a gun and a bomb shelter. Switzerland bristles with 600,000 rifles in homes and 12,000 heavy guns in place. Swiss vacuum-packed emergency army bread, which lasts two years, is also said to function as a weapon. Airstrips hide inside mountains behind Batmobile doors. With the push of a button, all road, rail, and bridge entries to the country can be destroyed, changing Switzerland into a formidable mountain fortress. Notice the innocent-looking but explosive patches checkerboarding the roads at key points like tunnel entrances and mountain summits (and hope no one invades until you get past). Sentiments are changing, and Switzerland has come close to voting away its entire military.

Shops throughout the land thrill tourists with carved, woven, and clanging mountain knickknacks, clocks, watches, and Swiss Army knives (Victorinox is the best brand).

Prices are high. More and more locals call sitting on the pavement around a bottle of wine "going out." Hotels with double rooms under $80 are rare. Even dormitory beds cost $20. If your budget is tight, be sure to chase down hostels (many with "family rooms") and keep your eyes peeled for *Matratzenlagers* (literally, "mattress dorms"). Hiking is free, though major Alpine lifts run $20 to $40.

The Swiss eat when we do and enjoy a straightforward, no-nonsense cuisine. Specialties include delicious fondue, rich chocolates, a melted cheese dish called *Raclette*, fresh dairy products (try *müesli* yogurt), 100 varieties of cheese, and *Fendant*, a good, crisp, local white wine, too expensive to sell well abroad and doled out by the pricey deciliter here. The Co-op and Migros grocery stores are the hungry hiker's best budget bet; groceries are only 50 percent higher than U.S.A. prices.

You can get anywhere quickly on Switzerland's scenic and efficient trains or its fine road system (the world's most expensive per mile to build). Drivers pay a one-time 40-SF fee for a permit to use Swiss autobahns. It's easy to slip across the border without buying one, but anyone driving on a Swiss autobahn without this tax sticker is likely to be cop-stopped and fined.

Tourist information offices abound. While Switzerland's booming big cities are cosmopolitan, the traditional culture survives in the Alpine villages. Spend most of your time getting high in the Alps. On Sunday you're most likely to enjoy traditional sports, music, clothing, and culture. August 1 is the festive Swiss national holiday.

# GIMMELWALD AND THE BERNER OBERLAND

Frolic and hike high above the stress and clouds of the real world. Take a vacation from your busy vacation. Recharge your touristic batteries up here in the Alps, where distant avalanches, cowbells, the fluff of a down comforter, and the crunchy footsteps of happy hikers are the dominant sounds. If the weather's good (and your budget's healthy), ride a gondola from the traffic-free village of Gimmelwald to a hearty breakfast at Schilthorn's 10,000-foot revolving Piz Gloria restaurant. Linger among Alpine whitecaps before riding, hiking, or hang gliding down (5,000 feet) to Mürren and home to Gimmelwald. Your gateway to the wonderfully mountainous Berner Oberland is the grand old resort town of Interlaken. Near Interlaken is Switzerland's open-air folk museum, Ballenberg, where you climb through traditional houses from every corner of this diverse country.

Ah, but the weather's fine and the Alps beckon. Head deep into the heart of the Alps and ride the gondola to the stop just this side of heaven—Gimmelwald.

## Planning Your Time

Rather than tackling a checklist of famous Swiss mountains and resorts, choose one region to savor—the Berner Oberland. Interlaken is the administrative headquarters (fine transportation hub, banking, post office, laundry, shopping). Use it for business and as a springboard for Alpine thrills. With decent weather, explore the two areas (south of Interlaken) which tower above either side of the Lauterbrunnen Valley: Kleine Scheidegg/Jungfrau and Schilthorn/Mürren. Ideally, home-base three nights in the village of Gimmelwald and spend a day in each area. On a speedy train trip, you can overnight into and out of Interlaken. For the fastest look, consider a night in Gimmelwald, breakfast at the Schilthorn, an afternoon doing the Männlichen-to-Wengen hike, and an evening or night train out. For a nature lover not to spend the night high in the Alps is Alpus-interruptus.

## Getting Around the Berner Oberland

For more than 100 years, this has been the target of nature-worshiping pilgrims. And the Swiss have made the most exciting Alpine perches accessible by lift or train. Part of the fun (and most of the expense) of the area is riding the many lifts. Generally scenic trains and lifts are not covered on train passes (but a Eurail or Europass gets you a 25 percent discount on even the highest lifts). Ask about discounts for earlybirds, youths, seniors, groups, and those staying awhile. A Family Card gives traveling families enough of a discount to pay for itself on the first hour of trains and lifts; children under 16 travel free with parents, children 16 to 23 pay half-price (20 SF at any Swiss train station but not gondola stations). Get a list of discounts and the free fare and time schedule at any train station or in Interlaken. Study the "Alpine Lifts in the Berner Oberland" chart in this chapter. Lifts generally go at least twice an hour, from about 7:00 to about 20:00.

## INTERLAKEN

When the 19th-century Romantics redefined mountains as something more than cold and troublesome obstacles, Interlaken became the original Alpine resort. Ever since then, tourists have flocked to the Alps "because they're there." Interlaken's glory days are long gone, its elegant old hotels eclipsed by the new, more jet-setty Alpine resorts. Today its shops are filled with chocolate bars, Swiss Army knives, and sunburned backpackers.

## Orientation (tel. code: 033)

Efficient Interlaken is a good administrative and shopping center. Take care of business, give the town a quick look, view the live TV coverage of the Jungfrau and Schilthorn weather in the window of the Schilthornbahn office on the main street (at Höheweg 2), and head for the hills. Stay in Interlaken only if you suffer from alptitude sickness (see Sleeping, below).

# Interlaken

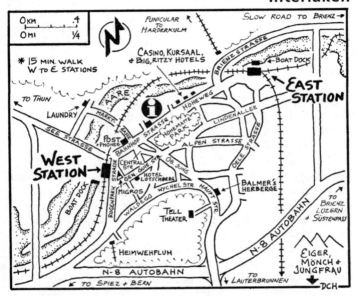

**Tourist Information:** The TI has good information for the whole region, advice on Alpine lift discounts, and a room-finding service (July–September Monday–Friday 8:00–12:00 and 13:30–18:30, Saturday 8:00–17:00, Sunday 17:00–19:00; off-season weekdays 8:00–12:00 and 14:00–18:00, Saturday 8:00–12:00, closed Sunday, tel. 033/822-2121). It's on the main street, a five-minute walk from the West station. While the Jungfrau region map costs 2 SF, a perfectly good mini-version of it is in the free Jungfrau region train timetable. Pick up a Bern map if that's your next destination.

**Arrival in Interlaken:** Interlaken has two train stations. Most major trains stop at the Interlaken-West station. The station's train information desk will also answer tourist questions and has an exchange desk with fair rates (daily 8:00–12:00 and 14:00–18:00). Ask at the station about discount passes, special fares, Eurail discounts, and schedules for the scenic mountain trains (tel. 033/826-4750). An open-late Migros supermarket is across the street with a self-service cafeteria upstairs (Monday–Thursday 8:00–18:30, Friday 8:00–21:00, Saturday 7:30–16:00, closed Sunday).

It's a pleasant 15-minute walk between the West and East stations, or an easy, frequent train connection. From the Interlaken-East station, private trains take you deep into the mountainous Jungfrau region (see Transportation Connections, below).

## Helpful Hints

**Telephone:** Phone booths cluster outside the post office in the center of town. Inside the office, you'll find metered phone booths (talk first, pay later; Monday–Friday 7:45–18:15, Saturday 8:30–11:00, closed Sunday).

**Laundry:** Helen Schmocker's Wascherei Laundry has a change machine, soap, English instructions, and a pleasant riverside place in which to hang out (daily 7:00–22:00 for self-service, 11 SF to wash and dry 10 pounds; Monday–Saturday 8:00–12:00 and 13:30–18:00 for full service: Drop off 10 pounds and 12 SF in the morning and pick up clean clothes that afternoon; from the post office, follow Marktgasse over two bridges to Beatenbergstrasse, tel. 033/822-1566).

**Activities:** For the adventurer with money, Alpin Raft offers high-adrenalin trips such as rafting, canyoning (rappeling down watery gorges), bungee jumping, and paragliding (Postfach 78, tel. 033/823-4100, Web site: www.alpinraft.ch).

## GIMMELWALD

Saved from developers by its "avalanche zone" classification, Gimmelwald is one of the poorest places in Switzerland. Its economy is stuck in the hay, and its farmers, unable to make it in their disadvantaged trade, are subsidized by the Swiss government (and work the ski lifts in the winter). For some travelers, there's little to see in the village. Others enjoy a fascinating day sitting on a bench and learning why they say, "If heaven isn't what it's cracked up to be, send me back to Gimmelwald."

Take a walk through the town. This place is for real. Most of the 130 residents have the same last name. They are tough and proud. Raising hay in this rugged terrain is labor-intensive. One family harvests enough to feed only 15 or 20 cows. But they'd have it no other way and, unlike absentee landlord Mürren, Gimmelwald is locally owned. (When word got out that urban planners wished to develop Gimmelwald into a town of 1,000, locals pulled some strings to secure the town's bogus "avalanche zone" building code.)

## Lauterbrunnen Valley: West Side Story

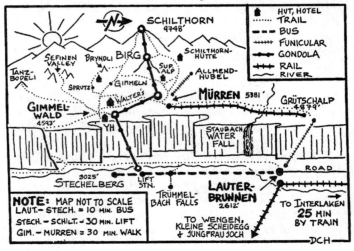

Notice the traditional log-cabin architecture and blond-braided children. The numbers on the buildings are not addresses, but fire insurance numbers. The cute little hut near the station is for storing and aging cheese, not hostelers. In Catholic-Swiss towns, the biggest building is the church. In Protestant towns, it's the school. Protestant Gimmelwald's biggest building is the school (one teacher, 17 students, and a room that doubles as a chapel when the pastor makes his monthly visit). Do not confuse obscure Gimmelwald with touristy and commercialized Grindelwald just over the Kleine Scheidegg ridge.

Evening fun in Gimmelwald is found at the youth hostel (lots of young Alp-aholics and a good chance to share information on the surrounding mountains) and up at Walter's Hotel Mittaghorn (see Sleeping, below).

Walter's bar is a local farmer's hangout. When they've made their hay, they come here to play. They look like what we'd call "hicks" (former city-slicker Walter still isn't fully accepted by the gang), but they speak some English and can be fun to get to know. Sit outside (benches just below the rails, 100 yards down the lane from Walter's) and watch the sun tuck the mountaintops into bed as the moon rises over the Jungfrau.

## Alpine Hikes

There are days of possible hikes from Gimmelwald. Many are a fun combination of trails, mountain trains, and gondola rides. Don't mind the fences, cross at will; a hiker has the right of way in Switzerland. But as late as May, snow can curtail your hiking plans.

▲▲▲**Hike 1: The Schilthorn: Hikes, Lifts, and a 10,000-foot Breakfast**—If the weather's good, have breakfast atop the Schilthorn, in the slowly revolving, mountain-capping restaurant (of James Bond movie fame). The early-bird-special gondola tickets (rides before 9:00) take you from Gimmelwald to the Schilthorn and back at a discount. Nag the Schilthorn station in Mürren for a gondola souvenir decal (Schilthorn info: tel. 033/231-444).

Breakfast costs from 13.50 SF to 22 SF. Expect slow service and ask for more hot drinks if necessary. If you're not revolving, ask them to turn it on. Linger on top. Piz Gloria has a souvenir shop, the rocks of the region on the restaurant wall, telescopes, and a "touristorama" film room showing a multi-screen slide show and explosive highlights from the James Bond thriller that featured the Schilthorn (free and self-serve; push the button for slides or, after a long pause for the projector to rewind, push for 007).

Watch hang gliders set up, psych up, and take off, flying 30 minutes with the birds to distant Interlaken. Walk along the ridge out back. This is a great place for a photo of the "mountain-climber you." For another cheap thrill, ask the gondola attendant to crank down the window, stick your head out, and pretend you're hang gliding, ideally over the bump going down from Gimmelwald.

Lifts go twice an hour, and the ride (including two transfers) to the Schilthorn takes 30 minutes. Watch the altitude meter in the gondola. (The Gimmelwald–Schilthorn hike is free, if you don't mind a 5,000-foot altitude gain.) You can ride up to the Schilthorn and hike down, but I wouldn't (weather can change; have good shoes). For a less scary hike, go halfway down by cable car and walk down from the Birg station. Buy the round-trip excursion early-bird fare (cheaper than the Gimmelwald–Schilthorn–Birg ticket) and decide at Birg if you want to hike or ride down.

Hiking down from Birg is very steep and gravelly. Just below Birg is the Schilthorn-Hutte. Drop in for soup, cocoa,

## Berner Oberland

NOTE: THIS BIRD'S EYE VIEW LOOKS SOUTH...

EIGER 13026'  MONCH 13449'  JUNGFRAU 13642'  SCHILT-HORN 9748'

JUNG-FRAU-JOCH

TUNNEL

KLEINE SCHEIDEGG 6762'

GIMMEL-WALD 4593'

BIRG 8784'

HIKE #1

GRINDEL-WALD 3393'

HIKE #2

MÄNN-LICHEN 7317'

MÜRREN 5381'

W-ALP

STECHEL-BERG 3025'

← NICE WALK

GRUND

GRÜTSCHALP 4879'

WENGEN 4180'

LAUTERBRUNNEN 2612'

↗TO FIRST

ISENFLUH

HIKE #3

WILDERSWIL 1916'

SCHYNIGE PLATTE 6454'

ISELT-WALD

SPIEZ

TO LUZERN

E.    W.

LAKE BRIENZ

INTER-LAKEN 1860'

LAKE THUN

TO BERN

BRIENZ    • BALLENBERG

—•—  PRIVATE RAIL – EURAIL NOT VALID
—+—  OTHER RAIL – EURAIL VALID
o—o  MTN. LIFTS
- - -  BUS
•••  BOAT
•••••  TRAIL

NOT TO SCALE!

—DCH—

or a coffee schnapps. You can spend the night in the hut's crude loft (40 mattresses; a ridiculous 60 SF for bed, breakfast, and dinner; open July–September, tel. 033/855-1167). Youth hostelers scream down the ice fields on plastic-bag sleds from the Schilthorn. (English-speaking doctor in Mürren.)

The most interesting trail from Birg to Gimmelwald is the high one via Grauseewli Lake and Wasenegg Ridge to Brünli, down to Spielbodenalp, and the Sprutz waterfall. From the Birg lift, hike towards the Schilthorn, taking your first left down to the little, newly made Grauseewli Lake. From the lake a gravelly trail leads down the rough switchbacks until it levels out. When you see a rock painted with arrows pointing to "Mürren" and "Rotstockhütte," follow the path to "Rotstock-hütte," traversing the cow-grazed mountainside. Follow Wasenegg Ridge left/down and along the barbed wire fence which dead-ends at Brünli below. (For maximum thrills, stay on the ridge and climb all the way to the knobby little summit

## Alpine Lifts in the Berner Oberland

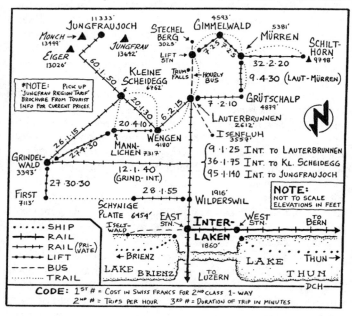

where you'll enjoy an incredible 360-degree view and a chance to sign your name on the register stored in the little wooden box.) A steep trail winds directly down from Brünli towards Gimmelwald, soon hitting a bigger, easy trail. The trail bends right (just before the popular restaurant/mountain hut at Spiel-bodenalp) leading to Sprutz. Walk under the Sprutz waterfall, and a steep wooded trail deposits you in a meadow of flowers at the top side of Gimmelwald. For any hike, get local advice and believe it more than me.

For an expensive thrill, you can bungee-jump from the Stechelberg–Mürren service gondola: 129 SF for a 330-foot drop, 259 SF for 590 feet, drop head-first or feet-first, tel. 033/826-7711).

▲▲▲**Hike 2: The Männlichen–Kleine Scheidegg Hike—**
This is my favorite easy Alpine hike, entertaining you all the way with glorious Jungfrau, Eiger, and Mönch views. (That's the Young Maiden being protected from the Ogre by the Monk.)

If the weather's good, descend from Gimmelwald bright

and early. Catch the post bus to the Lauterbrunnen train station (or drive, parking at the large multi-storied pay lot behind the station). Buy a ticket to Männlichen and catch the train. Ride past great valley views to Wengen, where you'll walk across town (buy a picnic, but don't waste time here if it's sunny), and catch the Männlichen lift (departing every 15 minutes) to the top of the ridge high above you.

From the tip of the Männlichen lift, hike 20 minutes north to the little peak for that king- or queen-of-the-mountain feeling. It's an easy hour's walk from there to Kleine Scheidegg for a picnic or restaurant lunch. (For accommodations, see Sleeping, below.) If you've got an extra 100 SF and the weather's perfect, ride the train from Kleine Scheidegg through the Eiger to the towering Jungfraujoch and back. Check for discount trips up to Jungfraujoch (three trips a day—early or late, tel. 033/826-4750, weather info: tel. 033/855-1022). Jungfraujoch crowds can be frightening. The price has been jacked up to reduce the mobs, but sunny days are still a mess.

From Kleine Scheidegg, enjoy the ever-changing Alpine panorama of the north face of the Eiger, Jungfrau, and Mönch, probably accompanied by the valley-filling mellow sound of Alp-horns and distant avalanches, as you ride the train or hike downhill (30 gorgeous minutes to Wengeralp, 90 more steep minutes from there into the town of Wengen). If the weather turns bad, or you run out of steam, catch the train early at the little Wengeralp station along the way. After Wengeralp, the trail to Wengen is steep and, while not dangerous, requires a good set of knees. Wengen is a fine shopping town. (For accommodations, see Sleeping, below.) The boring final descent from Wengen to Lauterbrunnen is knee-killer steep, so catch the train. Trails may be snowbound into early June. Ask about conditions at the lift stations or local TI. If the Männlichen lift is closed, take the train straight from Lauterbrunnen to Kleine Scheidegg. Many take the risk of slipping and enjoy the Kleine Scheidegg-to-Wengeralp hike even with a little snow.

▲▲Hike 3: Schynige Platte to First—The best day I've had hiking in the Berner Oberland is the demanding six-hour ridge walk high above Lake Brienz on one side and all that Jungfrau beauty on the other. Start at Wilderswil train station (just above Interlaken), where you catch the little train up to Schynige Platte (2,000 meters). Walk through the Alpine flower display garden and into the wild Alpine yonder. The high point is Faulhorn (2,680 meters, with its famous mountaintop hotel). Hike to a chairlift called First (2,168 meters), where you descend to Grindelwald and catch a train back to your starting point, Wilderswil—or, if you have a regional train pass or no car but endless money, return to Gimmelwald via Lauterbrunnen from Grindelwald over Kleine Scheidegg.

▲▲**Hike 4: Cloudy Day Lauterbrunnen Valley Walk**—For a smell-the-cows-and-flowers lowland walk, ideal for a cloudy day, weary body, or tight budget, follow the riverside trail 5 kilometers from Lauterbrunnen's Staubach Falls (just after the town church) to the Schilthornbahn station at Stechelberg. Detour to Trümmelbach Falls en route (see below).

If you're staying in Gimmelwald: To get to Lauterbrunnen, walk up to Mürren (30 min), walk or ride the train to Grütschalp (60 min hike), ride the funicular down to Lauterbrunnen (10 min), walk through town, and take the riverside trail ending up at Stechelberg (75 min) where you can ride the lift back up to Gimmelwald (10 min).

▲**Other Hikes near Gimmelwald**—For a not-too-tough three-hour walk (there's a scary 20-minute stretch that comes with ropes) with great Jungfrau views and some mountain farm action, ride the funicular from Mürren to Allmendhübel (1,934 meters), and walk to Marchegg, Saustal, and Grütschalp (a drop of about 500 meters), where you can catch the panorama train back to Mürren. An easier version is the lower "Bergweg" from Allmenhübel to Grütschalp via Winteregg. For an easy family stroll with grand views, walk from Mürren just above the train tracks to either Winteregg (40 min, restaurant, playground, train station) or Grütschalp (60 min, train station) and catch the panorama train back to Mürren. An easy, go-as-far-as-you-like trail from Gimmelwald is up the Sefinen Valley. Or you can wind from Gimmelwald down to Stechelberg (1 hour).

You can get specifics at the Mürren TI. The TI, Guesthouse Belmont, and Hotel Mittaghorn each have a "Hiking Possibilities: Schilthorn—Panoramaland" flier that describes 12 recommended hikes. The 3-D map of the Mürren mountainside, which includes hiking trails, makes a useful, attractive souvenir (2 SF at TI and lift station). For an extensive rundown on the region, get Don Chmura's fine 5-SF Gimmelwald guidebook (includes info on hikes, flora, fauna, culture, and travel tips; available at Hotel Mittaghorn).

## Rainy Day Options

If clouds roll in, don't despair. They can roll out just as quickly, and there are some good bad-weather options. There are easy trails and pleasant walks along the floor of the Lauterbrunnen Valley (see above). If all the waterfalls have you intrigued, sneak a behind-the-scenes look at the valley's most powerful one, **Trümmelbach Falls** (10 SF, daily April–October 9:00–18:00, on the Lauterbrunnen–Stechelberg road, tel. 033/855-3232). You'll ride an elevator up through the mountain and climb through several caves to see the melt from the Eiger, Mönch, and Jungfrau grinding like God's bandsaw through the mountain at the rate of up to 20,000 liters a second (nearly double the beer consumption at Oktoberfest). The upper area, "chutes 6 to 10," are the best, so if your legs ache, you can skip the lower ones and ride the lift down.

Lauterbrunnen's **Heimatmuseum** shows off the local folk culture (3 SF, mid-June–September, Tuesday, Thursday, Saturday, and Sunday 14:00–17:30, just over the bridge).

Mürren's slick **Sports Center** (Sportzentrum) offers a world of indoor activities (12 SF for use of the swimming pool and whirlpool, 7 SF for Mürren hotel guests, pool open Monday–Saturday afternoon, mid-June–October). Mürren also has plenty of shops, bakeries, banks, a TI, and accommodations (see Sleeping, below).

**Boat Trips from Interlaken**—From Interlaken (which means "between the lakes"), you can take daily boat trips on the lakes it's between (8/day, fewer off-season, free with Eurail). The Lake Thun boat stops at Beatushöhlen (interesting caves, 30 min from Interlaken) and two visit-worthy towns: Spiez (1 hr from Interlaken) and Thun (1.75 hrs away). The Lake Brienz boat stops at the super-cute and quiet village of Iseltwald (45 min away), and Brienz (1.25 hrs away, near Ballenberg Open-Air Folk Museum). Get the latest schedule at the TI.

▲▲**Swiss Open-Air Folk Museum at Ballenberg**—Near Interlaken, the Swiss Open-Air Museum of Vernacular Architecture, Country Life and Crafts in the Bernese Oberland is a rich collection of traditional and historic farmhouses from every region of the country. Each house is carefully furnished, and many feature traditional craftspeople at work. The sprawling 50-acre park, laid out roughly as a huge Swiss map, is a natural preserve providing a wonderful setting for this culture-on-a-lazy-Susan look at Switzerland.

The Thurgau house (#621) has an interesting wattle-and-daub (half-timbered construction) display and house #331 has a fun bread museum. Use the 2-SF map/guide. The more expensive picture book is a better souvenir than guide. (14-SF entry, half-price after 16:00, daily mid-April–October 10:00–17:00, houses close at 17:00, park stays open later, craft demonstration schedules are listed just inside the entry, tel. 039/511-123.) There's a reasonable outdoor cafeteria inside the west entrance, and fresh-baked bread, sausage, mountain cheese, and other goodies on sale in several houses. Picnic tables and grills with free firewood are scattered throughout the park. The little wooden village of Brienzwiler (near the east entrance) is a museum in itself with a lovely little church. Trains run frequently from Interlaken to Brienzwiler, an easy walk from the museum.

## Sleeping in the Berner Oberland
**(1.5 SF = about $1, tel. code: 033)**
Sleep Code: **S**=Single, **D**=Double/Twin, **T**=Triple, **Q**=Quad, **b**=bathroom, **t**=toilet only, **s**=shower only, **CC**=Credit Card (**V**isa, **M**asterCard, **A**mex), **SE**=Speaks English, **NSE**=No English. Unless otherwise noted, breakfast is included.

### *Sleeping in Gimmelwald*
*(4,500 feet, tel code: 033, zip code: 3826)*
To inhale the Alps and really hold it in, sleep high in Gimmelwald. Poor but pleasantly stuck in the past, the village has a happy hostel, a comfy B&B, a decent pension, and a creaky hotel. The bad news is that the lift costs 7.20 SF each way to get there.

**Hotel Mittaghorn**, the treasure of Gimmelwald, is run by Walter Mittler, a perfect Swiss gentleman. The hotel is a classic, creaky, Alpine-style place with memorable beds, ancient down comforters (short and fat; wear socks and drape the blanket over your feet), and a million-dollar view of the Jungfrau Alps. The loft has a dozen real beds on either side of a divider, with several sinks, down comforters, and a fire ladder out the back window. The hotel has one shower for ten rooms (1 SF for five minutes). Walter is careful not to let his place get too hectic or big and enjoys sensitive Back Door travelers. He runs the hotel by himself, keeping it simple, but with class. This is a good place to receive mail from home (check the mail barrel in entry hall).

To some, Hotel Mittaghorn is a fire waiting to happen—with a kitchen that would never pass code, lumpy beds, teeny towels, and nowhere near enough plumbing—run by an eccentric grouch. These people enjoy Interlaken, Wengen, or Mürren, and that's where they should sleep. Be warned, you may meet more of my readers than you hoped for, but it's a fun crowd—an extended family (D-60–70 SF, T-85 SF, Q-105 SF, loft beds-25 SF, all with breakfast, CH-3826 Gimmelwald/ Bern, tel. 033/855-1658, SE). Reserve by telephone only, and then you must reconfirm by telephone the day before your arrival. Walter usually serves a cheap, simple spaghetti or soup supper. Off-season only, lofters pay just 20 SF for a bed with breakfast and can eat their evening picnic in the bar with a free pot of coffee or tea, courtesy of Walter. The hotel is closed mid-November through early May.

**Mountain Hostel** is goat-simple, as clean as its guests, cheap, and very friendly. Its 50 dorm beds are often taken in July and August, so call ahead (easy same-day telephone reservations, call after 10:00). The hostel has low ceilings, a self-serve kitchen (pack in groceries), and new plumbing. Petra Brunner has filled the place with flowers. This relaxed hostel survives with the help of its guests. Please read the signs, respect its rules, and leave it cleaner than you found it. Guests are asked to do a small duty. The place is one of those rare spots where a family atmosphere spontaneously combusts, and spaghetti becomes communal as it softens (15 SF per bed in six- to 15-bed rooms, showers-1 SF, no breakfast, hostel membership not required, 20 yards uphill from the lift station, tel. & fax 033/855-1704, SE).

Next door, **Pension Restaurant Gimmelwald** serves meals and offers pleasant rooms (D-90 SF, Db-110 SF) and sheetless dorm beds (20 SF on top floor, 25 SF in smaller rooms), including breakfast. It's closed in November and the first half of May (a minute's walk from gondola station, non-smoking, CC:VM, tel. & fax 033/855-1730, Nicole SE).

**Maria and Olle Eggimann** rent out three rooms in their Alpine-sleek chalet. These are the most comfortable rooms in town, but they're tough to get in the summer. Twelve-year town residents Maria and Olle, who job-share the village's only teaching position and raise three young children of their own, offer visitors a rare inside peek at this community (D-100 SF, Db with kitchenette-60 SF apiece for two or three people, optional breakfast 15 SF, last check-in 18:30, three-night minimum for advance reservations; from the gondola station, continue straight for 100 yards past the town's only intersection, B&B is on your left, CH-3826 Gimmelwald, tel. 033/855-3575, e-mail: oeggimann@bluewin.ch, SE fluently).

**Schalf im Stroh** ("Sleep in Straw") offers exactly that, in an actual barn. After the cows head for higher ground in the summer, the friendly von Allmen family hoses out their barn and fills it with straw and budget travelers. Blankets are free, but bring your own sheet, sleep sack, or sleeping bag. No beds, no bunks, no mattresses, no kidding (19 SF, 13 SF for kids under 12, breakfast included, showers-2 SF, open mid-June–mid-October, depending on grass and snow levels; from the lift, continue straight through the only intersection, barn marked "1995" is on your right, tel. 033/855-3381, fax 033/855-4681, NSE). The family also rents two of the town's cheapest double rooms (St-30 SF, Dt-55 SF, across from post office, shower in the barn a block away). The nicer rooms upstairs (with bath) require a four-night minimum stay.

**Eating in Gimmelwald:** Gimmelwald feeds its goats better than its people. The hostel has a decent members' kitchen but serves no food. There are no groceries in town. The wise and frugal pack in food from the Co-ops in Mürren or Lauterbrunnen or the Migros in Interlaken. Hostelers enjoy the communal kitchen followed by an evening of conversation, wine, and occasional local music in the hostel dining room. Walter's guests are best off eating at Walter's. Follow dinner with a Heidi Cocoa (cocoa *mit* peppermint schnapps) or Virgin Heidis. Affordable Swiss meals are also served at Pension Gimmelwald next to the hostel.

### Sleeping in Mürren
*(5,500 feet, tel. code: 033, zip code: 3825)*
Mürren is as pleasant as an Alpine resort can be. It's traffic-free, filled with bakeries, cafés, souvenirs, old-timers with walking sticks, GE employees enjoying incentive trips, and Japanese making movies of each other with a Fujichrome backdrop. Its chalets are prefab-rustic. Sitting on a ledge 2,000 feet above the Lauterbrunnen Valley, surrounded by a fortissimo chorus of mountains, it has all the comforts of home and then some, with Alp-high prices. Mürren's TI can find you a room, give hiking advice, rent mountain bikes (20 SF/half day, 30 SF/full

day), and change money. It's located in the Sportzentrum (TI open mid-July–mid-September 9:00–12:00 and 13:00–18:30, Thursday until 20:30, Saturday 13:00–18:00, Sunday 13:00–17:30, less off-season, tel. 033/856-8686, Web site: www.muerren.ch, e-mail: info@muerren.ch).

**Guesthouse Belmont** offers some of Mürren's best budget rooms. This is a friendly home away from home (S-45 SF, D-90 SF, Db-130 SF, includes breakfast, 35-SF beds in four-person dorms, closed November, CC:VMA, across from the train station, tel. 033/855-3535, fax 033/855-3531, SE).

The nearby **Hotel Alpenblick** (Db-130–140 SF, closed off-season; exit right from station, walk two minutes downhill, tel. 033/855-1327, fax 033/855-1391) and cliff-hanging **Hotel Alpina** (exit left from station, walk two minutes downhill, tel. 033/855-1361) also have affordable rooms.

**Chalet Fontana**, run by an Englishwoman, Denise Fussell, is worn and basic but a rare budget option in Mürren (35–45 SF per person in small doubles or triples with breakfast, 5 SF cheaper without breakfast, one three-bed room with kitchenette-45 SF per person, open mid-May–October, across the street from the Stägerstübli restaurant in the town center, tel. 033/855-2686, e-mail: 106501.2731@compuserve.com). If no one's home, check at the Ed Abegglen shop next door (tel. 033/855-1245, SE).

**Hotel Jungfrau** has pricey, plush rooms (Sb-90–115 SF, Db-140–190 SF) and also offers cheaper, slightly worn rooms in its neighboring lodge (Db-110–140 SF). Many rooms have views (elevator, includes free entrance to pool, CC:VMA, near TI and Sportzentrum, tel. 033/855-4545, fax 033/855-4549, Web site: www.muerren.ch/jungfrau, e-mail: jungfrau@muerren.ch).

**Hotel Alpenruh** is expensive and yuppie-rustic, but it's the only hotel in Mürren that's open year-round. Run by Andreas and Anne Marie Goetschi, former travelers with a great Back Door perspective, this hotel's comfortable rooms come with views and some balconies (Sb-80–100 SF, Db-160–200 SF depending on season, elevator, attached restaurant, sauna, free tickets for breakfast atop Schilthorn, CC:VMA, 10 yards from gondola station, tel. 033/855-1055, fax 033/855-4277).

**Eating in Mürren:** For a rare bit of ruggedness, eat at the Stägerstübli (10–30 SF lunches and dinners, closed Tuesday).

For picnic fixings, shop at the Co-op (normally open 8:00–12:00 and 14:00–18:30, closed afternoons on Tuesday and Saturday and all day Sunday).

## Sleeping in Wengen
### (4,200 feet, tel. code: 033, zip code: 3823)

Wengen, a fancy Mürren on the other side of the valley, has more tennis courts than budget beds. This traffic-free resort is an easy train ride above Lauterbrunnen and halfway up to Kleine Scheidegg and Männlichen.

**Hotel Bernerhof** has double rooms and dorm beds (D-90 SF, Db-130 SF, includes breakfast, dorm bed-20 SF, BYO sheet, tel. 033/855-2721, fax 033/855-3358). **Chalet Bergheim,** open June through mid-October, has reasonable doubles and six 20-SF dorm beds (plus 6 SF for sheets and 15 SF for breakfast, tel. 033/855-2755), and **Chalet Schweizerheim Garni** is decent (Db-120 SF, summer only, tel. 033/855-1581).

**Hotel Eden** has comfy rooms, an inviting breakfast room, and views (S-62 SF, D-116 SF, Db-144 SF, dorm beds-26 SF, breakfast for dormers-15 SF, tel. 033/855-1634, fax 033/855-3950, Kerstin Bucher SE). The same hotel runs **Eddy's Hostel**, a block away, with 33-SF dorm beds. Prices include 7-SF surcharge for one- to two-night stays.

## Sleeping in Kleine Scheidegg
### (6,762 feet, tel. code: 033, zip code: 3801)

For dorm beds with breakfast high in the mountains, sleep at Kleine Scheidegg's **Bahnhof Buffet** (38 SF per bed, tel. 033/855-1151) or at **Restaurant Grindelwaldblick** (32 SF for bed in 12-bed room, no sheets, open June–October, tel. 033/855-1374). Confirm price and availability before ascending.

## Sleeping near the Stechelberg Lift
### (2,800 feet, tel. code: 033, zip code: 3824)

The local **Naturfreundehaus Alpenhof**, at the far end of Lauterbrunnen Valley, is a rugged Alpine lodge for hikers (60 coed beds, four to eight per room, 17.50 SF per bed, two D-80 SF, breakfast-8 SF, dinner-14 SF, no sheets, closed November, get off bus at "Hotel Stechelberg" stop, tel. 033/855-1202). The neighboring **Hotel Stechelberg** has 20 clean and quiet rooms (S-45 SF, D-74–100 SF, Db-112–132 SF, CC:VMA, tel.

033/855-2921, SE). **Klara von Allmen** rents out three rooms in a quiet, scenic, and folksy setting (S-27 SF, D-50 SF, minimum two nights, just over the river behind the Stechelberg post office at big "Zimmer" sign, get off bus at "Stechelberg Post" stop, tel. 033/855-3930, some English spoken).

**Mountain Hotel Obersteinberg**, a 2.5 hour hike from Stechelberg, is primitive: no shower, hot water, or electricity. Candles light up the night (dorm beds-57 SF, S-74 SF, D-148 SF, open June–September, mules carry your bags if you're staying for a week, tel. 033/855-2033).

### Sleeping in Lauterbrunnen
*(2,600 feet, tel. code: 033, zip code: 3822)*
**Masenlager Stocki** is a great value (12 SF a night with sheets in an easygoing little 30-bed coed dorm with a kitchen, closed November–mid-December, across the river, take the first left, tel. 033/855-1754). **Chalet im Rohr** offers 26-SF beds in one- to four-bed rooms (near the church, tel. 033/855-1507). Hotel Jungfrau's fine 12-SF breakfast buffet is open to the public.

Two campgrounds just south of town work very hard to provide 15- to 25-SF beds. They each have dorms, two-, four-, and six-bed bungalows, no sheets, kitchen facilities, and big English-speaking tour groups. **Camping Jungfrau**, romantically situated just beyond the stones hurled by Staubach Falls, is huge and well-organized, with a Heidi Shop and clocks showing the time in Sydney and Vancouver (tel. 033/855-2010). It also has fancier cabins and trailers for the classier camper (18 SF per person). **Schützenbach Campground**, on the left just past Lauterbrunnen toward Stechelberg, is much simpler (tel. 033/855-1268).

### Sleeping in Isenfluh
*(3,560 feet, tel. code: 033, zip code: 3807)*
In the tiny hamlet of Isenfluh, which is smaller than Gimmelwald and offers even better views, **Pension Waldrand** rents six reasonable rooms (tel. 033/855-1227; hourly shuttle bus from Lauterbrunnen).

### Sleeping in Interlaken
*(tel. code: 033, zip code: 3800)*
I'd head for Gimmelwald. Interlaken is not the Alps. But if you

must stay, here are some good choices.

**Hotel Lotschberg**, with easy parking and a sun terrace, is run by English-speaking Susi and Fritz (Sb-98 SF, Db-135–180 SF, cheaper off-season, elevator, bar, laundry service-3 SF, free to check e-mail, CC:VMA, free pick-up from station or four-minute walk from the West Station, look for the wall painting on hotel, General Guisanstrasse 31, tel. 033/822-2545, fax 033/822-2579, Web site: www.beoswiss.ch/lotschberg, e-mail: lotschberg@InterlakenTourism.ch). They also run **Guest House Susi's B&B** in their backyard, which has simple, cozy, cheaper rooms (Sb-85 SF, Db-105 SF, apartments with kitchenettes for two people-100 SF; for four to five people-165 SF, cheaper off-season).

**Hotel Beau-Site** has bright, airy rooms and a large yard with deck chairs. Well-maintained with flowers and personal touches, this is a fine splurge (S-75 SF, Sb-130–158 SF, small D-110 SF, Db-200–250 SF, extra bed-45 SF, cheaper off-season, great views, free parking, CC:VMA, four-minute walk from West train station: following "Spital" signs from station, turn left on Bahnhofstrasse, cross the tracks and bridge, and turn left on Seestrasse, tel. 033/826-7575, fax 033/826-7585, run by the Ritter family).

**Happy Inn Lodge** has cheap rooms a five-minute walk from the West Station (D-60–74 SF, dorm bed-20 SF, breakfast-8 SF, their bar is a dive, Rosenstrasse 17, tel. 033/822-3225, fax 033/822-3268).

Backpackers enjoy **Balmer's Herberge**. This Interlaken institution is run by creative tornadoes of entrepreneurial energy, Eric and Katrin Balmer. With movies, ping-pong, a laundromat, bar, restaurant, secondhand English book-swapping library, tiny grocery, bike rental, currency exchange, rafting excursions, shuttle-bus service into the mountains, plenty of tips on budget eating and hiking, and a friendly, hardworking, mostly American staff, this little Nebraska is home for those who miss their fraternity (19–20 SF for dorm beds, 22–28 SF in doubles, triples, and quads, 12 SF in over-flow on-the-floor accommodations, all with breakfast, open year-round, CC:VMA, Haupstrasse 23, in Matten, a 15-minute walk from either Interlaken station, tel. 033/822-1961, fax 033/823-3261, SE). They recently opened up **Balmer's Tent** about 3 blocks away; you can stay in the huge tent for dorm prices.

## Transportation Connections—Interlaken

**By train to: Spiez** (2/hr, 15 min), **Brienz** (hrly, 20 min), **Bern** (hrly, 1 hr). While there are a few long trains from Interlaken, you'll generally connect from Bern.

**By train from Bern to: Lausanne** (hrly, 70 min) **Zurich** (hrly, 75 min), **Salzburg** (4/day, 8 hrs, transfers include Zurich), **Munich** (4/day, 5.5 hrs), **Frankfurt** (hrly, 4.5 hrs, transfers in Basel and Mannheim), **Paris** (4/day, 4.5 hrs).

**Interlaken to Gimmelwald:** Take the train from the Interlaken-East station to Lauterbrunnen, then cross the street to catch the funicular to Mürren. You'll ride up to Grütschalp, where a special scenic train (*Panorama Fahrt* in German) rolls you along the cliff into Mürren. From there, either walk an easy, paved 30 minutes downhill to Gimmelwald or walk ten minutes across Mürren to catch the gondola (7.20 SF and a five-minute steep uphill backtrack) to Gimmelwald. A good bad-weather option (or vice versa) is to ride the post bus from Lauterbrunnen (leaves at five minutes past the hour) to Stechelberg and the base of the Schilthornbahn (a big, gray gondola station, tel. 033/823-1444 or 033/555-2141).

By car, it's a 30-minute drive from Interlaken to Stechelberg. The pay parking lot (5 SF/day) at the gondola station is safe. Gimmelwald is the first stop above Stechelberg on the Schilthorn gondola (7.20 SF, two trips/hour at :25 and :55; get off at first stop, walk into the village, hard right at PTT, signs direct you up the path on a steep 300-yard climb to the chalet marked "Hotel"). This is my home in Switzerland, Walter's Hotel Mittaghorn. Note that for a week in early May and from mid-November through early December, the Schilthornbahn is closed for servicing.

# APPENZELL

Welcome to cowbell country. In moo-mellow and storybook-friendly Appenzell, you'll find the warm, intimate side of the land of staggering icy Alps. Savor Appenzell's cozy small-town ambience.

Appenzell is Switzerland's most traditional region—and the butt of much local humor because of it. This is "Landsgemeinde" country, where entire villages would meet in town squares to vote (featured on most postcard racks). Until 1991, the women of Appenzell couldn't vote on local issues.

A gentle beauty blankets the region overlooked by the 8,200-foot peak, Säntis. As you travel, you'll enjoy an ever-changing parade of finely carved chalets, traditional villages, and cows moaning "milk me." While farmers' daughters make hay in bikinis, old ladies walk the steep roads with scythes, looking as if they just pushed the Grim Reaper down the hill. When locals are asked about their cheese, they clench their fists as they answer, "It's the best." It is, without any doubt, the smelliest.

If you're here in early September, there's a good chance you'll get in on—or at least have your road blocked by—the ceremonial procession of flower-bedecked cows and whistling herders in traditional, formal outfits. The festive march down from the high pastures is a spontaneous move by the herding families, and when they finally do burst into town (a slow-motion Swiss Pamplona), the people become children again, dropping everything and running into the streets.

The center of the Appenzell region is Appenzell town. The nearby hut at Ebenalp, snuggled into a cliff, is my top choice for a home base.

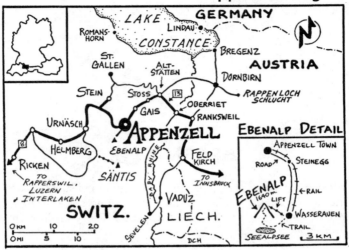

## Planning Your Time

The area's charms are subtle, prices are brutal, and its public transportation a little disappointing. For many on a fast trip with no car, the area is not worth the trouble. But by car it's a joy. And anyone hoping to get a broad feel for Switzerland has to stop here.

Ideally it's an interesting way for drivers to connect Tirol and Bavaria with the Berner Oberland (Jungfrau region): Drive in from Tirol in time to get up the lift to Ebenalp, descend the next morning and spend the day sampling the small town charms of Appenzell, and get to the Interlaken area that night.

## Getting Around Appenzell

Those with a car have the region by the tail. Those without will need more time and patience. An hourly train connects Appenzell with Wasserauen (20 min) and Herisau (40 min), from where bigger trains go hourly to St. Gallen (20 min) and Luzern (2 hrs). Regional buses connect all towns several times a day.

## Sights—Appenzell Region

**Appenzell Town**—In this traditional town, kids play "barn" instead of "house" while mom and dad watch yodeling on TV.

The tourist information office is on the main street, Haupt-gasse, next to the City Hall (TI open Monday–Friday 9:00–12:00 and 14:00–18:00, Saturday 9:00–12:00 and 14:00–17:00, tel. 071/788-9641). Ask about an Appenzeller folk evening (most nights, July–September, often free, dinner sometimes optional). The new folk museum next to the TI is good. Ride the elevator up to the sixth floor and work your way down through traditional costumes, living rooms, art, and crafts (5 SF, daily 10:00–12:00 and 14:00–17:00, ask for free loaner book in English). The Appenzeller beer is famous, good, and about the only thing cheap in the region. (For accommodations, see Sleeping, below.)

▲**Ebenalp**—This cliff-hanging hut is a thin-air alternative to Appenzell town. Ride the lift from Wasserauen, 5 miles south of Appenzell town, to Ebenalp (5,000 feet). On the way up, you'll get a sneak preview of Ebenalp's cave church and the cliffside boardwalk that leads to the guest house. From the top, enjoy a sweeping view of the entire region all the way to Lake Constance (Bodensee).

From the top of the lift, take a 12-minute hike downhill through a prehistoric cave (it's dark—descend holding the rail-ing and you'll come to daylight), past a hermit's home (now a tiny museum, always open) and the 400-year-old Wildkirchi cave church (hermit monks lived there from 1658–1853), to a 150-year-old guest house built precariously into the cliffside. Originally used by pilgrims who climbed here to have the her-mit pray for them, Berggasthaus Ascher now welcomes tourists (see Sleeping, below).

From Ebenalp's sunny cliff perch, you can almost hear the cows munching on the far side of the valley. Only the parasailers, like neon jellyfish, tag your world 20th-century. In the distance, nestled below Säntis Peak, is the Seealpsee (lake). The interesting 1.5-hour hike down to the lake is steep but a pleasure.

The Ebenalp lift runs twice an hour until 19:00 in July and August, 18:00 in June and September; otherwise, the last lift is at 17:00 (21 SF round-trip, 17 SF one-way, pick up the free one-page hiking map, tel. 071/799-1212).

▲**Stein**—In the town of Stein, the Appenzell Showcase Cheese Dairy (Schaukäserei) is open daily from 8:00 to 19:00 (cheese-making normally 9:00–14:00). It's fast, free, and well-explained in a 15-minute English video and the free English brochure (with cheese recipes). The lady at the cheese counter loves to cut it so you can sample it. They also have yogurt and cheap boxes of cold iced tea for sale. Stein's TI and a great folk (*Volkskunde*) moo-seum are next door. This cow-culture museum with old-fashioned cheese-making demonstrations, peasant houses, fascinating and complex embroidering machinery, lots of cow art, and folk craft demonstrations is not worth the 7 SF if you've seen the similar museum in Appenzell (Monday 13:30–17:00, Tuesday–Sunday 10:00–12:00 and 13:30–17:00, may open a little early if you ask nicely, closed in winter, tel. 071/368-5056).

▲Urnäsch—This appealing one-street town has my nomination for Europe's cutest museum. The Appenzeller Museum, on the town square, brings this region's folk customs to life. Warm and homey, it's a happy little honeycomb of Appenzeller culture (4 SF, daily in summer 13:30–17:00, less in spring and fall, closed in winter, good English description brochure, will open for groups of five or more if you call the director at 071/364-1487 or 071/364-2322). Gasthaus Ochsen is a fine traditional hotel with good food, low ceilings, and wonderful atmosphere (D-80 SF, three doors down from the museum, tel. 071/364-1117). Peek into its old restaurant.

## Sleeping in Appenzell
**(1.5 SF = about $1, tel. code: 071, zip code: 9050)**
Sleep Code: **S**=Single, **D**=Double/Twin, **T**=Triple, **Q**=Quad, **b**=bathroom, **t**=toilet only, **s**=shower only, **CC**=Credit Card (**V**isa, **M**asterCard, **A**mex), **SE**=Speaks English, **NSE**=No English. My top choice for a place to stay is Ebenalp (below).

### Sleeping in the Town of Appenzell
The town is small but quite touristy. Hotels are expensive; the Zimmer are a 6-block walk from the center.

**Gasthaus Hof** offers the best cheap beds in town in its modern *Matratzenlager* (25 SF per bed in six- to eight-bed rooms with breakfast, sheets-6 SF, centrally located just off the Landsgemeindeplatz, tel. 071/787-2210, Herr Dörig). Outside of peak times, you'll be sleeping alone in a warehouse of bunkbeds. They also have a few reasonable doubles. Gasthaus Hof serves a 20-SF *Rösti*, the area's cheesy potato specialty.

**Hotel Adler**, above a delicious café in a fine location, offers three kinds of rooms: modern; newly refurbished traditional Appenzeller; or old and basic (D-100 SF, Db-130–140 SF, elevator, CC:VMA, a block from the TI, just over the bridge, tel. 071/787-1389, fax 071/787-1365, e-mail: adlerhotelappenzell@bluewin.ch, Franz Leu SE). **Hotel Taube** is also good (D-120 SF, Db-140 SF, CC:VM, between the station and the main street, Hirschengasse 8, tel. 071/787-1149, fax 071/787-5633). The only inexpensive hotel in town, **Pension Union**, is a peaceful, grandfatherly old place (D-70 SF, Db-80 SF, between the station and the main street, tel. 071/787-1420, NSE).

**Haus Lydia** is an Appenzell-style home filled with tourist information and a woodsy folk atmosphere, on the edge of town with a garden and a powerful mountain view. This wonderful six-room Zimmer is run by friendly Frau Mock-Inauen (D-75 SF, great breakfast; east of the center over the bridge, past the Mercedes-Esso station, take next right; Eggerstandenstrasse 53, CH 9050 Appenzell, tel. 071/787-4233). **Gastezimmer Koller-Rempfler** is a stern place a few blocks before Haus Lydia (D-72 SF, Db-82 SF for one night stays, Eggerstandenstrasse 9, tel. 071/787-2117). **Johann Ebneter** runs a friendly and modern Zimmer in the same area (D-80 SF, Mooshaldenstrasse 14, tel. 071/787-3487, SE).

### Sleeping in Ebenalp

There's no reason to sleep in Appenzell town. The Ebenalp lift, across from the tiny Wasserauen train station, is a few minutes' drive (or a 20-minute bus ride) south. For a memorable experience, stay in **Berggasthaus Ascher**. Their 150-year-old house has only rainwater and no shower. Friday and Saturday nights are crowded and noisy with up to 40 people (literally four hikers to three mattresses) and parties going into the wee hours. Otherwise you'll normally get a small woody dorm to yourself. The hut is actually built into the cliffside; its back wall is the rock. From the toilet you can study this Alpine architecture. Sip your coffee on the deck, behind drips from the gnarly overhang a hundred yards above. The goats have their cliff hut adjacent. The guestbook goes back to 1941, and the piano in the comfortable dining/living room was brought in by helicopter. For a great 45-minute pre-dinner check-out-the-goats hike, take the high trail towards the lake; circle clockwise back up the peak to the lift and down the way you originally came. Claudia can show you the rock-climbing charts (15 SF for a dorm bed, blankets but no sheets required or provided, 10 SF for breakfast,

14-SF Rösti dinners, open daily May–October, 12 minutes by steep trail below top of lift, 9057 Weissbad, tel. 071/799-1142, run by Claudia and Bennie Knechtle-Wyss, their five little children, two pigs, and 40 sheep).

Less atmospheric and more normal is the **Berg Gasthaus Ebenalp**, just above the lift. It's booked long in advance on Saturdays but wide open otherwise (25-SF dorm bed with blankets but no sheets, breakfast included, D-80 SF, coin-op shower, tel. 071/799-1194, Sutter family). From Wasserauen at the base of the lift, you can drive up the private road to **Berggasthaus Seealpsee**, situated on an idyllic Alpine lake by the same name (D-80 SF, loft dorm beds with sheets-12 SF plus 10 SF for breakfast, 9057 Weissbad, tel. 071/799-1140, Dörig family).

## Route Tips for Drivers

**Hall to Appenzell (130 miles):** From the Austria/Switzerland border town of Feldkirch, it's an easy scenic drive through Altstätten and Gais to Appenzell. At the Swiss border you must buy an annual road-use permit for 40 SF (or the AS equivalent). Anyone driving on a Swiss autobahn without this tax sticker is likely to be fined.

From picturesque Altstätten, wind up a steep mountain pass and your world becomes HO gauge. The Stoss railroad station, straddling the summit of a mountain pass, has glorious views. Park here, cross to the chapel, and walk through the meadow—past munching cows, to the monument that celebrates a local Appenzeller victory over Habsburg Austria. From this spectacular spot, you can see the Rhine Valley, Liechtenstein, and the Austrian Alps—and munch a memorable picnic.

**Side Trip through Liechtenstein?** If you must see the tiny and touristy country of Liechtenstein, take this 30-minute detour: From Feldkirch south on E77 (follow "FL" signs), drive through Schaan to Vaduz, the capital. Park near the City Hall, post office, and tourist office. Passports can be stamped (for 2.50 SF) in the tourist office. Stamp collectors make a bee-line for the post office across the street, while the prince looks down on his 4-by-12-mile country from his castle, a 20-minute hike above Vaduz (it's closed but offers a fine view; catch the trail from Café Berg). Liechtenstein's banks (open until 16:30) sell Swiss francs at uniform and acceptable rates. To leave, cross the Rhine at Rotenboden, immediately get on the autobahn heading north from Sevelen to the Oberriet exit, and check another country off your list.

**Appenzell to Interlaken/Gimmelwald (120 miles):** It's a three-hour drive from Appenzell to Ballenberg and another hour from there to the Gimmelwald lift. Head west out of Appenzell town on the Urnäsch road, taking the first right (after about 2 miles, easy to miss, sign to Herisau/Wattwil) to Stein. In Stein, "Schaukäserei" signs direct you to the big, modern cheese dairy. From there, wind scenically south to Urnäsch and down the small road (signs to Hemberg) to Wattwil. Somewhere along the Urnäsch–Hemberg road, stop to ask an old local if this is the way to Wattwil (or San Jose)—just to hear the local dialect and to see the healthy outdoor twinkle in his or her eyes. Drive through Ricken, into the town of Rapperswil. Once in Rapperswil, follow green signs to Zurich over the long lake bridge, and southward, following signs to Einsiedeln and Gotthard. You'll go through the town of Schwyz, the historic core of Switzerland that gave its name to the country.

From Brunnen, one of the busiest, most expensive to build, and most impressive roads in Switzerland wings you along the Urnersee. It's dangerously scenic, so stop at the parking place after the first tunnel (on right, opposite Stoos turnoff), where you can enjoy the view and a rare Turkish toilet. Follow signs to Gotthard through Flüelen, then autobahn for Luzern, vanishing into a long tunnel that should make you feel a little better about your 40-SF autobahn sticker. Exit at the Stans-Nord exit (signs to Interlaken). Go along the Alpnachersee south toward Sarnen. Continue past Sarnensee to Brienzwiler before Brienz. A sign at Brienzwiler will direct you to the Ballenberg Freilicht (Swiss Open-Air Museum)/Ballenberg Ost. You can park here, but I prefer the west entrance, a few minutes down the road near Brienz.

From Brienzwiler, take the new autobahn to Interlaken along the south side of Lake Brienz. Cruise through the old resort town down Interlaken's main street from the Ost Bahnhof, past the cow field with a great Eiger-Jungfrau view on your left and grand old hotels, the TI, post office, and banks on your right, to the West Bahnhof at the opposite end of town. Park there. Gimmelwald is a 30-minute drive and a five-minute gondola ride away.

# WEST SWITZERLAND

Enjoy urban Switzerland at its best in the charming, compact capital of Bern. Ramble the ramparts of Murten, Switzerland's best-preserved medieval town, and resurrect the ruins of an ancient Roman capital in nearby Avenches. The Swiss countryside offers up chocolates, Gruyères cheese, and a fine folk museum. On Lake Geneva, the Swiss Riviera, explore the romantic Château Chillon and stylishly syncopated Montreux.

South of Murten, the predominant language is French, *s'il vous plaît*, and, as you'll see, that means more than language.

## Planning Your Time

The region doesn't merit a lot of time on a quick trip. Bern, Lake Geneva, and Murten are each worth half a day. Bern is easily seen en route to Murten—*Morat*, if you're speaking French. I'd establish a home base in Murten from which to explore the southwest in a day by car. Without a car, use a better transportation hub such as Bern, Montreux, or Lausanne.

For a day by car from Murten: 8:45-depart; 10:00-tour Château Chillon; 11:30-quick visit or drive through Montreux, Vevey, and the Corniche de Laveau; 14:00-cheese-making demo in Gruyères or Moleson; 15:30-Gruerien folk museum in Bulle; 18:00-Roman ruins in Avenches; 19:00-home in Murten for salad by the sea.

## BERN

Stately but human, classy but fun, the Swiss capital gives you the most (maybe even the only) enjoyable look at urban Switzerland. User-friendly Bern is packed into a peninsula bounded by the Aare River.

## West Switzerland

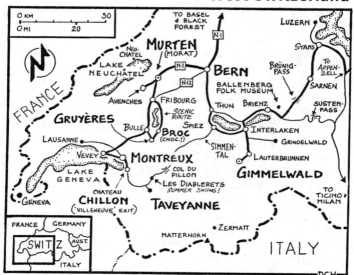

## Orientation

**Tourist Information:** Start your visit at the TI inside the train station (daily 9:00–20:30, until 18:30 in winter, tel. 031/311-6611). Pick up a map of Bern (and any other Swiss cities you'll be visiting), a list of city sights, and information on the Parliament tour, the clock, or other sights.

**Getting Around Bern:** Bern is easy. From the train station it's all downhill through the heart of town to the bear pits and Rose Garden (a 30-minute stroll), then catch trolley #12 back up to the station (buy the cheapest ticket from the machine at the stop, 1.50 SF). *Zeitung*, the city newspaper, offers loaner 21-speed bikes (free, leave passport and 20 SF for deposit, Zeughausgasse 14, in the old town, tel. 031/327-1191, NSE).

## Sights—Bern

▲▲**The Old Town**—Window-shopping and people-watching through dilly dally arcaded streets and busy market squares are Bern's top attractions. There are over 3 miles of arcades in this tiny (130,000 people) capital. This is my kind of shopping town: Prices are so high there's no danger of buying. Shops are open Monday through Friday from 9:00 to 18:00, Thursday until 21:00, Saturday from 8:00 to 16:00, and closed Sunday.

**Clock Tower (Zytglogge-turm)**—The clock performs a few minutes before each hour. Apparently this slowest-moving five-minute non-event in Europe was considered entertaining in 1530. To pass the time during the performance, read the TI's brochure explaining what's so interesting about the fancy old clock. Enthusiasts can tour the medieval mechanics daily at 16:30 (6 SF at the TI or on the spot, May–October).

**Cathedral**—The 1421 Swiss late-Gothic *Münster*, or cathedral, is worth a look (Tuesday–Sunday 10:00–17:00, closed Monday, shorter hours off-season). Climb the spiral staircase 100 yards above the town for the view, exercise, and a chance to meet a live church watchman. Peter Probst and his wife, Sigi, live way up there, watching over the church, answering questions, and charging tourists 3 SF for the view.

**Parliament (Bundeshaus)**—You can tour Switzerland's imposing Parliament building (free 45-minute tours most days at 9:00, 10:00, 11:00, 14:00, 15:00, and 16:00; closed most of March, June, September, and December when in session, tour canceled if less than five people show up, tel. 031/322-8522 to confirm). Don't miss the view from the Bundeshaus terrace. You may see some national legislators, but you wouldn't know it—everything looks very casual for a national capital.

**Einstein's House**—Einstein did much of his most important thinking while living in this house on the old town's main drag. It was just another house to me, but I guess everything's relative (2 SF, Tuesday–Friday 10:00–17:00, Saturday 10:00–16:00, closed Sunday, Monday, December, and January, Kramgasse 49).

**▲Bear Pits and Rose Garden**—The symbol of Bern is the bear, and some lively ones frolic their days away (8:00–18:00) to the delight of locals and tourists alike in the big, barren, concrete pits (*Graben*) just over the river. Up the paved pathway is the Rosengarten and a restaurant—worth the walk for the great city view.

**▲▲The Berner Swim**—For something to write home about, join the local merchants, legislators, publishers, students, and carp in a lunchtime float down the Aare River. The Bernese, proud of their very clean river and their basic ruddiness, have a tradition—sort of a wet, urban paseo. On hot summer days, they hike upstream five to 30 minutes and float back down to

# Bern

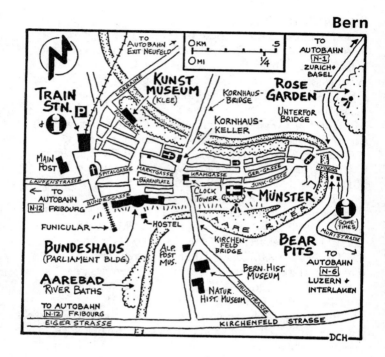

the excellent (and free) riverside baths and pools (*Aarebad*) just below the Parliament building. While the locals make it look easy, this is dangerous—the current is swift, and if you miss the last pole, you're history. If the river is a bit much, you're welcome to enjoy just the Aarebad. If the river is not enough, a popular day trip is to raft all the way from Thun to Bern.

▲▲**Museum of Fine Arts (Kunstmuseum)**—While it features 1,000 years of local art and some Impressionism, the real hit is its fabulous collection of Paul Klee's playful paintings. If you don't know Klee, I'd love to introduce you (6 SF, Tuesday 10:00–21:00, Wednesday–Sunday 10:00–17:00, closed Monday, 4 blocks from station, Holdergasse 12, tel. 031/311-0944).

**Other Bern Museums**—Across the bridge from the Parliament building on Helvetiaplatz are several museums (Alpine, Berner History, Postal) that sound more interesting than they are. Nearly all are open from 10:00 to 17:00 and closed on Monday.

## Sleeping in Bern
**(1.5 SF = about $1, tel. code: 031)**

Sleep Code: **S**=Single, **D**=Double/Twin, **T**=Triple, **Q**=Quad, **b**=bathroom, **t**=toilet only, **s**=shower only, **CC**=Credit Card (Visa, MasterCard, Amex), **SE**=Speaks English, **NSE**=No English. These are in the old town, about a ten-minute walk from the station.

**Hotel National** has bright, well-furnished rooms with big windows and street noise (S-60–75 SF, Sb-85–110 SF, D-100–120 SF, Db-120–150 SF, apartment-170–260 SF, elevator, CC:VMA, near station and old town, Hirschengraben 24, 3011-Bern, tel. 031/381-1988, fax 031/381-6878).

**Hotel Goldener Schlüssel** is an old, basic, comfortable, crank-'em-out hotel in the center (S-75 SF, Sb-98 SF, D-110 SF, Db-139 SF, Tb-178 SF, elevator, CC:VMA, Rathausgasse 72, 3011 Bern, tel. 031/311-0216, fax 031/311-5688).

**Hotel Zum Goldenen Adler**, in the old town, has comfy (but worn and smoky) rooms with all the amenities (Sb-100–130 SF, Db-130–180 SF, elevator, Gerechtigkeitsgasse 7, 3011 Bern, tel. 031/311-1725, fax 031/311-3761).

Bern's big, newly renovated, sterile, well-run **IYHF hostel** has four- to 26-bed rooms and provides an all-day lounge, laundry machines, and cheap meals (dorm beds-18 SF, non-members-23 SF, breakfast 6-SF, office open 7:00–9:30 and 15:00–24:00, down the stairs from the Parliament building, by the river at Weihergasse 4, 3005 Bern, tel. 031/311-6316).

## Transportation Connections—Bern

**By train to: Murten** (hrly, 30 min, change in Kerzers), **Lausanne** (2/hr, 70 min), **Interlaken** (hrly, 1 hr), **Zurich** (2/hr, 75 min), **Fribourg** (2/hr, 30 min), **Munich** (4/day, 5.5 hrs), **Frankfurt** (4.5 hrs), **Paris** (4/day, 4.5 hrs).

# MURTEN

The finest medieval ramparts in Switzerland surround the 4,600 people of Murten. We're on the lingua-cusp of Switzerland: 25 percent of Murten speaks French; a few miles to the south and west, nearly everyone does. Murten is a mini-Bern with three parallel streets, the middle one nicely arcaded with breezy outdoor cafés and elegant shops (closed Monday). Its castle is romantically set, overlooking the Murtensee and the rolling vineyards of gentle Mount Vully in the distance. Try some Vully wine. Murten is touristic but seems to be enjoyed mostly by its own people. Nearby Avenches, with its Roman ruins, glows at sunset.

The only required sightseeing is to do the rampart ramble (free, always open, easy stairway access on east side of town). Notice the old town clock reconstructed in the base of the tower (behind the Hotel Ringmauer) and be glad you have a watch. The town history museum in an old mill is not quite worth a look (closed Monday).

The lakefront offers a popular but pricey restaurant (Des Bains), a swimming pool with a sauna, a lovely promenade path along the lake, and one-hour lake cruises (free with train passes, daily in summer at 15:40). Rent a bike at the train station for a lakeside ride (17 SF/half day, 21 SF/full day).

## Orientation (tel. code: 026)

**Tourist Information:** Murten's TI tries to be helpful, but there's not much to say (April–October Monday–Friday 10:00–12:00 and 14:30–18:00, Saturday 10:00–12:00, closed Sunday, tel. 026/670-5112). Ask about their free town walks (10:30 in the summer).

**Arrival in Murten:** Exit right from the station, angle left uphill on Bahnhofstrasse, and turn right through the town gate (a three-minute walk).

## Sights—Avenches, Near Murten

Avenches, 4 miles south of Murten, was Aventicum, the Roman capital of the Confederation Helvetica. Back then its population was 50,000. Today it could barely fill the well-worn ruins of its 15,000-seat Roman amphitheater. You can tour the Roman museum (Tuesday–Sunday 10:00–12:00 and 13:00–17:00, closed Monday, near the dinky amphitheater in the town center), but the best experience is some quiet time at sunset at the evocative Roman amphitheater in the fields, a half-mile walk out of town (free, always open). Avenches, with a pleasant, small-French-town feel, is a quieter place to stay than Murten. It also makes an easy day trip. The TI is a seven-minute uphill walk from the station (TI tel. 026/675-1159).

# Sleeping and Eating in Murten and Avenches
**(1.5 SF = about $1, tel. code: 026)**

## *Sleeping and Eating in Murten*
**Hotel Ringmauer** (German for "ramparts") is characteristic, a block from the center, with showers and toilets within a dash of each room (S-60 SF, D-105 SF, attached restaurant, near wall on the side farthest from the lake, CC:VM, Deutsche Kirchgasse 2, tel. 026/670-1101, fax 026/672-2083).

**Hotel Murtenhof** is a worthwhile splurge with all the comforts and a lake view (Sb-90–155 SF, Db-130–210 SF, extra person-50 SF, CC:VMA, next to castle on Rathausgasse, tel. 026/670-5656, fax 026/670-5059, SE).

I eat on Hotel Murtenhof's terrace every night for their salad bar (summer only): 7.50 SF for a small plate, 15 SF for the big one; the small one—carefully stacked—is plenty, and comes with wonderful bread and a sunset over the lake. The small plate is meant as a side dish (no bread), but, if you can handle the ridicule and don't mind being seated in back or outside, the big boss assured me you can eat just a small salad plate stacked high and the waiters will even bring you a piece of bread and free water. The romantic terrace is a good place to try the Vully wine—just point to the vineyards across the lake (restaurant open 6:30–23:30 and closed Monday).

**Hotel Bahnhof**, just across the street from the train station, is a last resort (S-60 SF, Ss-70 SF, D-100 SF, Ds-120 SF, CC:VMA, Bahnhofstrasse 14, tel. 026/670-2256, NSE).

The Migros and Co-op supermarkets, just outside three of the town gates, have cafeterias (closed Sunday).

## *Sleeping in and near Avenches*
The Avenches **IYHF hostel**, the only hostel in the area, is a beauty. It's run by the Dhyaf family, with four- to eight-bed rooms, a homey TV room, ping-pong, a big backyard, and a very quiet setting near the Roman theater (23 SF for bed, sheets, and breakfast, more for non-members, office open 7:00–9:30 and 17:00–22:30, 3 blocks from the center at the medieval *lavoir* or laundry, Rue du Lavoir 5, 1580 Avenches, tel. 026/675-2666, fax 026/675-2717).

Friendly **Elisabeth Clement-Arnold** rents out a room in her house (Sb-30 SF, Db-50 SF, rue Centrale 5, 1580 Avenches, tel. & fax 026/675-3031).

**Auberge de l'Ecusson Vaudois** is the only hotel in the small village of Oleyres, 3 km from Avenches (Sb-60 SF, Db-92 SF, dorm bed-24 SF, all with breakfast, 1589 Oleyres, tel. & fax 026/675-1087). It's run by Madame Glauser, a big Elvis fan who makes frequent trips to Memphis.

## Tranportation Connections—Murten
**By train to: Avenches** (hrly, 10 min), **Bern** (hrly, 30 min, change in Kerzers), **Fribourg** (hrly, 30 min), **Lausanne** (hrly, 75 min, transfer in Fribourg).

# SOUTHWEST SWISS COUNTRYSIDE
The French Swiss countryside is sprinkled with tasty chocolates, summer skiing, smelly cheese, and sleepy cows. If you're traveling between Murten, Montreux, and Interlaken, take in a few of the countryside's sights, tastes, and smells.

## Getting Around the Countryside
Cross-country buses use Fribourg and Bulle as hubs. For example: **Bulle–Gruyères** (7/day, 15 min), **Fribourg–Bulle** (hrly, 45 min), **Avenches–Fribourg** (7/day, 30 min), **Murten–Fribourg** (hrly, 30 min).

## Sights—Swiss Countryside
**Caillers Chocolate Factory**—The town of Broc is chock full of mourning chocoholics. The last great Swiss chocolate factory tour is now dead . . . for hygienic reasons. While you can no longer drool in front of a molten river of your favorite chocolate, you can see a 40-minute movie and stuff yourself with free melt-in-your-hands samples at Caillers, the smell of which dominates the town (free, Monday–Friday, April–June and August–mid-November, closed July, follow signs to Nestlé and Broc Fabrique, call one day in advance to reserve, tel. 026/921-5151). Broc town is just the sleepy, sweet-smelling home of the chocolate-makers. It has a small, very typical hotel, the Auberge des Montagnards (D-70 SF, great Gruyères view, elegant dining room, tel. 026/921-1526). From Bulle, trains run hourly to Broc (10 min).

▲▲**Musée Gruèrien**—Somehow the unassuming little town of Bulle built a refreshing, cheery folk museum that manages to teach you all about life in these parts and leave you feeling very good. It's small and easy (4 SF plus 1 SF for the excellent

English guidebook; Tuesday–Saturday 10:00–12:00 and 14:00–17:00, Sunday 14:00–17:00, closed Monday, tel. 026/912-7260). When it's over, the guide reminds you, "The Golden Book of Visitors awaits your signature and comments. Don't you think this museum deserves another visit? Thank you!"

▲**Gruyères**—This ultra-touristy town, famous for its cheese, fills its fortified little hilltop like a bouquet. Its ramparts are a park, and the ancient buildings serve the tourist crowds. The castle is mediocre, and you don't need to stay long, but make a short stop for the setting. Minimize your walk by driving up to the second parking lot. Hotels in Gruyères are expensive.

▲▲**Gruyères Fromagerie**—There are two very different cheese-making exhibits to choose from. Five miles above Gruyères, a dark and smoky 17th-century farmhouse in Moleson gives a fun look at the old and smelly craft (3 SF, daily 9:30–18:30, mid-May–mid-October, TI tel. 026/921-2434). Closer, slicker, and very modern, the cheese-production center at the foot of Gruyères town (follow "Fromagerie" signs) opens its doors to tourists with a good continuous English audiovisual presentation (free, daily 8:00–18:30). Cheese is made at each place (usually 10:00–11:00 and 15:00–16:00). The cute cheese shop in the modern center has lunches and picnic stuff (closed from 12:00–13:30).

**Glacier des Diablerets**—For a grand Alpine trip to the tip of a 10,000-foot peak, take the three-part lift from Reusch or Col du Pillon. A quick trip takes about 90 minutes and costs 40 SF. You can stay for lunch. From the top, on a clear day, you can see the Matterhorn and even a bit of Mont Blanc, Europe's highest mountain. This is a good chance to do or watch some summer skiing. Normally expensive and a major headache, it isn't bad here. A lift ticket and rental skis, poles, boots, and a heavy coat cost about 65 SF. The slopes close at 14:00. The base of the lift is a two-hour drive from Murten or Gimmelwald. From Montreux, it's a two-hour bus ride (7/day, transfer in Gstaad Bahnhof).

▲▲**Taveyanne**—This enchanting and remote hamlet is a huddle of log cabins used by cowherds in the summer. These days the hamlet's old bar is a restaurant serving a tiny community of vacationers and hikers. Taveyanne is 2 miles off the main road between Col de la Croix and Villars. A small sign points down a tiny road to a jumble of huts and snoozing cows stranded at 5,000 feet. The inn is Refuge de Taveyanne (1882

Gryon), where the Seibenthal family serves hearty meals in a prize-winning rustic setting with no electricity, low ceilings, and a huge charred fireplace. Consider sleeping in their primitive loft. It's never full (10 SF, five mattresses, access by a ladder outside, urinate with the cows, open May–October, closed Tuesday except in July and August, tel. 024/498-1947). A fine opportunity to really know bell prize-winning cows.

## LAKE GENEVA (LAC LEMAN)
This is the Swiss Riviera. Separating France and Switzerland, surrounded by Alps, and lined with a collage of castles, museums, spas, resort towns, and vineyards, Lake Geneva's crowds are understandable. This area is so beautiful that Charlie Chaplin and Idi Amin both chose it as their second home.

## Getting Around Lake Geneva
Buses connect towns along Lake Geneva every 15 minutes. Boats carry visitors comfortably to all sights of importance. The boat ride from Lausanne to Chillon takes two hours with stops in Vevey and Montreux (19 SF, 5-SF supplement for steamers, Eurailers sail free, four trips daily in each direction, tel. 021/617-0666). The short Montreux–Château Chillon cruise is fun even for those with a car (6 SF, 20 min). Trains connect Lausanne, Montreux, and Villeneuve hourly.

## Sights—Lake Geneva
▲▲▲Château Chillon—This wonderfully preserved 13th-century castle, set wistfully at the edge of Lake Geneva, is a joy. Follow the free English brochure from one fascinating room to the next, enjoying tingly views, the dank prison, battle-scarred weapons, mobile furniture, and 700-year-old toilets. The 130-step climb to the top of the keep (#25 in the brochure) isn't worth the time or sweat. Curl up on a windowsill to enjoy the lake (7.50 SF, 1.50 SF extra to join a tour, private tours for 40 SF, daily 9:00–18:15, less off-season, easy parking, tel. 021/963-3912, call to see if an English tour group is scheduled). Coming by train, get off at Veytaux-Chillon and walk a few minutes along the lake to the castle.
Villeneuve—This is a relatively run-down little resort a 30-minute walk beyond Château Chillon. The train station is a block from the beach promenade, main street (Grand–Rue), and TI (Monday 13:30–18:00, Tuesday–Friday 9:00–12:30 and

13:30–18:00, Saturday 9:00–12:30, closed Sunday, tel. 021/960-2286). Visit here only if you need an affordable place to sleep (see Sleeping, below).

**Montreux**—This expensive resort has a famous jazz festival each July. The Montreux TI has a list of moderate rooms in the center (TI tel. 021/962-8484). Hotel-Restuarant du Pont offers decent rooms and great spaghetti (Db-120 SF, Rue du Pont 12, tel. 021/963-2249).

**Vevey**—Near Montreux, Vevey is a smaller and more comfortable resort town.

**Corniche de Lavaux**—The rugged Swiss Wine Road swerves through picturesque towns and the stingy vineyards that produce most of Switzerland's tasty but expensive *Fendant* wine. Hikers can take the boat to Cully and explore on foot from there. A car tour is quick and frightening (from Montreux, go west along the lake through Vevey, following blue signs to Lausanne along the waterfront, taking the Moudon/Chexbres exit). Explore some of the smaller roads.

**Geneva**—This big city bores me. It's sterile, cosmopolitan, expensive, and full of executives, diplomats, and tourists.

## LAUSANNE

This is the most interesting city on the lake. Peek in its impressive cathedral and stroll through the hilly, colorful old town—the ritzy shopping street is Rue Bourg and the liveliest square is Place de la Palud (the mechanical puppet show above the *Pharmacie* tells a story in French on the hour). Open-air markets sprawl every Wednesday and Saturday morning from St. Francis Church to the town hall. Climb up to the 13th-century cathedral for the view (2 SF to climb the tower, but the view from the terrace is free).

### Orientation (tel. code: 021)

**Tourist Information:** Lausanne has two TIs, one in the train station (Monday–Friday 9:00–20:00, weekends 10:00–19:00) and the other at Ouchy, on the shorefront (Monday–Friday 8:00–19:00, weekends 9:00–18:00, tel. 021/613-7321). Skip the museum pass. Ask if there are free concerts at the cathedral and any walking tours in English (the twice-daily walking tours offered May–September are "subject to the availability of an English-speaking guide," 10 SF, tel. 021/321-7766).

**Helpful Hints:** The Laundromat closest to the train station is Quick-Wash (open Monday–Saturday 8:00–21:30, Sunday 11:00–21:00, Boulevard de Grancy 44).

## Getting Around Lausanne

The city is steeper than it is big. A five-stop metro connects the upper part of Lausanne (called the old town, *vielle ville*, or *centre ville*) with the train station (about mid-way) and ends at Ouchy (OO-shee), the lakefront district. The cost is 2.20 SF (tickets good for one hour on buses, too). You can walk, but even locals use the metro. Buy your ticket from the ticket window. The train station's metro stop is directly across the street from the station. If you take a bus, buy your ticket from the yellow machine at the bus stop before boarding (2.20 SF; the cheaper 1.30-SF ticket is good for only three stops). The day pass, which covers both the metro and the bus, is a good deal if you take three trips or more (6.5 SF).

The train station rents bikes (17 SF/half day, 21 SF/full day, plus 6 SF to drop off at another station, no deposit needed except address and passport number).

## Sights—Lausanne

**Collection de l'Art Brut**—This fascinating and thought-provoking collection of art was produced by those who have been labeled criminal or crazy by society (6 SF, Tuesday–Sunday 11:00–13:00 and 14:00–18:00, closed Monday, bus #3 from the station, follow signs to Palais de Beaulieu, 11 Avenue des Bergieres, tel. 021/647-5435).

**Olympics Museum**—This new high-tech museum includes an extensive film archive of thrilling moments in the history of the games (14 SF, daily 10:00–19:00, Thursday until 21:30).

**City History Museum**—This museum is notable for its 1:200-scale model of Lausanne in the 17th century, accompanied by an audiovisual presentation. Before paying the 4-SF admission, ask when the next English showing is scheduled (Tuesday–Sunday 10:00–18:00, Thursday until 20:00, closed Monday). The museum is right next to the cathedral and the viewpoint terrace.

## Sleeping in Lausanne

**(1.5 SF = about $1, tel. code: 021, zip code: 1007)**
Breakfast is included unless otherwise noted.

**Jeunotel**, with concrete walls and cell-block rooms, is astonishingly stark, but clean and affordable. The main difference between this hotel and a minimum-security prison is that you've got the key (dorm bed=26 SF, S-65 SF, Sb-75 SF, D-74 SF, Db-92 SF, T-78 SF, breakfast-3 SF, some rooms with fridges, easy parking, any age welcome, attached restaurant, CC:VMA, Chemin du Bois-de-Vaux 36, tel. 021/626-0222, fax 021/626-0226, SE). From the train station, take the metro to Ouchy, then bus #2 to the Bois-de-Vaux stop (you'll see signs for the hotel, which is just a block from the stop, near the lake). The Roman museum next door is not worth the 4-SF entry fee.

**Hotel Regina,** on a pedestrian street in the old town, has comfortable rooms. Run by the same family since 1953, it feels cared for (S-65–75 SF, Sb-90–110 SF, D-90–100 SF, Db-120–140 SF, cheaper off-season, CC:VMA, Rue Grand Saint-Jean 18, tel. 021/320-2441, fax 021/320-2529, SE).

**Hotel du Raisin,** with dingy, faded furnishings, has a great but noisy location on a popular square in the old town (S-60 SF, D-120 SF, attached restaurant with sidewalk café, CC:VMA, Place de la Palud 19, tel. & fax 021/312-2756, SE).

**Hotel du Port,** in a peely building, has small rooms but some lakefront views (S-42 SF, Sb-60–85 SF, D-75 SF, Db-80–106 SF, Tb-130 SF, breakfast-12 SF, CC:VMA, Place du Port 5, tel. 021/616-4930, fax 021/616-8368, NSE). It's a block from the Ouchy metro stop (turn left as you exit).

## Sleeping in Villeneuve, near Montreux and Château Chillon
### (1.5 SF = about $1, tel. code: 021, zip code: 1844)

The town of Villeneuve, 3 miles east, has the same palmy lakeside setting without the crowds or glitz. Its main drag runs parallel to the shore, 1 block in. Stroll the waterfront promenade to the château (30 min walk). Don't count on speaking English at these hotels—zees ees a French city. As you exit the train station, take a left on main street to find the TI and first two hotels, or walk straight ahead to find the lakefront listing.

**La Romantica,** with dark, narrow, cheap-feeling rooms, is a decent value with a frumpy, very French bar scene downstairs (Sb-40 SF, Db-80F–90 SF, breakfast-5 SF, CC:VMA, Grand-Rue 34, tel. 021/960-1540, fax 021/960-3791). Even the stools are overstuffed.

**Hotel du Soleil** is an expensive but comfortable place (Sb-70 SF, Db-100–120 SF, CC:VMA, Grand-Rue 20, tel. 021/960-4206, fax 021/960-4208). **Hotel du Port** is the town's affordable, pleasant hotel on the waterfront (Db-140 SF, family deals, elevator, CC:VMA, Rue du Quai 6, tel. 021/960-4145, fax 021/960-3967, Msr. Raneda SE).

**Haut Lac hostel** is at the edge of Montreux, on the lake, a ten-minute stroll north of the château and a long stroll from the fun of Montreux (dorm bed, sheets, and breakfast-27.40 SF, D-73 SF, non-members pay 5 SF extra, closed 10:00–16:00, cheap meals served, Passage de l'Auberge 8, 1820 Territet town, tel. 021/963-4934). Train noise can be a problem.

**Hotel-Restaurant du Pont** offers decent rooms and great spaghetti (Db-120 SF, Rue du Pont 12, tel. 021/963-2249).

## Transportation Connections—Lake Geneva
**Lausanne by train to: Montreux** (hrly, 20 min), **Geneva** (3/hr, 50 min), **Bern** (hrly, 70 min), **Basel** (2/hr, 2.5 hrs), **Milan** (hrly, 3.5 hrs).

## Route Tips for Drivers
**Interlaken to Bern to Murten (50 miles):** From Interlaken, catch the autobahn (direction: Spiez, Thun, Bern). After Spiez, the autobahn takes you right to Bern. Circle the city on the autobahn, taking the fourth Bern exit, Neufeld Bern. Signs to "Zentrum" takes you to Bern Bahnhof. Turn right just before the station into the Bahnhof Parkplatz (two-hour meter parking outside, all-day lot inside, 2 SF per hour). You're just an escalator ride away from a great TI and Switzerland's compact, user-friendly capital. From the station, drive out of Bern following Lausanne signs, then follow green signs to Neuchatel and Murten. The autobahn ends about 20 minutes later in Murten.

Parking in Murten is medieval. Ask about parking at your hotel. If you have a dashboard clock, you can try the blue spots near the Ringmauer Hotel, but there are large free lots just outside either gate. Walk in to Murten. It's a tiny town.

**Murten to Lake Geneva (50 miles):** The autobahn from Bern to Lausanne/Lake Geneva makes everything speedy. Murten and Avenches are ten minutes from the autobahn. Broc, Bulle, and Gruyères are within sight of each other and the autobahn. It takes about an hour to drive from Murten to Montreux. The autobahn (direction: Simplon) takes you high above Montreux (pull off at the great viewpoint rest stop) and Château Chillon. Take the first exit east of the castle (Villeneuve). Signs direct you along the lake back to the castle.

# APPENDIX

## Let's Talk Telephones

Smart travelers use the telephone every day—to make hotel reservations, call tourist information offices, and phone home. In Europe, card-operated public phones are speedily replacing coin-operated phones. Each country sells telephone cards good for use in its country. Get a phone card at any post office. To make a call, pick up the receiver, insert your card in the slot, dial your number, make your call, then retrieve your card. The price of your call is automatically deducted from your card as you use it. If you have phone-card phobia, you'll usually find easy-to-use "talk now, pay later" metered phones in post offices. Avoid using hotel room phones for anything other than local calls and calling-card calls (see below).

### Calling Card Operators

Calling home from Europe is easy from any type of phone if you have a calling card. From a private phone, just dial the toll-free number to reach the operator. Using a public phone, first insert a small-value coin or a German, Austrian, or Swiss phone card. Then dial the operator, who will ask you for your calling-card number and place your call. You'll save money on calls of three minutes or more. When you finish, your coin should be returned (or, if using a card, no money should have been deducted). Your bill awaits you at home (one more reason to prolong your vacation). For more information, see Introduction: Telephones and Mail.

|             | AT&T          | MCI           | SPRINT        |
|-------------|---------------|---------------|---------------|
| Austria     | 022-903-011   | 022-903-012   | 022-903-014   |
| Germany     | 0130-0010     | 0130-0012     | 0130-0013     |
| Switzerland | 0800-89-0011  | 0800-89-0222  | 0800-89-9777  |

### Dialing Direct

**Calling Between Countries:** First dial the international access code, then the country code, the area code (if it starts with zero, drop the zero), and then the local number.

**Calling Long Distance Within a Country:** First dial the area code (including its zero), then the local number.

**Some of Europe's Exceptions:** A few countries lack area codes, such as Denmark, Norway, and France. You still use the above sequence and codes to dial, just skip the area code. In Spain, area codes start with nine instead of zero (just drop or add the nine instead of a zero).

## International Access Codes
When dialing direct, first dial the international access code of the country you're calling from.

| | | |
|---|---|---|
| Austria—00 | Germany—00 | Russia—810 |
| Belgium—00 | Ireland—00 | Spain—07 |
| Britain—00 | Italy—00 | Sweden—009 |
| Czech Republic—00 | Latvia—800 | Switzerland—00 |
| Denmark—00 | Lithuania—810 | U.S.A./Canada—011 |
| Estonia—800 | Netherlands—00 | |
| Finland—990 | Norway—00 | |
| France—00 | Portugal—00 | |

## Country Codes
After you've dialed the international access code, then dial the code of the country you're calling.

| | | |
|---|---|---|
| Austria—43 | Germany—49 | Russia—7 |
| Belgium—32 | Ireland—353 | Spain—34 |
| Britain—44 | Italy—39 | Sweden—46 |
| Czech Republic—42 | Latvia—371 | Switzerland—41 |
| Denmark—45 | Lithuania—370 | U.S.A./Canada—1 |
| Estonia—372 | Netherlands—31 | |
| Finland—358 | Norway—47 | |
| France—33 | Portugal—351 | |

## Directory Assistance
Austria: national–16, international–08
Switzerland: national–111, international–191
Swiss info for Germany/Austria: 192
Germany: national–01188, international–00118
German tourist offices: local code then 19433
German train information: local code then 19419

# Metric Conversions (approximate)
| | |
|---|---|
| 1 inch = 25 millimeters | 32 degrees F = 0 degrees C |
| 1 foot = 0.3 meter | 82 degrees F = about 28 degrees C |
| 1 yard = 0.9 meter | 1 ounce = 28 grams |
| 1 mile = 1.6 kilometers | 1 kilogram = 2.2 pounds |
| 1 centimeter = 0.4 inch | 1 quart = 0.95 liter |

1 meter = 39.4 inches     1 square yard = 0.8 square meter
1 kilometer = .62 mile     1 acre = 0.4 hectare

## Numbers and Stumblers

- Europeans write a few of their numbers differently than we do.
  1 = 1, 4 = 4, 7 = 7. Learn the difference or miss your train.
- In Europe, dates appear as day/month/year, so Christmas is
  25/12/98.
- Commas are decimal points, and decimals are commas. A
  dollar and a half is 1,50 and there are 5.280 feet in a mile.
- When pointing, use your whole hand, palm downward.
- When counting with fingers, start with your thumb. If you
  hold up your first finger to request one item, you'll get two.
- What we Americans call the second floor of a building is the
  first floor in Europe.
- Europeans keep the left "lane" open for passing on escalators
  and moving sidewalks. Keep to the right.

## Climate

The first line indicates average daily low. The second line
indicates average daily high. The third line indicates days per
month of no rain.

| | J | F | M | A | M | J | J | A | S | O | N | D |
|---|---|---|---|---|---|---|---|---|---|---|---|---|
| **Frankfurt** Germany | 29° | 31° | 35° | 41° | 48° | 53° | 56° | 55° | 51° | 43° | 36° | 31° |
| | 37° | 42° | 49° | 58° | 67° | 72° | 75° | 74° | 67° | 56° | 45° | 39° |
| | 22 | 19 | 22 | 21 | 22 | 21 | 21 | 21 | 21 | 22 | 21 | 20 |
| **Vienna** Austria | 26° | 28° | 34° | 41° | 50° | 56° | 59° | 58° | 52° | 44° | 36° | 30° |
| | 34° | 38° | 47° | 57° | 66° | 71° | 75° | 73° | 66° | 55° | 44° | 37° |
| | 23 | 21 | 24 | 21 | 22 | 21 | 22 | 21 | 23 | 23 | 22 | 22 |
| **Geneva** Switzerland | 29° | 30° | 35° | 41° | 48° | 55° | 58° | 57° | 52° | 44° | 37° | 31° |
| | 39° | 43° | 51° | 58° | 66° | 73° | 77° | 76° | 69° | 58° | 47° | 40° |
| | 20 | 19 | 21 | 19 | 19 | 19 | 22 | 21 | 20 | 20 | 19 | 21 |

# German Survival Phrases

| Hello (good day). | Guten Tag. | **goo**-ten tahg |
| Do you speak English? | Sprechen Sie Englisch? | **shprekh**-en zee **eng**-lish |
| Yes. / No. | Ja. / Nein. | yah / nīn |
| I'm sorry. | Entschuldigung. | ent-**shool**-dee-goong |
| Please. / Thank you. | Bitte. / Danke. | **bit**-teh / **dahng**-keh |
| Goodbye. | Auf Wiedersehen. | owf **vee**-der-zayn |
| Where is...? | Wo ist...? | voh ist |
| ...a hotel | ...ein Hotel | īn hoh-**tel** |
| ...a youth hostel | ...eine Jugend-herberge | ī-neh **yoo**-gend-hehr-behr-geh |
| ...a restaurant | ...ein Restaurant | īn res-tow-**rahnt** |
| ...a supermarket | ...ein Supermarkt | īn **zoo**-per-markt |
| ...the train station | ...der Bahnhof | dehr **bahn**-hohf |
| ...the tourist information office | ...das Touristen-informationsbüro | dahs **too**-ris-ten-in-for-maht-see-**ohns**-bew-roh |
| ...the toilet | ...die Toilette | dee toh-**leh**-teh |
| men / women | Herren / Damen | **hehr**-ren / **dah**-men |
| How much is it? | Wieviel kostet das? | vee-**feel kos**-tet dahs |
| Cheap / Cheaper. | Billig / Billiger. | **bil**-lig / **bil**-lig-er |
| Included? | Eingeschlossen? | **īn**-geh-shlos-sen |
| Do you have...? | Haben Sie...? | **hah**-ben zee |
| I would like... | Ich hätte gern... | ikh **het**-teh gehrn |
| ...just a little. | ...nur ein bißchen. | noor īn **bis**-yen |
| ...more. | ...mehr. | mehr |
| ...a ticket. | ...ein Karte. | īn **kar**-teh |
| ...a room. | ...ein Zimmer. | īn **tsim**-mer |
| ...the bill. | ...die Rechnung. | dee **rekh**-noong |
| one | eins | īns |
| two | zwei | tsvī |
| three | drei | drī |
| four | vier | feer |
| five | fünf | fewnf |
| six | sechs | zex |
| seven | sieben | **zee**-ben |
| eight | acht | ahkht |
| nine | neun | noyn |
| ten | zehn | tsayn |
| At what time? | Um wieviel Uhr? | oom vee-**feel** oor |
| now / soon / later | jetzt / bald / später | yetzt / bahld / **shpay**-ter |
| today / tomorrow | heute / morgen | **hoy**-teh / **mor**-gen |

For more survival phrases, check out *Rick Steves' German Phrase Book and Dictionary* or *Rick Steves' French, Italian & German Phrase Book and Dictionary.*

## Faxing Your Hotel Reservation

Most hotel managers know basic "hotel English." Faxing is the preferred method for reserving a room. It's more accurate and cheaper than telephoning and much faster than writing a letter. Use this handy form for your fax. Photocopy and fax away.

### One-Page Fax

To: _____ @ _____
         *hotel*                                    *fax*

From: _____ @ _____
           *name*                                  *fax*

Today's date: ___ / _____ / ___
                    *day*  *month*  *year*

Dear Hotel _____,

Please make this reservation for me:

Name: _____

Total # of people: _____    # of rooms: _____    # of nights: _____

Arriving: ___ / _____ / ___   My time of arrival (24-hr clock): _____
              *day*  *month*  *year*   (I will telephone if I will be late)

Departing: ___ / _____ / ___
                *day*  *month*  *year*

Room(s):  Single___  Double___  Twin___  Triple___  Quad___

With:  Toilet___  Shower___  Bath___  Sink only___

Special needs:  View___  Quiet___  Cheapest Room___

Credit card:  Visa___  MasterCard___  American Express___

Card #: _____

Expiration Date: _____

Name on card: _____

You may charge me for the first night as a deposit. Please fax or mail me confirmation of my reservation, along with the type of room reserved, the price, and whether the price includes breakfast. Thank you.

_____
*Signature*

_____
*Name*

_____
*Address*

_____
*City*                        *State*        *Zip Code*      *Country*

# Road Scholar Feedback for Germany, Austria & Switzerland 1998

*We're all in the same travelers' school of hard knocks. Your feedback helps us improve this guidebook for future travelers. Please fill this out (attach more info or any tips/favorite discoveries if you like) and send it to us. As thanks for your help, we'll send you our quarterly travel newsletter free for one year. Thanks! Rick*

**I traveled mainly by:** ___ Car ___ Train/bus tickets
___ Railpass   Other (please list _____)

**Number of people traveling together:**
___ Solo ___ 2 ___ 3 ___ 4 ___ Over 4 ___ Tour

**Ages of traveler/s (including children):**

_____

**I visited _____ countries in _____ weeks.**

**I traveled in:** ___ Spring ___ Summer ___ Fall ___ Winter

**My daily budget per person (excluding transportation):**
___ Under $40 ___ $40–$60 ___ $60–$80 ___ $80–$120
___ over $120 ___ Don't know

**Average cost of hotel rooms:** Single room $_____
Double room $_____   Other (type _____) $_____

**Favorite tip from this book:**

_____

**Biggest waste of time or money caused by this book:**

_____

**Other Rick Steves books used for this trip:**

_____

**Other non–Rick Steves guidebooks used for this trip:**

_____

**Hotel listings from this book should be geared toward places that are:**

___ Cheaper     ___ More expensive     ___ About the same

**Of the recommended accommodations/restaurants used, which was:**

Best _____

    Why? _____

Worst _____

    Why? _____

**I reserved rooms:**

____from U.S.A.               ____in advance as I traveled

____same day by phone     ____just showed up

**Getting rooms in recommended hotels was:**

____easy          ____mixed          ____frustrating

**Of the sights/experiences/destinations recommended by this book, which was:**

Most overrated _____

    Why? _____

Most underrated _____

    Why? _____

**Best ways to improve this book:**

_____

**I'd like a free newsletter subscription:**

___ Yes     ___ No     ___ Already on list

Name

_____

Address

_____

City, State, Zip

_____

E-mail Address

*Please send to: ETBD, Box 2009, Edmonds, WA 98020*

# INDEX